Praise for *Survival of the Fastest*

"Flooring his racer on the back straight of the Indy 500 at the same time that his barge with 80 tons of pot bucks up waves along the California coast, Randy Lanier didn't let me go until the last page of his ripping, true saga."

—BRUCE PORTER, bestselling author of *BLOW: How a Small-Town Boy Made $100 Million with the Medellín Cocaine Cartel and Lost It All*

"Randy Lanier's need for speed was his true addiction. Part *Miami Vice* (1980s fast cars, fast money, cigarette boats), part *Talladega Nights* (as a 'gentleman driver' funding his race team with cash from his vast marijuana smuggling enterprise), and part *Blow* (fueled by adrenaline and humor and recklessness), Lanier's story perfectly illustrates why the War of Drugs was always doomed. The rewards for smuggling drugs are just too huge for wily-crazy operators like Lanier to resist. Like any self-respecting outlaw, Lanier has a hell of a time breaking the law, even as knuckleheaded hubris promises ruination, but you can't help but cheer for him as the glory and despair of the checkered flag of his rookie Indy 500 finish line and clanging prison doors loom on the horizon."

—GUY LAWSON, bestselling author of *War Dogs: How Three Stoners From Miami Beach Became the Most Unlikely Gunrunners in History*

"So the guy has become this international racecar driver, a star, rookie of the year at Indy and all that. So he has a secret, the fact that he's also a big-time international drug smuggler. So—cue the music—all this is taking place in the *Miami Vice* eighties with the cool clothes and the big hair and the FBI has taken notice and…Tell me you're not going to read this whopper of a true-life tale. Buckle your seat belts. This is one terrific ride."

—LEIGH MONTVILLE, bestselling author of *The Big Bam*

"As the test pilot for the world's most dangerous amusement park, I was thrust right back into those harrowing days as I read the story of Randy Lanier and his wild ride of a life from drug smuggler to race car driver. It's non-stop action and a thrill a minute. Strap in and blast off!"

—ANDY MULVIHILL, author of *Action Park: Fast Times, Wild Rides, and the Untold Story of America's Most Dangerous Amusement Park*

SURVIVAL OF THE FASTEST

SURVIVAL OF THE FASTEST

Weed, Speed, and the 1980s Drug Scandal that Shocked the Sports World

RANDY LANIER

WITH **A.J. BAIME**

hachette
BOOKS
New York

Hachette Books
Hachette Book Group
1290 Avenue of the Americas
New York, NY 10104
HachetteBooks.com
Twitter.com/HachetteBooks
Instagram.com/HachetteBooks

First Edition: August 2022

Published by Hachette Books, an imprint of Perseus Books, LLC,
a subsidiary of Hachette Book Group, Inc. The Hachette Books name and
logo is a trademark of the Hachette Book Group.

The Hachette Speakers Bureau provides a wide range of authors for
speaking events. To find out more, go to www.hachettespeakersbureau.com
or call (866) 376-6591.

The publisher is not responsible for websites (or their content) that are not owned
by the publisher.

All photos courtesy of the author unless otherwise noted.

Print book interior design by Jeff Williams.

Library of Congress Control Number: 2022936525

ISBNs: 978-0-306-82645-0 (hardcover), 978-0-306-82647-4 (ebook)

Printed in the United States of America

LSC-C

Printing 1, 2022

For Pam, Brandie, and Glen, and my mom
and my dad, may they rest in peace.

"It was written I should be loyal to the nightmare of my choice."

—JOSEPH CONRAD, *Heart of Darkness*

Contents

This is a true story.
Some of the names have been changed.

Prologue

On October 10, 1987, at sunrise, I stepped out of the salon and onto the rear deck of my custom-built sixty-foot Hatteras, a sport fishing vessel that I named *Reel Liv-In*. I stared out at the Caribbean. The sunrays bounced off the sapphire ocean, like the sea was boiling with diamonds. It was one of those halcyon tropical days where you feel like nothing could possibly go wrong. Slight breeze, scent of salt water, warm humid air.

I was anchored off the leeward side of Barbuda, the sister island of Antigua, and my three-person crew (two ship captains and a girlfriend I had with me) were readying a Zodiac, a motorized inflatable boat, to head for the grassy shallows. We were going to dive for our lunch—fresh seafood. I had my mask, my snorkel, my knife. Suddenly, I heard the sound of an engine buzzing overhead. I looked up.

"What the fuck do you think that plane is doing?" I said, turning to my main boat captain, Slick. "Why's that aircraft flying so low, so early in the morning?"

"Probably tourists," Slick said.

The little plane disappeared over a sandy beach and some palm trees on the island. "There must be an airstrip right over there," I said.

We launched the Zodiac and spent the morning pulling conch off the grassy seafloor and lobster out of the crevices in the coral reef close by. Afterward, we pulled anchor, turned the Hatteras, and made for port in Falmouth Harbor, Antigua.

I'd been on the run from the law by this time for ten months. Aside from the crew on my boat, nobody in the world knew where I was. I aimed to keep it that way. I was a fugitive, separated from my two children and their mother, Pam, my best friend. Up to this time, my life had been all about speed. I was a motor-racing international champion and an Indy 500 Rookie of the Year, crowned *the next big thing* at the temple of IndyCar racing. Now my life was dictated by a different kind of speed—always moving fast to stay one step ahead of the law.

Falmouth Harbor sits on the southern edge of Antigua. To get into the harbor, you line up with markers to steer safely through an inlet. On one side is a rocky cliff, and on the other, a coral reef that can tear the guts out of your vessel if you don't approach correctly. I was standing on the enclosed flybridge with Slick, holding binoculars as he steered the boat into this postcard beautiful harbor full of anchored sailboats. I did a full 360 with the binoculars, and that's when I saw this gray ninety-foot patrol boat by the rocky cliff to our port side. It looked like a navy ship.

"What do you think they're doing here?" I said, handing the binoculars to Slick.

"Shit," he said, "they might want to board the vessel and see our paperwork."

"I don't like this. Let's pivot the boat. Let's get the fuck out of here and head back out to sea."

The moment those words came out of my mouth, the patrol boat made its move. It motored toward the opening of the inlet, blocking the only way out of the harbor.

"Hell no!" I screamed. "They're here for me! Get the Zodiac in the water!"

I was wearing baggy shorts, no shirt, and no shoes. I had no identification on me. I didn't know where I was going. But I knew I had to get off this vessel, and there was no time to spare. I had a hundred grand in cash and a fake passport in the ship's stateroom, but I was in too much of a hurry to get it. My crew winched the Zodiac into the water, and I climbed down into this rubber vessel. I took off, weaving through anchored sailboats. When I made it to the harbor dock, I tied up the Zodiac, climbed out, and started running, down to the end and onto a dirt road.

As I barreled forward, I saw a cloud of dust in front of me, and through it came three Jeeps at high speed. I could see that the Jeeps were full of islander police officers with big guns. My heart started to beat so fast I felt like it was going to explode.

Turning right, I ran up a hill, clawing at the ground for traction. The rough terrain ripped the skin off my bare feet, and the sharp points of the palmetto bushes punctured my hands. I heard the words, "Halt! Or we'll shoot!" I was close to the peak of the hilltop. When I turned around, I saw police officers kneeling and aiming gun barrels at me.

"Don't shoot!" I shouted, lifting my hands up. "Don't shoot!"

I walked back down the hill, and the island policemen threw me against one of the Jeeps. One said, "You're under arrest, mon."

"What's this about!?!" I shouted. "You got the wrong guy!"

One of the cops grabbed me by my right wrist and held it up. He looked at my right hand, which was missing a finger.

"No, mon," he said. "We got the right guy. You're Randy Lanier. You're going to jail, mon."

They handcuffed me and pushed me into the back of one of the Jeeps. It was a madhouse inside. These guys didn't put their guns away; they all kept the barrels pointed at me. As we motored back to the end of the dock, I said, "Who's in charge here?"

"I am," said the guy driving.

"See that sixty-foot boat out in the harbor?" I said. "The Hatteras? You can have it and everything on it! Just let me go!"

He didn't say anything. Just kept driving.

When we reached the dock, I saw them: two white guys wearing sports jackets and aviator sunglasses, with clean-shaven pale faces. They stood with feet apart and hands clasped in front. "Oh shit!" I said. These guys were central casting law enforcement USA.

That little airplane I'd seen at sunrise, buzzing by over-head? FBI.

Thirteen months later, after a three-month court trial, with sixty-four witnesses and ten thousand pages of testimony transcript, I awoke on the morning of my sentencing in a cell at the supermax prison in Marion, Illinois. It was December 21, 1988. Marion was, at the time, the only supermax prison in the country, designed to hold the worst of the worst. The federal government opened this nightmare place when they shut down Alcatraz. It was home in the 1990s to the likes of John Gotti and various al-Qaeda operatives.

I was wearing a suit and tie when the US marshals came to get me that morning. They put me in a van and drove 100 mph with a squad car in front of us, its lights flashing. We were heading to the federal courthouse of the Southern District of Illinois. When we got there, I noticed officers standing on top of the building and officers surrounding the outside, all of them armed. I thought: What a fucking waste of taxpayer money.

When the marshals brought me into the courtroom, I already knew what I was facing. I'd been convicted of all three counts charged against me, all of which carried mandatory sentences. So there was no mystery around what was about to happen. I just had to go into the courtroom to hear the judge say the words out loud. I had asked my family—Pam, my kids, my mom—to remain absent. I did not want my loved ones to have to witness this.

"All rise," announced the bailiff.

My lawyer, Bob Ritchie, and I got up on our feet as James L. Foreman, United States judge of the Southern District of Illinois, walked into the room and sat down behind the bench, his silver hair side parted. He asked my lawyer if he had any final words, and my lawyer rose to address the court. All these years later, the words in the court transcript still ring in my ears.

"Who is this man?" he asked the judge. "Who is this man that the court is called upon to sentence? It's a complex picture. He has acknowledged his wrongdoing. He has acknowledged . . . that he went down a road he shouldn't have gone. . . . But you know, this court knows that there is another side to Randy Lanier that has not been fully addressed. He had, obviously, a strong bond between himself and his daughter, Brandie, now eight years old. . . .

"I'm not going to stand up here and say because he was a race car driver that that entitles him to any leniency. . . . But I think the court can also look to see if should anything happen in regard to this matter which would remove from him the specter of coming out of the penitentiary in a pine box, that there is a man here who is susceptible to rehabilitation, and susceptible to making a contribution, a positive contribution to society. . . . He went in the field of racing because of courage. . . . He had dedication. . . . He had things that could carry him far."

When he finished his appeal for mercy, Judge Foreman spoke, as my lawyer and I stood before him. "You are a very young man now," the judge said. "You are only thirty-four, isn't it? I guess?"

"Yes, sir," I said.

"You and Ben Kramer are almost identical in age," the judge said, referring to my lifelong business partner, now one of my codefendants. Judge Foreman moved his glasses to the end of his nose, so he could peer over them into my eyes from across the room. "The real basic purpose of punishment is the age-old, century-old idea of deterrence," he said. "We do have a war on drugs in this country. . . . The best answer that anybody has been able to come up with has been severity of punishment. Whether that's going to solve the problem or not, I don't know. But that is what Congress has spoken to. It's the law of the land." It didn't sound like he was swayed by my lawyer's plea.

He then read my sentence. Count 1, Continual Criminal Enterprise B: "Imprisonment for a term of life." Count 2, Conspiracy to Distribute Marijuana: "Imprisonment for a term of forty years." Count 3, Impeding the IRS: "Imprisonment for a term of five years." The jury determined that my partners and I were to pay a forfeiture of $150 million. It was the largest forfeiture ever ordered in an American courtroom at that time. My share was $60 million.

The judge peered at me again over the rim of his glasses and said that if he could give me a harsher sentence, he would. Therefore, he said, my sentences would run consecutively rather than concurrently. Meaning, technically, I was to serve the rest of my life in prison without a chance of parole, and if my sentencing was to be followed literally to the word, they were to leave my dead body behind prison bars, for another forty-five years.

I began my sentence in the St. Louis County Jail. The guards led me to a small cell with no bed, just a bench and a blanket. When I heard the steel door to my cage slam shut behind me, I felt myself shatter into a pile of pieces for somebody to sweep off the floor. The thought of failure in my family's eyes and the failure within myself—it was beyond heartbreaking. And I'd brought it all on myself.

My life was no longer going to be about being a father to my two children or a husband to the love of my life. It was no longer going to be about worshipping at the altar of speed. Now my life was going to be stripped down to the bare essentials of daily survival. I was left to wonder: *Would I ever find a way out, legally or illegally? Would I ever breathe a single breath of freedom again?*

I was a South Florida hippy kid who grew up with a dream. A construction worker who wanted to be a race car driver so bad I was willing to take incalculable risks. A guy who came from nothing and beat the Porsche factory racing team from Germany, the Jaguar factory team from Britain, and the Ford factory team from the US. A businessman who created an international empire outside the law because that was the only path I could find that would lead me to the place where my heart and soul told me I had to go: the winner's podium.

For the rest of my life, I'd hear one question over and over. Did I have any regrets? If I could do it all again, would I do it differently? To answer that one, I have to go back to the beginning, to the day I heard the sound of the Indy 500 for the first time on an AM radio. The sound of those roaring engines haunts me still, to this day.

1

Coming of Age

Virginia and Florida, 1950s and 1960s

South Florida came to define my life, but I didn't start there. I was born in Virginia in 1954. My family had a small house in a small town called Madison Heights, where my parents grew what we ate. A far cry from private planes and luxury yachts. We had chickens, and some of my earliest memories are of going to collect the eggs. I had three brothers and one sister, and we spent lots of our time running through the miles of woods behind the house, building forts, and having battles throwing mud balls across rambling creeks. We had swings on the front and back porch, and a clothesline in the back where we would hang our laundry to dry.

Across the street was a place called Bryant's Market where the old-timers sat out front chewing tobacco. At age five, I started going over there to help pump gas, at the only pump there was for miles in either direction on the main road. I couldn't wait to get out of bed in the morning so I could run across the street and get started. Sometimes I'd wait hours for a vehicle to pull up to the pump. I loved how every car was different. I'd observe the way they looked and smelled, delighting in the shiny chrome and the stink of the engine fumes. I was only a kid, but every time I filled a tank, I felt like a man.

Even then, cars were at the center of my dreams.

My mother was the most compassionate woman I've ever met. Her name was Elise Maude Elliott Lanier, and she worked at a state institution for mentally and physically disabled people. Sometimes we would pick her up from work, and I would see these young people struggling to walk. It was hard for me to understand why they were the way they were. My mom cared so much for these people, and they loved her back. All her life until she retired, that's what she did: be in service to others. My mom taught me that the greatest form of knowledge in our lives is empathy.

My dad, Noel Edward Lanier Jr., had no formal education beyond the sixth grade, but he could read and write blueprints, and he had a job at a pipe foundry. People called him Junior, and he could build anything. All over our house, there was stuff that he made out of wood with his hands—couches, potato bins, tables, and chairs. He had a Harley-Davidson with a suicide clutch—a shifter near the tank and a clutch pedal by his foot. On Saturdays, he would take one of us kids on a ride. I would get so excited when it was my turn. The motorcycle looked so huge, and the engine was so loud. He would pick me up and put me on the back and away we'd go, riding along the Blue Ridge Parkway in the Shenandoah Valley.

It felt like heaven, holding onto my dad and riding through this valley. Speed, open air, family. What else do you need?

My father had a dark side, however. He would drink, and a couple times I saw him beating my mother. I'd hear the screaming and run down the stairs, trying to stop him, and he would chase me back up. I'd huddle in my room with my younger brother Glen, trying to distract him so he wouldn't hear.

But mostly it was good times. Idyllic, even.

Every Sunday we'd go to my grandparents' house. Going for a car ride was a big adventure. Us kids would stand up on the floorboards looking over the driver's seat and out the windows. At my grandparents' house, we'd make homemade ice cream in the shade of a walnut tree. Unlike our home, my grandparents' house had no running water. They had a woodstove and, instead of a toilet, a well-beaten path outside with wooden planks leading through the overgrown weeds to what we called the johnny house.

My grandparents grew tobacco. Tobacco fields spread out as far as the eye could see. They had a big tobacco house where they dried the leaves, and this place was spooky. To me it was like a medieval castle. My senses were always alert when I went in there.

This one time, I walked inside and saw my uncle on a homemade bench, and there were some people around him. I saw a lot of empty beer cans. He had this AM radio, and the guys were listening to something turned all the way up. I was six years old at the time. I approached them, and the closer I got, the more I could hear what was coming out of the radio speaker. The announcers were calling the Indy 500. I believe it was 1961, the first year that A. J. Foyt won.

I'd never heard of the Indy 500 or any motor race. The announcers so excited, it sounded like they could barely catch their breath, and you could hear the engines thunder as the cars shrieked past. It was like the air in that tobacco house was electrified, and as I listened, I started to fantasize about what it would be like to drive a race car. It was a world so far away from mine, it might as well have been another planet. That I'd ever get to sit in one of these cars, or even meet A. J. Foyt—let alone race against him and beat him—seemed as likely as me landing on the moon. Still, I sat on a piece of wood holding my arms up with my hands clenched, clutching a phantom steering wheel, imagining myself piloting down a straightaway at terminal speed.

For me, that was the day the future was born.

One day when I was twelve, I was in the backyard working on a homemade go-kart when my father came to me, telling me to come inside the house for a family meeting. I thought I was in trouble because I needed wheels for my go-kart and so I'd taken my sister's roller skates apart without asking. Instead, at the dinner table, my father explained that we were moving to South Florida. He never told us why. He just said we were going.

Everything was changing, and I was nervous. My oldest brother, Steve, had gone off to Vietnam. I was going to have to leave my friends and my baseball team, which felt like my entire existence.

We sold our house for $6,000 and drove all the way to South Florida. In 1967, outside of Miami and Fort Lauderdale, South Florida was rural. But that was about to change. The whole peninsula was about to blow up with what would later be thought of as the great South Florida building boom.

Everyone wanted to be in South Florida, and why not? All the rich people from New York came down to drink champagne and see Frank Sinatra at the Fontainebleau in Miami, the city that was the gateway to the Caribbean islands. Others came because there was work. Home developments were going up all over, and the boating industry was exploding.

I couldn't know it at age twelve, but South Florida would become as much a part of me as my own skin. Looking back, I can't imagine what my life would have become if we hadn't moved there.

The first place we lived was a trailer park in the town of Hollywood, which bordered Fort Lauderdale to the south, at the corner of Johnson Street and US 441. There was a bowling alley, an A&P market, and honky-tonk cowboy bars. I'd watch my father down whiskey while he played poker with the guys in the trailer park. After a year or so, we moved into a nicer home. My father got a job doing home construction at Pasadena Lakes, a development west of Hollywood. My first job was washing dishes at an Italian restaurant, where I made $1.10 an hour. The summer after ninth grade, my father got me a job digging foundations for new houses. I started out at $1.65 an hour, shoveling dirt in brutally hot weather.

South Florida in 1968 was a wild place to come of age. Almost all the people that I met had families who had come here from somewhere else. There was an indescribable draw to this place, which lured creative, strange, edgy people. People with pasts they couldn't talk about. People who didn't care about tomorrow, only about today. People with no money. People with endless money. People who didn't give a shit about the way life was supposed to be lived; people who chose their own path. When I look back on it now, it was like coming of age in 1960s Haight-Ashbury—hippies everywhere. Only unlike San Francisco, the sunshine blazed, and there were beaches and boats everywhere, girls in bikinis, honky-tonk bars, and outdoor parks full of palm trees and rock 'n' roll bands jamming.

By that point, a lot of the kids at my school were already smoking weed, as most people called it back then. The first time I smoked a joint, it didn't do anything. Then one day a friend of mine told me that he knew two sisters who had some hash. We smoked some of it out of a pipe behind a farm supplies store. This time I did get high, and I liked it.

I had long hair, and I kept it in a ponytail. My dad was on me to cut it off. He was a country guy, and it drove him crazy. After a while, all he could talk about was that ponytail. So one of my closest friends, a guy named Alan Hollingsworth (with whom I'm still friends today), and I decided we were going to take a vacation. Without telling my parents, we met up and got a ride to the I-95 on-ramp. We had twenty dollars between us, a cardboard matchbox full of weed, two hits of LSD, and a bunch of clothes in a pillowcase. We stuck our thumbs out and hitchhiked all the way to Canada. We slept underneath bridges. We had no food, so we had to steal it.

So many crazy things happened that summer. The moon landing, Nixon and Vietnam, the Manson murders, the Miracle Mets. On the way to Canada, we heard about this rock 'n' roll festival happening in upstate New York. It was Woodstock, but we didn't stop; we kept on going. . . .

At one point I called my parents. They were furious. But my brothers had told them where I'd gone, so they hadn't called the police. When Alan and I finally got back to Florida after

about three weeks, my mom was thrilled I was back, but my
dad wouldn't even look at me. That was punishment worse
than being whipped. But you know what? They forgave me. I
still refused to cut my hair, though. I held my ground.

I went back to school and to working construction on weekends. Because I had a ponytail, all the construction workers
were always asking me the same questions:

Did I smoke weed?

Did I know how to get it?

One of my friends had a neighbor who had gone to Vietnam, and he was sending weed back. He would grind it up,
put it between two postcards, and glue the edges. It was that
easy. When this guy came back from the war, he had a source
who started sending weed in bigger quantities. So now I had
a way to get my hands on some.

I started selling four-finger lids (close to an ounce) for fifteen dollars to the construction workers so I could smoke for
free and make money at the same time. This was mostly Mexican weed and sometimes Jamaican weed. Big, dried, brown
and green buds with tons of stems and seeds, not as good as
the stuff we got from Vietnam. I was still fifteen, and I was
already making more money selling weed to the workers on
the construction site than I was for the job itself. I didn't even
need the job anymore, but I kept it because that's where I got
my clientele.

And that's how it all started. It was innocent enough, it
seemed to me. Smoking weed was a way of life. It bonded people together. It was a connection to nature. It was an instant
cure for boredom, a party in my pocket. When I looked at a
map of the United States on the wall of my history classroom,

the whole South Florida peninsula looked like a giant joint waiting to be torched.

Nobody was getting hurt, and nobody was getting arrested. It actually felt like I was helping people, turning them on, being of service—just like my mom had taught me.

My two biggest passions were weed and cars. All my heroes were race car drivers: A. J. Foyt, Gordon Johncock, Mario Andretti. So on my fifteenth birthday, I got my mother to drive me to the Florida Department of Motor Vehicles office early so I could be the first in line to get my driver's license. In Florida, at that time, you could get a restrictive license at fifteen. That meant you could drive, day or night, if you had an adult with you. I walked out of the Florida DMV that morning not just with a driver's license but with a whole new outlook on life. I was mobile.

That night, I asked my mom if I could use the car to go to a movie with a neighborhood friend.

"I'm picking up a friend who's eighteen so it'll be legal for me to drive," I told her.

She said yes. I had some friends—two sisters, plus one other guy—meet me at a movie theater. We were all lying to our parents. We weren't going to see any movie. We were heading to the beach with a six-pack, some Mexican shake, and rolling papers.

Later that night, I was lying on a blanket smoking a joint with one of the sisters, and I noticed headlights flashing. So I got up and went to check it out. A cop had pulled up, and he'd found one of the sisters with my other buddy in the back of my mother's car, parked under some pine trees. This officer saw me. He asked if this was my car, and I told him it was my mother's. He ordered my buddy and the two sisters into the back of his squad car. Then he turned back to me.

"Put your hands on the hood of the squad car, kid."

This was my first interaction with a police officer, and I was nervous as hell. I did what I was told. The red-and-blues were flashing, and I could hear the waves crashing on the sand, nearby. I had the bag of weed in my jockeys and was doing everything I could to hide my nerves. The cop searched me, but by some stroke of luck or providence, he didn't find it.

"Remain here with your hands on the hood of the car," he told me. Then he leaned into the back of the squad car to talk to my three friends. When he came back, he put one hand on my shoulder and his other right down my pants. I couldn't believe it! My friends had ratted me out. I guess they were scared of going to jail. The cop took the four of us to the Hollywood police station. The two sisters' parents got there before mine did, and when they walked into that room, I felt so little. Just worthless. Their dad leaned into my face.

"We don't ever want you in our house again," he said. "We don't ever want you to call our house again. We don't want to see you walking anywhere near our house. You understand?"

Then in came my dad, with smoke coming out his ears. He didn't say a word, and I was afraid to open my mouth. On the car ride home, it was like I wasn't even there, like I had never even been born. Because I was fifteen, the police dropped any charges. So the next day, I went back to school.

It was September of my tenth-grade year. I had acquired a rusted orange Harley-Davidson 250 with cash I'd made selling herb, and now that I was fifteen, I could ride the motorcycle to school. Before I could even get the kickstand down in the parking lot that morning, a kid I barely knew came up to me. "Oh man, I heard what happened to you!" he said. "Can you still get some grass?" A couple other kids walked up, and one said, "Hey man, I hear you're the man! Can you get us some weed?"

Another and another. It was bizarre. A crowd formed around me. I was bombarded before I even got to my locker.

I got so unnerved, I jumped on my Harley 250 and left school before my first class. I walked right out the door and went home, and I decided I didn't want to go back. That night, my mother and father came home from work, and I told them I wasn't going back to school. My father screamed at me.

"You're not going to be some bum! Some damn hippy! You're going to get your high school diploma!"

He couldn't force me back to that school. So we came to an agreement: I promised to get my General Equivalency Diploma (GED) as fast as I could, while still working construction.

I wasn't comfortable being in high school with a reputation as a marijuana salesman, with strangers coming up to me in the hallways all day long. But I started to think: All these people—they just wanted weed! The students. The construction workers. And I knew how to get it. What if I chose my own clients and kept it all on the down low?

Even then, I knew that finding a niche and filling it is one of many paths to success. I was thinking: *Maybe I'm onto something.*

2

From Ounces to Pounds

South Florida, late 1960s, early 1970s

At fifteen, I was the youngest guy in the adult education program. One day, one of the students, an older guy, came up to me outside after class. We got to chatting, and I told him I had quit school and was working construction.

"Hey," he said, "do you smoke weed?"

"I sure as hell do," I said.

"Do you know where I can buy some?"

"Matter of fact, I can. You're talking to the right guy. How much you want?"

I started selling him four-finger lids, bags full of big sticky buds, at fifteen dollars apiece, and soon he brought me more customers, other students from adult education. Between my customers at the construction job and these adult students, my business was crackling. Very quickly, I went from buying ounces to getting a half a pound, then a pound, then two pounds. I could clear about $300 profit per pound. Basically, doubling my investment. A lot of the weed was coming from the same guy who'd come back from Vietnam a year earlier.

He introduced me to one of his friends, another source, so now I could get quantities from two people.

All over my neighborhood in Hollywood, I was making connections, going over to their houses, sitting on beanbags and toking weed out of homemade bamboo bongs, cranking Jimi Hendrix on the eight-track. I was a popular guy.

Around this time, I met two people who were to have a profound influence on my life. One was Ben Kramer, a figure destined to leave his mark on South Florida criminal history. We would see each other at parties or at a local park we called the Hollywood Circle. He came from a Jewish family, and his father owned a lighting store in town. I didn't know any Jewish people besides Ben. He was destined to become (to my mind, at least) the heir apparent of Jewish South Florida gangsters in the lineage of Meyer Lansky and Abe Bernstein—only more badass, if such a thing were possible. (I've even heard that Ben was distantly related to Lansky.)

Ben's parents let him smoke dope in the house, so I was always there. He had wild bushy long hair, and he would pull it back into a ponytail, like me. We were the same age, and he just liked to hang out. But our relationship became something more important in the summer of 1971.

With my weed profits, I bought a van and had it painted lime green. I laid shag carpet in the back, popped in an eight-track player, and hung posters. That summer, I filled it with friends and drove to a music festival called the Celebration of Life, in a field north of Baton Rouge in Louisiana. For ten days we partied in the heat, dropping so much LSD I don't think any of us bothered with food for days. There were Hells Angels and Dead Heads and Bible thumpers and a lineup of the hottest musical acts of the day—Ike and Tina Turner, Sly and the Family Stone, Eric Clapton, Hot Tuna. On the ride home, I saw a couple guys on the side of the road hitchhiking. I recognized one of them; it was Ben.

"Hey, I'm going to stop and pick these guys up," I yelled.

"No, don't do that!" people were yelling from the back of the van. "There's no room in here!"

"Make room," I said. "That's Ben Kramer."

I picked up Ben, and that's when we really bonded.

Ben had a vibe about him that made some people nervous. A few years later, when *Star Wars* came out, people started calling him Darth Vader, and that about summed him up. At the time, nobody ever thought Ben and I would amount to anything. We were going to prove them wrong.

One night around this time, I went to see Grand Funk Railroad with Ben. The show was at Pirate's World, an amusement park in Dania, a town south of Hollywood. The band was playing, and we were packed in there, shoulder to shoulder in front of the stage. I saw this girl dancing. I'd seen her before, riding her bicycle around. She had thick brown curly hair, an olive complexion, and a thin athletic body. I remember passing her a joint at the show. A few days later, I was standing in the kitchen when my mother passed me the telephone.

"This is Pam," she said. I don't even know how she got my number.

"How you doing?" I said. "It was great seeing you the other night."

"I wanted to call you so I could wish you a happy birthday."

"I'm so glad you called. But I hate to tell you, it's not my birthday. My birthday is in September."

She knew it wasn't my birthday. She wanted a reason to call me, so she made one up.

We talked for a while. She was living in Hollywood Hills, a nice neighborhood. We didn't have those big homes and manicured lawns where I lived. Not that her family was wealthy. Her dad was a butcher. But their home was nice. They had a pool. We started seeing each other almost daily. I was sixteen, and she was two years younger than me.

Some people say that when you meet the love of your life, you know it right at that moment. Like a lightning strike, or Cupid's arrow. That didn't happen with us. It was more natural, gradual. Pam was a lot of fun, and she made me feel good just being in her presence. But there was a moment early in our relationship when we learned that we were meant to be together through whatever storm was coming our way. It wasn't a happy moment, though. It was completely terrifying.

When I was seventeen, I moved out of my parents' place and rented my first house. It was on the county line road in an unincorporated part of Lake Forest. South of the house was all this undeveloped land—lots of trails and trees. There were melaleuca trees, oak trees, sand pines, royal poinciana trees. With my weed profits, I bought dirt bikes for me and my little brother Glen. We'd ride through miles of sandy trails and never see a house anywhere. Like me, Glen was into motorcycles, and we were having the time of our lives. Outside of Pam, Glen was the closest person to me. He was my little bro, and I loved him.

Things were happening. I finished my GED. I became a vegetarian. I bought fifty-pound bags of carrots, and I drank so much carrot juice Pam joked I was turning orange. I was developing my weed business, so now I was getting shipments of ten or twenty pounds at a time. If Pam had any idea of what I was doing, she never said anything. She certainly didn't mind that I always had plenty of cash on me.

This one night, Pam and I were lying on my waterbed. Candles burning. Grateful Dead playing. I was expecting somebody to come by the house to pick up some weed. When I heard a knock on the door, I got up and put some clothes on. "Hang on a second, just wait here," I said. "There's something I got to do. Stay in the bedroom."

When I answered the door, the guy I was expecting was standing on my doorstep. But there was another guy too, a guy I didn't recognize. I shook his hand and turned to the guy I knew.

"Who's this?" I asked.

"Oh, this is my friend," he said. "I'm not really the guy buying the weed. This is the guy that's buying the weed."

I had this gut instinct, a voice in my head that said, *Don't let this stranger in the house. Don't do it.* There's a lot of truth to be found in gut instinct. But this time, I didn't listen. I took them into a spare bedroom where I kept the weed and shut the door. Out of nowhere, this stranger pulls a sawed-off shotgun out of his pant leg. The other guy takes out a knife. I got this shotgun aimed right at my face, the barrel so close I could smell it. It smelled like death.

"Anybody else in this house?" the stranger barked.

"Just my girlfriend," I said. As soon as the words came out of my mouth, I knew I'd made a mistake. Pam was lying naked on a waterbed. One of the guys left the room, and that's when I got really scared. There was no telling what these guys were going to do. But in just a few seconds, he returned holding her by the arm. She'd heard some noise, so she'd gotten dressed. The look on her face was indescribable.

"What the fuck is this!?!" she screamed.

"Get on your knees!" the stranger shouted.

He pulled out duct tape and bound my ankles, my wrists, and my mouth. Then he did the same to Pam. These guys kept yelling, "Anybody else in this house? Anybody else in this house?" I shook my head. No, no, no. "You stay in this room," the stranger said. He pointed to the door with the barrel of the gun and said, "You open this door and I'll blow your fucking head off."

They left the room and shut the door behind them. I could hear them ransacking the place. I was trying to get the tape off my wrists, and I kept looking at Pam, communicating with my eyes: *Everything is going to be OK.*

A half hour went by, and finally it got quiet in the house. I got my hands loose and pulled the duct tape off me, then freed Pam. I got down as low as I could, and with my head on the floor, I reached up to open that door. I was sure a shotgun blast was about to take my head off. I turned the handle as slowly and quietly as I could, and when I opened the door, the house looked empty, which it was. These guys had stolen all my weed and taken off.

I ran to the phone, but they'd ripped the cord out of the wall. I left in a hurry and jumped in my Volkswagen Beetle, which I had just bought used. But it wouldn't start. They had ripped the distributor cap off the engine. So I ran to the nearest pay phone, which was at a 7-Eleven. When I called my weed source to tell him what had happened, I could hear him breathing heavily into the phone. He was pissed. He'd recently gotten out of prison, and I was concerned that I wasn't going to be able to pay the money I owed him. I knew how badly he needed it. I was worried that he would threaten me if I didn't get him his money.

But he surprised me. "Randy," he said, "that's part of the game. You lose a load, you write it off. It's part of doing business." I described the two guys who'd stolen the weed, and my source said, "I know who those guys are. I'll take care of it. I'll tell you what: You just get out of town. I don't care where you go. Just leave and don't come back for at least a month."

Pam didn't speak a word to me for the rest of that night. She got a ride home, and when she left, I wondered if I would ever see her again.

The next morning, I fixed my car, packed up my stuff, drove to my parents' house to pick up some things, and off I went, headed west in the Beetle. I hid a personal stash—a pound of good weed—in the air-conditioning vents in case I got pulled over, and what I couldn't fit, I left for my little brother Glen to smoke. I didn't even know where I was going. The whole time I was thinking about Pam, how bad I felt that I'd gotten her mixed up in this mess. The farther I drove from South Florida, the more I missed her. Eventually, I ended up in Aspen, Colorado.

I rented a cheap apartment and called Pam. I asked her if she would come visit me. I was surprised and elated when she agreed. I'll never forget the way she looked when I picked her up at the airport, her skin golden from the sun and beautiful brown curls hanging over her eyes. She was excited to see me, and said she felt like she was on a thrilling adventure. She'd never been on an airplane before, and neither had I. Little did we know this was the beginning of a lifetime of adventures together.

She could only stay a week, she told me, because she had to go back to school. She was going into the eleventh grade. We spent the whole week hiking in those mesmerizing mountains. We would make love in the woods, by these beautiful rambling streams, and despite all the chaos of the last month, it felt right and good.

When she left, I stayed in Colorado for another couple months. That's when I started going to an ashram. There was a guru who taught meditation there. I started attending *satsangs*, open dialogues about spirituality. This wasn't about smoking weed. It was about getting high a whole different way.

That involvement put me on a new path. I would practice meditation for an hour every morning and an hour at night. There were times when I found myself looking down on my own body, detached from it, exploring the object of me and understanding how that was different from the spirit within me. I came to learn that we're all just particles of matter, and we're all created by the same energy; it is eternal, the only thing that never changes.

Meditation helped me handle the trauma of what had happened back in Florida. One day, it would help me stay calm driving over 200 mph with a world of chaos outside my window.

When I returned to Florida, I moved back into my parents' home and started working construction again. I wasn't selling weed. I spent all my time at a local ashram. I was living a clean, spiritual life, focusing on my higher power. But tragedy was about to change my trajectory again.

On the morning of March 3, 1974, I woke up and walked outside. It was a beautiful day—the air balmy, the sky that peculiar shade of crystal Florida blue. I got an idea to go on a motorcycle ride. Glen was working construction with me, and he'd put all his money into his 750cc Honda. He loved that motorcycle. That morning, I asked him if I could take it out for a ride. He said sure, so off I went. I rode all along the State Road A1A, along the coast, stopping to look at the beaches and the crashing waves. When I got home, I told Glen, "Man, it's a great day for a ride."

"Yeah," he said. "I'm going to go for a cruise myself."

"Enjoy the ride," I said.

Those were the last words I ever said to him. He got on his Honda and rode off.

I had a new dog that I named Kilo. I was driving an El Camino now, and I had to take Kilo to dog obedience school that morning. So I scooped him up, put him in the back of the El Camino, and left the house maybe twenty minutes after Glen did. I drove down Hallandale Beach Boulevard with Kilo in the back, and at an intersection, I saw that a cop car had blocked off a section of the road and nearby were more police cars and an ambulance. I thought, *Man, that looks like a serious accident.* When I got to the obedience school, I pulled into the parking lot, and this friend of Glen's pulled up beside me. He jumped out of his car, all agitated, and he said, "Man! Glen's been in an accident!"

"What!?"

That's when I realized that the ambulance I had seen was for my little brother.

I went straight to the only hospital in the area, Memorial Hospital, and I asked the nurse at the desk if Glen Lanier was in the emergency room. Apparently, he had no identification on him when they'd brought him in, so I had to explain to the doctors and nurses who he was. I called my parents, and I called Pam. They all came immediately.

So there we were, sitting in the hospital waiting room. Me, my mother, my father, Pam, and my youngest brother, Bobby. When a doctor finally came out, he said that the accident was so bad Glen's helmet had gotten knocked off his head. His head trauma was so severe, machines were keeping him alive.

"Your son is never going to wake up," the doctor told my parents. "I am sorry."

When the doctor asked if the hospital team could disconnect Glen from the machines and donate his organs, my mother fell to pieces. We all went into his hospital room to say good-bye. He had tubes sticking out of him. It was devastating to see him like that. My brother, my best friend. I couldn't get my head around the idea that somebody you loved so much could be gone in an instant, with no warning.

In the church on the day of his funeral, the place was too small for all Glen's friends. He was just sixteen, but he was a big guy, physically and spiritually. He had this energy that everyone wanted to be around. He was an amazing human being. I've never stopped missing him.

After Glen's death, everything changed. I stopped going to the ashram. I started eating meat again for the first time in two years. And I went back to selling weed. It happened so fast; I was on autopilot.

Before I knew it, I had cash stashed all over my parents' house. The beanbag in my room was stuffed with cash. I had so much cash I had to get a place of my own just to have somewhere to put it all. So I rented a house in Hallandale Beach and moved out of my parents' home again. The day Pam graduated high school, she came to my house and never went back home. I was still a teenager, and I had enough cash to buy anything I wanted. And I did what any guy in South Florida does with money: I bought a boat.

Buying my first boat was a pivotal moment. It was a seventeen-foot Checkmate ski boat, and I started spending all my days on it. I towed the boat behind my El Camino to a different launch spot every day, and we'd waterski for hours. There are miles of saltwater canals laid out like a circulatory system throughout Broward, Palm Beach, and Miami-Dade counties. Way back in the beginning of the century, developers had dug out all these canals for flood protection and for boat commerce. We would ski through the canals along the

Intracoastal Waterway around Fort Lauderdale and through the neighboring towns.

Some sections cut through residential neighborhoods with homes, docks, and boats. Other sections were entirely undeveloped, lined with mangrove forests filled with wild birds, the water boiling with jumping fish. There were industrial sections with work boats and cranes and factories. All of it spilled into the bay at Port Everglades, where years later the giant cruise ships and oil tankers came into the east coast of South Florida.

I learned the ins and outs of every section of canal until I could maneuver the boat anywhere I wanted to go, even at night with no lights. At one point, I was on a waterski and I had a thought: These canals would make a great place to bring in loads of grass and to off-load them. It occurred to me that if someone wanted to move weed from one place to another or to bring it in from a source far off somewhere and land it in South Florida, these canals were the place to do it.

The Florida canals were about to become the launching point for an international smuggling ring. It was time to scale up.

3

Launching the Operation

South Florida, Bahamas, 1970s

*I*n the early 1970s, Pam and I moved to North Miami to a house that was engulfed in bushes and flowers—so much tropical vegetation you couldn't even see the house itself. We had a roommate named Billy who went to Dade College and distributed weed for me on the campus.

Back then, Miami was different—not nearly as built up as it is today. Still, it was a party city, and it came alive at night. Prostitutes appeared in packs under streetlights while Lincolns and Cadillacs crisscrossed the intersections. Tourists flooded the Coconut Grove neighborhood to go to the Mayflower Club. If you wanted ritzy, you dined out at The Forge or Joe's Stone Crab. If you wanted seedy, you hit Tommy's Deck Bar, where the cops came 168 times in one year.

For me, the beating heart of the city was Thunder Boat Alley. To get there, you drove down this unassuming, industrial road toward the ocean—Northeast 188th Street in North Miami. When you neared the water, a row of boat factories lined both sides of the road, each with its own marina. There'd be forklifts buzzing around. Molds for hand-laid fiberglass boats were everywhere. You could smell the resin and fiberglass. One after another, you passed the Magnum boat factory, then Formula, then Donzi. And, at last, the crème de la crème: Cigarette, the fastest offshore boat in the world.

Most of these companies were the brainchild of Don Aronow, the king of Thunder Boat Alley and a legend in offshore boat racing. Aronow was Hollywood handsome and a brilliant guy—someone I deeply admired. There was an aura of greatness about him, and I loved that he'd devoted his life to the ocean and to speed.

One day in the early 1970s, I walked into the Magnum showroom on Thunder Boat Alley with a friend named Jeff. I was flush with cash as usual. We'd seen on the showroom floor a sleek twenty-seven-foot Magnum with a white deck and a red hull, its two Chevrolet 350s hidden under the engine compartment hatches. The boat looked like a bullet ready to fire. It had two seats up front—for the driver and navigator— with red and white stripes, and the seats sat on chrome shock absorbers that softened the waves out on the ocean. The back seats had red and white stripes too. There was a cuddy cabin with a V-shaped berth big enough for two people to sleep. I wanted that boat as much as anything I'd ever wanted anything in my life.

I asked the salesman, "Hey, how much for this Magnum Sport?"

"$20,000."

"I'll give you $18,000 cash, right now."

"Sold!"

We spent some time doing paperwork. "Get it ready and put it in the water," I told the salesman. "We'll be back in a couple of hours."

Jeff and I went to lunch, and when we came back, the Magnum was tied up at a dock, looking even better on water than it did on dry land. We jumped in, fired up those Chevrolet engines, and headed out of Thunder Boat Alley to Haulover Inlet, a man-made channel with a bridge over it, connecting Biscayne Bay to the Atlantic. Then, from there, out into the wide blue ocean.

There's no way to overstate the feeling of liberation and excitement, being nineteen in my own kick-ass boat with all that horsepower. We were riding the waves about a half mile from shore. The seas were three and a half to five feet. I was getting the hang of timing the throttle to accelerate up the crest of a wave and laying off the throttle at that split second when the whole twenty-seven-footer lifted off the water—becoming airborne—before crashing back down.

I'd never driven a boat like this before. This was freedom. This was balls-out fun. This was my ticket to anywhere.

Jeff screamed over the engines, "Lemme try it!" So I let him. Big mistake. Within a minute, Jeff hit a wave sideways with the throttle pinned and the boat did a 180-degree jolt. It happened so fast, my arm crashed right through the plexiglass windshield, and I got hurled into the sea.

When I came to the surface and looked up, I saw my boat turning in an arc and coming right for me, engines roaring, with no sign of anyone on board. I yelled "holy fuck!" so loud, they probably heard me in Manhattan. I dove underwater to try to escape the hull of the boat and its deadly propellers, and when I came up, the boat was headed straight for the shoreline and utter disaster. I kept treading water and thinking: *Damn! Jeff, where are you!?* I was hoping he didn't get thrown out of the boat like I did. Then I saw him get to his feet and grab for the throttle and the wheel.

I looked at my arm. Blood everywhere, and I was floating in the water like a piece of shark bait. It was a calamity. I made it back into the boat, and we limped to the dock with a full crack down the port side, a smashed windshield pane, and blood all over the place. Jeff was lying on the back seat moaning, bleeding from both nostrils. The salesman at Magnum couldn't believe his eyes.

He saw us and said, "What! The! Fuck?!"

I owned the boat all of one hour. Meanwhile, Jeff was badly hurt. I had to get him to the hospital because his back was in so much pain he couldn't stand up.

All the way to the hospital, I prayed for Jeff to be OK. But I couldn't get my mind off that boat. I had big plans. I was going to install better offshore bolster seats, a race-geared steering unit, flaps on the transom to handle the big seas, and of course, I needed the hull crack fixed. I was going to turn that twenty-seven-foot Magnum into an open-sea hot rod, the fastest Magnum of Thunder Boat Alley.

A few months later, the Magnum was fully refitted, ready for prime time. I was on board, kicking back one day at the Miami marina where I kept the boat, cold Heineken in my hand. A buddy came up to me asking if he could rent it. He had a friend coming in with a load of weed on a big mother ship, and he needed some smaller boats to load up the weed from the mother ship out on the ocean at night and then bring it into the South Florida canals.

"Not interested in renting it out," I said. "But I'll tell you what. *I* will run a load in."

"I don't know, Randy." His hesitation made sense; there'd be a lot riding on this, and if I screwed up, it'd all come back to him. But I knew my boat, and I knew the canals. I knew I could handle it.

"Trust me. Ayyyight?"

We negotiated a deal: I'd get 30 percent of the weed that I smuggled in. I'd get more than that, though, because I was going to sell the weed for him too. But first I had to come up with a game plan. How was I going to pull this off? Where was I going to stash the product when I got it on land? Selling it was the easy part; bringing it in required logistical planning. Once I got the loaded boat into the canals, I knew I'd be fine. But out on the open ocean, there was always a chance of getting pulled over and boarded by the US Coast Guard.

My old roommate Billy had moved out of the house where I was living with Pam and into a place in a suburban neighborhood that backed up to the Dania Cutoff Canal, one of the larger canals moving east and west through mainland Florida. I'd waterskied on this canal a thousand times. I offered Billy ten pounds of weed if I could use his house, and he agreed. The plan was for me to arrive at his dock in the middle of the night so his neighbors wouldn't see, and we'd unload into his home. Before sunrise, I'd use my lime-green van to move the weed out of there and sell it to my clientele.

At nineteen, I'd already been selling weed for four years. But this was my first smuggling score, a big step up. I needed help, and I recruited two friends to go on the boat with me as crew. One was Ben Kramer. The other was a guy we called Slick. I'd known Slick for four years, and I trusted him implicitly. He was dark haired, a little pudgy, and four years older than me. When Slick was in high school, both of his parents died, and he had come to live with my family for a while. We had a strong bond.

Slick was useful too—a genius with mechanical things, smart with boat navigation. And as it would turn out, he'd be one of my main boat captains until the very end.

The day of the exchange, while the sun was still out, Slick, Ben, and I drove the Magnum to Bimini, an island of the Bahamas. We had an Igloo cooler full of beer and not much else. It's a fifty-mile run to Bimini from Miami, and I'd driven it before. I had a compass right on the instrument panel, and if you come out of Port Everglades and set your compass to 110 degrees east, your ass is headed straight for Bimini. If you miss it, you won't miss it by far. Bimini had been an outlaw's paradise going way back. It was a favorite supply point for rumrunners during Prohibition, and Ernest Hemingway spent a good deal of time there back in the day. It had one marina, and that became our staging point.

After we topped off with gas at the marina, we waited for the sun to set. When it was nearing dark, we headed out to sea. We had coordinates where we expected to meet the mother ship. Sure enough, just before midnight, I saw a light on the horizon. There was nothing else out there but big ships moving over the shipping lanes. I reached out over marine radio with the code names we'd set up.

"Saddle calling the Sea Witch. Saddle calling the Sea Witch." I tried it again and again, hearing nothing but the water lapping at our boat hull. Then, finally, I got a response back: "This is Sea Witch. Sea Witch coming at you." Bingo! We'd made contact.

We tied our two boats together and went to work. The excitement I felt, the dopamine flooding my brain as we loaded bale after bale of weed, was beyond anything I'd felt before. I felt exhilarated, empowered, and I felt this bond between me and my partners, Ben and Slick. It felt like we were on fire, like nothing could stop us.

Within a short time, we'd loaded 750 pounds of weed into my Magnum under the moonlight. The operation required muscle and good sea legs. The bales weighed about 50 pounds each; they were burlap sacks lined with paper on the inside, about forty inches high, twenty-six inches wide, and about a foot thick. Each bale gave off a sweet, earthy perfume.

Once we had all 750 pounds stowed in the Magnum's cuddy cabin, we cruised through the night on flat seas all fifty miles back to Florida and through Port Everglades inlet. From there, we headed south and motored about a half mile, making a right into the quiet Dania Cutoff Canal. We reached my buddy's house, unloaded the weed, and moved it all out before sunrise.

It was easy, fun even. Nothing to it.

Seeing that much weed in one place gave me the same sensation I felt when I was a kid and I got ahold of *Playboy* magazine for the first time. What was even better? Holding twenty grand cash in my hand.

Now we had a system. Another opportunity came, then another. I bought a second boat—a thirty-six-foot Cigarette, the fastest brand of boat in the world. Then I bought a third—a thirty-eight-foot Sea Ray. Now we had a whole fleet. It was in my nature to be an empire builder, even though I was still a teenager. I liked fast cars, fast boats. Those things cost money.

I also wanted to help my family. My mom, my dad, my brothers, my sister—here was an opportunity to bring us all up in the world. We weren't the most financially secure family, and there was always this air of tragedy about us because of Glen's death. To be able to hand some cash over and make my family members smile? That felt good!

It sounds exotic, but building a smuggling operation wasn't all that different from building any company. You needed the right people with the right talents. You needed the right equipment. You needed leadership skills, you needed to be a risk-taker, and you needed a dash of luck. Only we weren't manufacturing wigs or fixing cars. We were running weed into South Florida. And from what I'd seen so far, I was pretty good at it. Our loads got bigger and bigger. So did the payouts. The money was insane. But what felt insane one day felt normal the next. There's always more to chase, more to achieve. A higher high. A bigger rush.

It wasn't always as easy as it was on our first score. You had to be on your toes in this business. Ready to improvise. Sometimes, things could go horrendously wrong.

On one run—I was twenty at the time—I went out to Bimini to fuel up with the two guys I knew I could count on, Ben and Slick. I was nervous because a storm was coming in. When we left Bimini that night to meet the mother ship, the sun was just starting to set. On one side of the boat was clear blue skies, but the other was a threatening dark gray.

"Look at that," I said to Slick.

"I see it," he said.

We didn't have foul-weather gear. We were wearing Top-Siders and shorts with T-shirts. It didn't matter the circumstances. It's like show business. No matter what, you had to go out and perform. People were counting on you.

Out on the water, the seas started getting choppy, especially when we hit the Gulf Stream. We met the mother ship on the Bahama Flats, an area of shallow water just past the Gulf Stream. By this time, the swells were huge, even in the shallows. We loaded two thousand pounds onto our boat. This was my biggest score yet, but a fraction of what we'd be doing in just a year's time. It was hard going, moving all those bales on rough seas. A tropical depression was brewing right above us. The salty air seemed electrically charged. You could smell the energy.

We set a course for Port Everglades, but now we were cresting twenty-five-foot waves. We were getting battered.

The wind gusts came so strong and loud, it felt like I was standing inside a jet engine. Seawater was coming over the bow and both sides of the vessel, soaking us. I worried that water would get in the engine compartment, at which point we would be entirely fucked. It was pitch black, and suddenly the sky opened up. It started raining so hard, I couldn't hear the sound of my own voice. We tried to cross the Gulf Stream, but the boat couldn't handle the seas. Waves crashed over our starboard side. If we continued on our course, we weren't going to make it. I had to make the call: we had to turn around.

Slick grabbed me and pulled my face close to his so I could hear him over the wind. "Hey man," he shouted. "We could fucking die out here! We need to call for help!"

"We got two thousand pounds of weed on this fucking boat, ayyyight?" I screamed back. "There's no calling for help. We're going to make it!"

Ben knew of an abandoned lighthouse on a coral outcropping called Great Isaac Lighthouse, eighteen miles north of Bimini. We set a course in that direction, working the throttle softly but firmly, trying not to get pitched into the trough of a monster wave. The boat's cabin was loaded with bales of weed all the way to the ceiling, so while the product would stay dry, we had no shelter. The rain was coming in sheets, and we were cold, wet, and miserable.

We found the Great Isaac Lighthouse and anchored right off the abandoned island, on the leeward side. We had no food or water, and we waited all night in pounding rain and gusting winds, using whatever we could to collect drinking water. I was worried the anchor wouldn't hold, and if it let go, we'd be totally at the mercy of a merciless sea. Those were some of the longest hours of my life.

In the morning, it was still storming, and I heard the groaning engines of an airplane. Sure enough, a Coast Guard patrol plane flew over at a suspiciously low altitude.

"Shit!" I yelled. "They know we're here!"

We waited it out. After an hour, a helicopter arrived and hovered right over us. There was nothing else around except that rusted, abandoned lighthouse on the coral outcropping. I could see that inside the helicopter's cockpit the pilot was studying our vessel and talking into a radio microphone. He must have noticed our boat was sitting low in the water, and he had to be wondering why we weren't taking shelter inside the boat's cabin. When that chopper left, I figured the pilot had called all his pals. The hunters were coming for us. This was the first time in my life I felt like the law was closing in on me. It wouldn't be the last.

"Let's go!" I shouted. "Pull anchor! We gotta get the fuck out of here!"

Bimini was eighteen miles away from the lighthouse, pretty much straight south. The seas were coming in from the northeast, so we were moving in the direction of the waves. We had to climb up these twenty-five-foot waves and dive down the other side, with all the weight in the bow due to the weed. Every time we crested a wave and came crashing down, I felt like we were motoring straight into hell. It was the middle of the day now, and it took us hours to get to Bimini. But we made it. When we tied up at a dock, we were all famished.

"Wait here," I told the crew. "I'm going to get us something to eat."

I walked through the pouring rain to this rusted shack in front of a big game fishing club and got us a bunch of conch fritters and Cokes. I was walking back to the boat when that same helicopter appeared again, hovering over us low enough now that the rotor blades made ripples in the bay. Nothing I could do, so I stood there like an idiot in the rain, waving to the guy. He stared at me through sunglasses, helmet on, talking into his radio. I was thinking that the Bahamian police were going to show up at any moment, so I calmly had the crew take the lines off the pilings.

We had to move again. We found an old rickety dock by a patch of thick pine trees at another part of the island. Luckily, the chopper didn't follow us. We waited. It was quiet. Too quiet. The rain finally started to ebb. The sun set, bringing on the darkness and the mosquito swarms. Until you see mosquitoes in the Bahamas, you don't know how big mosquitos can get. These motherfuckers are as big as cats. We were drenched and shivering in the cold, getting eaten alive.

I was worried that in the morning Bahamian Customs officials would corner us and ask to search the vessel. So we walked the bales down the dock and hid them in the woods, tiptoeing under the cover of darkness. All two thousand pounds! My guys were not happy.

To top it all off, now I was worried about our stash house. Even if we were able to get the weed to the stash house on the Dania Cutoff Canal, we would be days late. The owner of the house had sent his wife out of town to her mother's place, and the wife had no idea of our plans. With our delay, she was probably back in the house now, and that was going to be a problem.

I left Ben and Slick and got a Chalk's flight on a twin-engine seaplane out of Bimini first thing in the morning. Chalk's was a tiny airline that flew tourists from Miami to the Bahamas and back every day. The airport consisted of a boat ramp, a dock, and a small hangar, right on the edge of the water in Bimini's only harbor. When we took off, I looked out the starboard side window for any island police. I didn't see any.

The Chalk's flight took only twenty-five minutes, though it felt like longer. I went to my buddy's house on the canal where we were supposed to unload and explained that he had to tell his wife to leave again. Which she did. I was supposed to meet my crew that night at the opening of the Dania Cutoff Canal. I told them to look out for a dude fishing there in the darkness in a dinghy, under the first bridge after the canal's opening. The first night I went out, they didn't show up, but sure enough, on the second night, I was out there fishing under the bridge, and I could hear those engines from a mile away.

I climbed aboard and met my crew. "The fish are biting tonight," I said, trying to be funny.

"Where's this fucking house?" Ben snapped.

"Good to see you guys too," I said. "How you doing, Slick?"

"Hmm," he answered. "Lemme think about that. I'm fucking tired. I'm cold. I'm wet. I'm hungry. I'm fucking angry, Randy."

"Bro, we're almost home."

We headed west down the canal. We were almost to the stash house, motoring quietly in darkness past houses on both sides with their lights out, looking for the small canal we were supposed to turn into. Suddenly, we ran aground. "What the fuck is this?" I said. I realized that the storm surge had accumulated sand in a place I wasn't expecting to find it. We'd hit a sandbar.

The three of us jumped into the water, and now we were desperately trying to push a thirty-two-foot boat loaded with two thousand pounds of marijuana off a sandbar. We tried shaking the bow while one of us gunned the engines. A house light on the canal popped on, and I realized that if someone called the cops, that'd be it: game over. We were helpless. So we shut the engines off. We ended up waiting all night into the morning for the tide to come in and lift the boat off the sand.

That whole operation tested the limits of my patience and stamina. It had been a headache alright—a very, very profitable headache. But we'd survived. We were in business, and business was good.

4

Muscle Billy

February 1976

I needed my own stash house, somewhere rural to store weed and cash. I had a close friend named Charles Podesta, and one day I met up with him at a Fort Lauderdale diner. "Charles," I said, "I could use your help. I need to rent this house I found." Of course, I couldn't put it in my own name. "Would you go rent it for me?" I asked him.

"Sure, Randy. No problem."

Charles came from an Italian family, and he worked in the family business in high-end food brokerage. He was always dressed nicely, and he carried himself with an elegance that was totally disarming. He was a perfect front: he knew exactly what we were doing, and he was on board with it. He rented the house, which was set back on eight acres at the end of a dirt road, and he lived there with his girlfriend so nothing would look suspicious when cars were coming and going. I bought some seven-foot-tall gun safes, and we started using those to store money. We stored the weed in bedrooms, stacking bales from floor to ceiling.

The system worked like this: I'd bring in a load aboard one of my boats, unload it at a house on one of the canals, and take it to the stash house in one of my vehicles. I also took in loads from other guys, which I would then distribute for them. They would instruct me that they were leaving a van in a parking lot at a Kmart shopping center or a Denny's restaurant, and they'd leave the key on the right rear wheel. I'd show up with my driver, pick up the van, and bring everything back to the stash house.

It was important to keep everything compartmentalized, with as little human contact as possible. All communications occurred through beepers and pay phones. I never met or was even seen by anybody I did not personally know. The stash house had a two-car garage, so we could do all the loading and unloading out of sight. As soon as I could, I got ahold of a second stash house, this one for money, because I never wanted the weed and the cash in the same place.

The operation kept growing. I had one childhood friend move to New York City, and he became a distributor for me there. Another friend moved to Michigan. Another, New Orleans. The distributors would come down to the stash houses in all kinds of camouflage vehicles. One guy had a welding truck with secret compartments welded into the chassis. Another used vans that he'd ingeniously fill with two-by-fours, only the two-by-fours were only six inches long, so when you opened the van's back doors, you'd see the ends of two-by-fours stacked floor to ceiling, and it looked like the van was packed to the gills with wood. But in fact, the van could carry over a thousand pounds of grass behind those six-inch two-by-fours.

The distributors were the ones who got the weed onto the street through their networks of dealers, in New York, in Michigan, in Louisiana, in Pennsylvania. Then, a little later, in Kentucky and Georgia. For me, a pound would cost about $150 (my cut per pound was roughly $25 to $50). On the street, that same pound could bring in $250. So every person involved—down to the dime bag salesman—was making good money.

People trusted me, so I often got my weed up front. Other times I'd pay a downstroke—some money up front. I'd sell the weed to the distributors, collect the cash, and pay the bill, holding onto my cut. One day, the stash house would be full of weed. The next, empty. Charles Podesta was in charge of the accounting. He was good at it.

It all made good business sense. If you can consistently produce a product that's reasonably priced, if you're reliable and trustworthy, if there's no drama—then your business grows. But I was also in the right place at the right time. In the mid-1970s, weed was going from a counterculture thing to the mainstream. *High Times* magazine ran photos of buds like *Playboy*-style centerfolds. The Grateful Dead spread the gospel in never-ending tours across the nation. The first Cheech and Chong records were selling as fast as they could be stamped. Weed was becoming a pop culture sensation, and the nationwide demand was insatiable.

I married the love of my life on Valentine's Day, 1976. It was one of the proudest moments of my life, but also a time when, looking back, I should've seen how fucked up my priorities were becoming. By this time, Pam was fully aware of my line of business. But I don't think she understood the degree to which I was *all in* and the speed at which my operation was growing.

Five days before the wedding, a friend called and asked if I wanted to take 350 pounds off him. It was a typical piece of business, and I was up for it—not just because he was a stand-up guy but because he had the right connections. I knew it was going to be good weed. I thought I could do the deal, flip the product fast, and go off on my honeymoon with an extra fifteen grand in my pocket. I met up with my buddy, and together, we went out to the source's house in my El Camino. That's when I met Muscle Billy.

Muscle Billy lived in Davie, just north of Miami, in a big ranch house set on a bunch of acres. There wasn't much in Davie at the time except ranches, cow pastures, and orange groves. I pulled up at his house, which was set at the end of a dirt road behind wooden farm fences, with pit bulls running all around. A guy came out to open the gate. As I drove through, I took a look at him. He had scars across his face like he'd gotten in a fight with a blender. Not a good-looking guy. He told me to pull the El Camino around back of the house so we could load. Behind the house sat a Formula 40 Performance cruising boat on a trailer. Then I saw Muscle Billy for the first time, walking out of the house.

"Hey," he said, "I'm Bill."

"Yeah, I know. Randy."

We shook hands, and when I say his hand was like a vise, I mean that literally.

There was a reason people called him Muscle Billy. He was a big dude, in every possible way. He was well known locally as a bodybuilder and an offshore powerboat racer, a legitimate sport that was taking off big-time in South Florida at that time. His race boat was a sleek black forty-foot Cigarette called *Longshot*. Even if you didn't know Muscle Billy, if you lived in South Florida, you knew who he was. What you might not have known was that Billy was a smuggler.

We walked into the house, and I took a look at the weed. Some bales were stacked on his kitchen floor, and one was busted open. The stuff was fresh and sticky, just like I thought it would be. Around this time, the brown, dried-out product that was coming in from Mexico—full of stems and seeds— was getting replaced by higher-quality cannabis out of Colombia. It was beautiful—big, round, tight red nuggets with red-orange threads woven through and some crystals around the outside that made it glow in the light from a nearby lamp. Looking at this stuff, I didn't know whether I wanted to smoke it or make love to it.

I weighed out 350 pounds on an industrial scale in Billy's kitchen. His wife was there, and together they looked like Brutus and Olive Oil from the *Popeye* cartoons—he was massive, she was tiny. The thought of a physical relationship between these two humans put a smile on my face. Just as I was finishing weighing the last bale, someone came rushing into the room. I looked over; it was the guy who had opened the gate for me, scarface. I realized I knew who this guy was. People called him Jake the Snake, and I'd heard nothing good about him.

"Hey, the cops are out front!" he shouted.

I hustled over and looked out the front window. There was a sheriff's car at the gate.

"Let's get the fuck out of here!" Billy said.

We all ran out the back door into the melaleuca trees behind his house. We stayed crouched in the woods for about fifteen minutes. Eventually, Muscle Billy went out front and came back. He told us the cop was gone and that he was probably just turning around because the house was at the end of a dirt road.

I loaded up the El Camino and took off.

There was a problem, though. When I got to the stash house and unloaded in the garage, I was one eighty-pound bale short. Something had gotten messed up due to the frenzy over that cop car. This was a serious problem, because that eighty pounds was going to cut deep into my profits.

Any business phone calls I had to make, I made from pay phones. So I drove to the nearest pay phone I could find and called my connection, the middle man who'd introduced me to Muscle Billy. I explained the situation.

"Look," he said, "these guys are gangsters. You're shit out of luck. You bought it, you weighed it, you paid for it. You got to eat it."

I answered, "I ain't eating shit. I am getting my weed."

Now I was in a dilemma. I didn't want to lose my money, and I didn't want to be disrespected. Still, I was five days away from my wedding. We had a reception booked, flights to Hawaii for the honeymoon, hotels booked on all the islands. This was no time to get caught up in anything nasty. But I was bent out of shape, and I wouldn't let it go. I was on autopilot. I had a nine-millimeter Glock semiautomatic, which I had fired a few times for fun, but I'd never brought it to any business meeting, let alone used it for real. I put fourteen shots in the clip and one in the chamber. Then I drove out to Muscle Billy's house.

When I arrived, Billy and Jake the Snake were leaving and locking the gate to the driveway behind them. I was driving a beige 1974 Mercedes 450 SL that night, another one of my cars, and I had the gun on the driver's seat. Billy got out of his car, came over, and when he looked through the window, he saw the gun lying on the passenger seat. The look on his face changed instantly.

"What the fuck is this about?" he said.

Still sitting behind the wheel, I explained the situation. He said he didn't know anything about it. "You weighed it!" he said. "This is *your* problem." He said he'd go back in the house and see if there were any bales of weed, as a courtesy to me. Jake the Snake followed him in. When they came out again, I knew they were armed. They'd gone into the house not to look for cannabis but to get a weapon. Muscle Billy said, "There's no bale of weed in that house. I can't motherfucking help you. Do you want to take this any further?"

I looked into Muscle Billy's eyes and glanced over at Jake the Snake. There was no bluffing with these guys. I drove off, and while I headed back toward Miami, I decided to call Ben Kramer. Ben had connections that I didn't have. So I pulled over and found a pay phone. Ben listened. He said, "Let me make some calls, see what I can find out."

That night, I stood outside by a pay phone anxiously waiting for it to ring. I tried calling Ben again, but he didn't pick
up. It seemed like hours had passed, but when I checked my
watch, it was only thirty minutes. I was pissed off. I was nervous. I didn't want any trouble, but I was ready for anything.

Finally, the pay phone rang. Ben told me he'd set up a
meeting for the next night at Far Away Joe's, an Italian restaurant and bar in Hallandale. This place was known to be mob
owned. Ben said I was going to meet a guy called Skinny
Louie. I knew Skinny Louie was connected to an organized
crime family.

When I showed up the next night at Far Away Joe's, Ben
and his connection were waiting for me. Skinny Louie was
very tall and very skinny, with a full head of black hair. He had
a brother with him who looked the opposite—overweight, not
so tall, and balding. This was my first experience with anyone
mob connected, and I knew that when you're dealing with
men like these, you have to be prepared for whatever comes
next. When the mob gets involved, people can get hurt. People can get killed. I had to show no fear, no second-guessing—
none of what I was really feeling.

In the movie *Goodfellas*, the character Henry Hill defines
the mafia as "a police force for wise guys," for people who
need protection but can't go to the police. That was me, in
a nutshell. I explained my dilemma and Skinny Louie said,
"I know Muscle Billy. I'll set up a sit-down."

The next day, Skinny Louie and I drove out to Muscle Billy's
house. Only now, Billy was a different man. Couldn't have

been nicer. We were sitting in the house, getting served drinks by Mrs. Muscle Billy.

"Listen, Billy, this is my friend Randy," Louie said. He stared into Billy's eyes without blinking. "If he tells you he's missing a bale, he's missing a bale. We want peace but we also want us all to do the right thing. If my family has to come up and get involved, it's not going to go well for you."

Muscle Billy got up, walked out of the room, and came back with an eighty-pound bale of weed. When I picked it up, something felt off. It was damp. But I didn't think about that at the time. I was just grateful, and I wanted to get the fuck out of there as fast as possible.

When I got it home, however, I realized the weed was all wet. I figured that it'd been dropped in the ocean during a smuggling operation. I had to get this weed dried out before I went on any honeymoon or else it would mold, and I would have to eat the money after all. So I spread paper towels across my pool table and dumped it all out. Pam saw what I was doing and screamed at me.

"Randy! What are you doing? My bridesmaids are coming over to the house right now!"

"No bridesmaids are coming into this house," I told her. "And unfortunately, another thing. We are not going on any honeymoon until I get this weed dry and out the door."

We ended up having a beautiful wedding. Although I postponed our honeymoon a few days, we made it to Hawaii. Pam was pissed, but she took it in stride. I spent the entire fifteen grand from the Muscle Billy score on champagne and room service. That was the beginning of our married life. It was only going to get crazier.

5

Becoming a Race Car Driver

South Florida, late 1970s

One day in 1977, I was at the Miami International Auto Show perusing the latest machinery when I saw a booth for the Sports Car Club of America. The SCCA is one of the main sanctioning bodies for amateur club racing. I took home some literature—"Join Now!"—and left it on my kitchen table. For the next few days, every time I came home, those brochures were staring at me. Finally, I called the 800 number. I needed to take a classroom test and a road test, I was told. I'd need to find myself a car I could take onto a racetrack and have it tech inspected. Then I could get my competition license and compete in club racing.

Sports car racing is the most popular and accessible form of motor sport seen around the world. Other types include stock car racing (like NASCAR), various types of motorcycle racing, and open-wheel racing (which includes IndyCar and Formula 1). Stock car racing on oval speedways is a purely American phenomenon, meant to pit real American customer (stock) cars against each other (although the cars have evolved over the years in NASCAR and aren't really stock anymore at all). Sports car racing is a far more international game, held on twisty and hilly circuits, using sports cars built in the United States, Europe, and Japan.

I was twenty-three, and I'd been dreaming of motor racing ever since I heard the Indy 500 on that tinny AM radio all those years ago. It's a sport so remote for most people, simply because of the cost. I never dreamed I'd actually be able to do it. But now, I had cash coming out of my nostrils.

I started scouring the classifieds looking for the right vehicle. I had a buddy named Joe who was the best mechanic I knew, so when I found a 1957 Porsche 356 Speedster in Tennessee, Joe was nice enough to go inspect the convertible and then trailer it back to Florida for me. I paid $7,000 for it. I also acquired a Chevy Silverado dually pickup (two wheels on each side in the back), and I was going to use that to tow the 1957 Porsche on a trailer to races.

When I got the car back to my house, I circled it and literally kicked the tires. It was in rough shape. It still had its original drum brakes from 1957. Someone had reworked the wiring with lamp cord. The floorboards were rusted out so you could sit in the driver's seat and touch the pavement with your feet like Fred Flintstone.

Time to roll up the sleeves.

I was going to spare no expense to turn this busted old Porsche into a kick-ass race car. And money wasn't an issue, anyway. I installed several safes in my house and one in my parents' house and each held as much as $500,000. So whenever I needed money, I just went to my own little private bank.

I rented a single-bay, thousand-square-foot warehouse in Davie, and my friend Joe and I went to work. We'd put Jimi Hendrix on, smoke a joint, and the hours would fly by. We redid the wiring, replaced sheet metal, and fitted the car with modern disc brakes. We welded a full roll cage in, which protects the driver in the event of a crash, and stiffened the chassis to improve the car's handling. I had a custom trailer made, with a rack up front for tires.

Meanwhile, while I was building the car, Pam got pregnant with our first child. It was an exciting time for our little family.

I took the Porsche to the first open track weekend I could, with the Sports Car Club of America, at Sebring International Raceway, two hours from my house. I planned on practicing all weekend long and then testing for my competition license at the end. I did some classroom instruction at the track, most of it on safety but also on proper technique—how to attack a corner (slow in, fast out) and how to find the apex of a turn so you can maximize your speed through it, no matter its shape or the camber of the pavement. The first time I took the car out, I was every bit a novice.

Driving a car on a racetrack is kinda like golf; it looks so easy on TV, but in fact, it requires tremendous skill and endless practice. I started lapping and lapping, taking different lines through turns, exploring the limits of what the car could do. Always building speed, always testing the strength of my own nerve.

How much speed was too much? Where was the limit? To find it, you have to reach further, take more and more risk. Practice creates confidence. Confidence gives you the ability to tap into your reserves, a place where balance is right on the edge. And when you find that balance, it all comes together and you feel it in your soul. This is when you shine.

At one point that weekend, I blew out my clutch, and I didn't have the part I needed to fix it. One of the other Porsche drivers, who also had a 356, said he had the part at his shop in Fort Lauderdale. But we were in Sebring, 150 miles away.

"I'll charter a plane," I said. "I'll go get it and be back by tonight."

"You're fucking crazy!" he said. "It's gonna cost you all this money, and this is just a practice weekend. It's an eighty-dollar part. We'll just come back in a couple of weeks."

"No way," I said. "I want my competition license *now*."

So I chartered a small plane, flew out of Sebring to Fort Lauderdale, got the part, and flew back that same day. That was my mind-set at the time. I had the money; I had the drive. Let's get this done! By the end of that weekend, I had my license.

I was ready to go racing.

My first real competition was at Palm Beach Raceway, my home track. I loved this place, not just because I'd seen a lot of races here. It was here, back in 1969, where I ate LSD and saw Janis Joplin and the Rolling Stones. Now, in 1978, I was twenty-four years old. I figured if I could finish the race without smashing the car or breaking any bones, that would be a victory.

Pam and I drove out together in her Mercedes, and Joe trailered my Porsche to the track. My mother, my father, my brothers, and some friends all came. We turned the weekend into a big barbecue party. I was competing in what they called E Production, a class of cars that included vintage Triumphs, Alfa Romeos, and Austin-Healeys. This was sports car racing— basically, vintage street legal showroom cars loaded up with aftermarket speed and safety equipment, on a racetrack with right and left turns and elevation changes, up and down. Palm Beach is a two-mile track with ten turns. It was hot asphalt with a lot of barriers and pine trees around the perimeter, stuff you didn't want to run into at speed. I qualified in the middle of the pack—nothing impressive.

On the eve of the race, Joe and I worked all night long to make the car bulletproof, and it occurred to me that racing a car wasn't so different from bringing in a load of weed. You're relying on your machinery to be fast and reliable, and you're relying on yourself to have the nerve to do what has to be done, to push the machinery as hard as it can go. It occurred to me that the same will to succeed and to take risks in smuggling applied at the track. Which meant maybe I had a shot at this.

When I climbed into the car on race day, helmet on, I strapped my five-point harness over my chest and thighs. My heart was revving harder than the car's engine. I was nervous, but I knew how to handle it; I was used to the adrenaline— addicted to it, even. I had number 57 painted on the side of my car, a nod to my 1957 Porsche. I heard the announcer call for E Production cars, so I motored out of pit lane and onto the track.

We did a warm-up lap behind a pace car and then came around the last corner heading for the flag stand. When the steward waved the green flag, all the engines thundered, and the whole pack took off. On the first lap, my RPM gauge cable broke, so I had no tachometer. I had to improvise—just like you do when you're hauling loads out on the water. Think fast! Problem-solve! I could gauge the revs on the engine by ear and shift gears accordingly.

This was my first time in wheel-to-wheel close combat. It's all about concentration, supreme focus, and the stamina to remain at that level of focus over a long period of time. All the stresses of life, all the inner dialogue—all of that disappears. This is where my meditation skills came in. I could get in a flow state and stay there. I communicated with the car with my hands and my feet, and the car responded with noises and smells and smoke and speed.

Hit every corner apex the best you can.

Brake late in tight corners. Brake slow and smooth in faster corners. Get on the gas as early as possible coming out of every corner.

Quick gear shifts and smooth clutch work. No mistakes.

Drive with confidence. Believing in yourself goes a long way on the racetrack.

There's a natural gyroscope inside your brain that guides you so that you can *feel* the corners rather than just see them. It's like you're existing in an entirely separate plane of understanding. The balance in your ears becomes the balance of the car, and all you have to do is stay focused and let your instinct do the work.

This was a sprint race—about twenty minutes long. Nearing the end, I was trailing a Triumph and snapping at its tail.

Turn ten is a long, fast, sweeping switchback that leads onto the front straightaway. I knew I could take that Triumph if I positioned the car tightly on the inside line coming out of that corner, if I could get on the gas early enough. But if I got on it too early, I'd risk hitting him and knocking us both off track.

I flew into that corner, my nose inches behind the Triumph. I waited . . . waited . . . then made my move, hammering the throttle. When I shot down the straightaway, that Triumph was fading in my rearview.

Two laps later I saw the checkered flag waving in the wind. The rush was indescribable.

No racer can ever forget the first victory—especially if it's the driver's first race. When I made it back into the pits and got out of that car, my whole family was there. The look of pride on my father's face, the smile on Pam's lips, the hug from my mother—this was living. It even felt like my kid brother Glen was there in spirit. It was just unreal. I remember thinking: *If winning a little race in Palm Beach could feel this good, what would it feel like to win the Indy 500?*

After that, I was going to racetracks every chance I could get. I was hooked, and Pam could see it. It was all I wanted to talk about—that and the baby coming. Whether you're learning to put oil paint on a canvas, ski black diamond runs, or smuggle millions of dollars of illegal cannabis, if you want to be good at something, you have to put in the time and effort, always paying attention to the details.

But racing was also like smuggling in another particular regard. The first time you hold $20,000 in cash, you get a killer rush. The next time? It's normal, and you want more. Same with speed. You hit 120 mph, and you're white-knuckling the wheel, your ass cheeks clenched so tight they're sore for days. The next time you hit 120 mph, that speed feels normal. You start chasing 130 mph, 140 mph. You're hunting the intangible, breaking the laws that control the universe. That's the kind of thing that can either drive you to the top or get you in big trouble—or both.

Even when I wasn't behind the wheel, I was working on my craft. I could think through a racetrack and drive phantom laps while sitting in a bathtub, thinking my way through a particularly hard corner or thinking about how the weight of a car can be transferred quickly from front to back and side to side, according to where the car is placed at any split second, in a particular part of a turn, or according to the camber of the pavement.

Nothing in a race car at speed is ever stagnant. Everything is always moving, a constantly evolving and limitless set of dynamics. The most important engine in the car is not the one making the horsepower. It's always the one in your skull, and after that, the one in your chest.

Part of learning anything is making mistakes. Only when you make a mistake in a race car, it can happen in a flash, and the consequences can be your life.

One time, I was at a practice session at Palm Beach, and I pushed hard into turn five. I carried too much speed into the right-hand corner and lost my grip. I was reaching for that limit! But I went too far. The car spun on me, and off I went through a thick patch of saw grass.

Once you've lost control of a car, and you know there's no chance of getting it back, time slows to a crawl and all you can do is pray that you're not going to hit something hard. On the other side of the saw grass was a lake. I didn't even know it was there because I couldn't see through this thick overgrowth.

Splash!

Now I was sitting in my Porsche, in the middle of a lake. The car was filling with water, and I got myself out of there as fast as I could.

Embarrassed? You bet. I made sure to get a picture of the car in the lake, sunk up to the top of the doors, before the tow truck hauled it out of there. The look on Pam's face when she saw that photo? Un-fucking-believable.

One evening, we were preparing for a race at Palm Beach International Raceway. I was taking Pam out to dinner and on the way, we stopped by my race shop to make sure everything was ready to go. Joe and I had put in long hours to rebuild the Porsche after its unfortunate lake swim. The car was really coming together.

I was wearing a suit and tie, and Pam was in a nice dress, as we were headed to a fine French restaurant. She was very pregnant with our first child. I'd bought us a blue Mercedes 380 SEL, a big sedan for our growing family. I was proud of that car; it screamed *success*. At the race shop, I stepped out of the Mercedes to talk to Joe while Pam waited in the car. (I'd hired Joe by this time, so he was actually working for me as my mechanic.)

The dually Chevy Silverado was there, hooked up to the trailer carrying the Porsche 356. The tire rack was full of racing tires, giving off that wonderful fresh rubber smell. Joe had loaded it all up, and he was spraying down the shop floor with a hose. Out in front of the shop was another Mercedes. He was in the process of rebuilding this car for a friend.

"Everything's ready to go," Joe assured me, then added, "Hey, would you give me a hand with this Mercedes?"

He wanted me to help him push it into the race shop, to lock it up for the night. He opened up the driver's door and put his hands on the steering wheel. I reached under the rear bumper to push.

What I didn't know was that he had the back of the car up on jack stands, and the back wheels were off. Joe must have just forgotten. When we started pushing, the car fell off those jack stands and crashed down on my right hand, on the middle two fingers. I felt instant panic and searing pain.

"Oh fuck! I cut my finger off! I cut off my fucking finger!"

Joe said, "No, you didn't."

I held up my maimed hand. Blood shot up three feet in the air.

"Shit! You did!"

I started dancing around, trying to figure out what to do with my hand. Joe yelled, "We got to go to the hospital!"

I ran over to my car. Pam was in the passenger seat. I opened her door.

"What happened?"

"I cut my finger off!"

I held up my hand to show her and blood sprayed all over the inside of the windshield. She let loose a shriek and then started crying. "Get out of the car!" I shouted. "Get out of the car! You got to drive!"

So she got out and waddled over to the driver's side as fast as her pregnant body could take her. I got in the passenger seat and heard Joe yell, "Hold on! Wait!" He came running over and opened Pam's door. He handed her my severed finger, and Pam let loose that shriek again. She wouldn't take the finger.

"Put it on the back seat, Joe!" I yelled. So he threw it on the back seat. I realized that Pam was in no shape to drive. "Get in the car!" I told him. "You drive!"

It was like the bloodiest game of musical chairs in history. Pam got back out and waddled over to the passenger seat. Joe got in the driver's seat, and I got in back. Joe hit the throttle hard, and my finger rolled from the back seat onto the floorboard, right between my feet. When Joe hit the brakes at a stop sign, the finger rolled under the front seat. When he hammered the gas, it rolled back between my feet. I watched that finger roll back and forth all the way to the hospital.

When we got to the emergency room, the inside of the car looked like the set of a Hollywood slasher film. I marched into the ER, wearing my nice suit. We finally got to see a doctor, and Joe handed him my severed digit. Talk about giving someone the finger. He scrutinized it closely and said, "I'm sorry, there's no saving this thing." So now I was missing half of my right ring finger.

I never did make it to the race in Palm Beach that weekend. Instead, I got a bottle of Quaaludes and I hit the couch. I could never imagine how that missing finger would later play a role in my ultimate arrest and demise, years in the future.

As soon as I could, however, I had the bandages off and I was back with Joe in the shop, working on the Porsche, and back at the track, doing laps. Holding the wheel with a hand with four fingers took some getting used to, but I made it work. The 1979 season was ending, but I was already looking forward. The SCCA had regional championships and a national championship. I had enough laps under my belt by this time that I felt comfortable on the track, and I was ready to start winning at a higher level. I wanted that national championship in 1980. I was also thinking about the next car.

I was spending thousands and thousands of dollars on racing. But what might my situation look like, I wondered, if I spent tens of thousands? Or hundreds of thousands? If I needed more money, I knew how to get it. The more I grew my business, the faster I could go.

6

Motor Races and Gun Battles

1980

*E*verything changed in 1980. Everything in my life started to happen at a higher speed or in much larger volumes. Meanwhile, America was on the brink of a profound cultural shift that would have drastic effects on my life and livelihood. It was an election year. The arrival of the Reagan era was about to slam a door shut on the biggest decade-long party humanity had ever known.

The 1970s were gone. A war on drugs was on the horizon.

Pam was getting ready for the baby to come. It was the most exciting thing that had ever happened to us. One day I was driving through Davie, and I saw a house for sale by the owner. It was beautiful, set on 4.5 acres. I knocked on the door, and a guy answered.

"I'd like to make an appointment to see the inside of the house," I said.

"Why don't you come in right now?"

The place was perfect. I offered $250,000, which was a lot of money at that time and probably more than what the house was worth. The owner and I worked out a deal where I paid him in cash under the table and he held onto the mortgage. That way, this big purchase wouldn't set off any alarm bells at the IRS. I immediately set about renovating the place. I also launched a legitimate business for the first time—Sun Coast Jet Ski Rental, on the beach in Fort Lauderdale. Now at least I had something on paper to show the feds at tax time.

When our daughter was born—that was the peak moment of my life. We named her Brandie, but I called her Sweet Pea (and, occasionally, Boodle Doodles). The house was ready, and we took her home from the hospital to begin our new life as a family. Becoming a father should've been a moment to rethink the way I was living my life. But it didn't happen. The smuggling business just kept growing. I now had three rented stash houses. We were throwing wild parties at the new house in Davie. Let me tell you, when the Eagles put out that song "Life in the Fast Lane," they could have written it for Pam and me.

Meanwhile, I was getting ready for my first full season of SCCA racing.

One winter day early in 1980, I walked into General RV, located at Florida State Road 84, right off the exit ramp of I-95. I needed a motor home, so I could bring Pam and Brandie to racetracks where I'd be competing. General RV was the biggest RV dealership in Florida. It was owned by Bill, Don, and Dale Whittington.

The Whittington brothers had an incredible story and a huge reputation in South Florida. They were the sons of a former racing champion turned rich businessman who raised his boys to be uber-competitive. "Dad had us competing against each other," Don later told a reporter. "We had motorcycles almost as soon as we could walk. We've raced horses, bikes, boats, airplanes, anything that moves and always fought each other to win."

In the mid-1970s, the Whittington brothers set up a Learjet leasing franchise in Fort Lauderdale. In 1978, they bought the Road Atlanta racetrack. In 1979, the year before I met them, they flew to France for the 24 Hours of Le Mans, the most important sports car race in the world by far. They tried to talk their way onto the Kremer sports car racing team as drivers. This team was affiliated with Porsche, and it was among the best sports car endurance outfits out there. Legend has it, Kremer refused to let the Whittingtons compete at Le Mans, so the brothers made a phone call, came to the track with a bag full of money, and bought out the entire team the day before the race started.

True? Beats me. What is definitely true, however, is that the Whittington brothers, as codrivers along with the German ace Klaus Ludwig, went out and won the 24 Hours of Le Mans. They became legends overnight.

Now eight months later, I was in their RV dealership hunting for a motor home.

The first of the three Whittington brothers I met was Dale. He was the salesman, so we walked around the lot together. I picked out a motor home, and we took it out for a test drive. Right away we hit it off. Dale was the most easygoing of the three brothers. I used to call him Youngblood because his energy was effusive and electric.

I was driving along in this huge motor home, which had every amenity, top of the line, and I asked Dale, "You smoke weed?"

"Yeah."

"Can we smoke one in here? I got a joint right here in my pocket."

"Hell, yeah. Spark it up."

"I want to buy this here motor home," I told him.

"OK, let's go back to the office, and you'll meet my older brother, Bill. We'll talk over the financing."

"There ain't going to be any financing," I said in between tokes. "I'll buy this thing in cash."

"Cash?"

"Cash."

So we headed back to the dealership, and in the offices, I first met Bill. He was a good bit taller than me. Dirty blond hair, side parted with a receding hairline, big smile. Good-looking guy.

"I want to pay cash for that motor home," I told him. "But I want a good deal. What can you do for me?"

The two brothers went into an office, shut the door behind them, talked for two minutes, and then came back out. They made me a good offer, and I took it. "Clean it up and have it ready," I said. "I'll be back in an hour."

As promised, I came back an hour later with an attaché case holding tens of thousands of dollars. I plopped it onto Bill's desk. He opened it, smelled that fresh green cash, and howled, "Damn, Randy! What the hell kind of business did you say you were in?!"

"Jet ski rental," I said, smiling.

We became fast friends, right there. The Whittington brothers also introduced me to a guy named Marty Hinze, another race car driver who was working with them. The more we all got to know each other, the more we liked each other, and the more we were willing to reveal about ourselves. Turned out, the Whittington brothers and Marty Hinze were in the same businesses I was—smuggling weed and racing cars— and we started doing a little bit of business together. Here and there, they'd have a big load, and I'd help them with my distributors. We were all making so much money, we didn't see each other as competition, and in fact, it was only a matter of time before we would team up in an attempt to conquer the motorsport world.

Off we went in our new motor home—Pam, Sweet Pea Brandie, and I. Joe drove the pickup pulling the trailer with the Porsche. We were racing nearly every weekend, and Pam loved it. She was my rock—always up for whatever came next, full of vibrance and energy. We went to Savannah, to Charlotte, and to the Texas World Speedway, north of Houston. We hit all three major racetracks in South Florida—Palm Beach, Sebring, and Daytona International Speedway.

There's also a lot of downtime in racing, and Pam and I were making the most of it, playing with the baby, having a good time when Brandie napped, barbecuing with our friends. It was a way of life that I loved, hanging around with all these people you meet on the road, who, like you, share this love of racing, competition, and camaraderie. It's a love so deep you commit yourself and your family to traveling thousands of miles and showing up, ready to give 100 percent and to grab whatever glory you can. You come to love the sounds, the smell of oil and gas, and especially the people, because you all share that passion.

Then, when it's your turn, you get in the car and go like hell. Your friends become your competitors. Until the race is over, and then they're your best friends again.

In my first full season, I won enough points to capture the E Production class championship for the Sports Car Club of America Southeastern division—top-flight amateur racing. The national SCCA runoffs—what we thought of as the Olympics for amateur racing—took place in 1980 at Road Atlanta, the racetrack owned by the Whittington brothers. It was a full weekend with any number of different classes of cars. It was also a weekend-long party.

I met Paul Newman that weekend, a man who truly loved motor racing just the way I did. He was competing in the C Production class in the national championship runoffs, driving a Nissan 280ZX race car. Yeah, he was a Hollywood superstar, but once he slipped on his racing suit and covered that million-dollar face behind a helmet shield, he was just another competitor like any of the other guys. I think he loved that about racing.

Road Atlanta was one of the most challenging tracks in America. It featured an extremely fast four-thousand-foot back straight that led to a downhill dip at the end with an uphill blind right-hand turn on off-camber pavement. There were severe elevation changes, left- and right-hand switchbacks, and terrifying blind turns, all laid out across seven hundred acres of rolling Georgia hills.

What are those blind turns like? Imagine driving into a blind corner that you approach at very high speed. You enter the turn, which is structured such that you can't see what's on the other side until you're already there. If there's an obstruction (say, a car that has crashed), a flag man is there waving a caution flag so you know to slow up and be careful. Otherwise, you have to dig up the nerve to enter that turn with the throttle down, even though you can't see what's on the other side.

It's like closing your eyes halfway through a screaming fast corner, then opening them two seconds later. It takes practice. It requires nerves of steel. Total commitment to speed.

The day before my national championship race, I was fooling around with a three-wheel motorcycle, doing wheelies in this area where all the motor homes were parked. This guy came out of his motor home looking ticked off. As I zoomed by shirtless on my motorcycle, having a good time, he stopped me and pointed to a bunch of stuff under an awning near his motor home. He had a race car and a moped and some other stuff.

"Hey asshole, you see that stuff!?" this stranger yelled at me. "That's my stuff. You hit any of that stuff, and I'm going to hit you. You understand me!?"

This dude had a temper. My older brother, Steve, was with me. He was a Vietnam vet. To say he didn't take shit from anybody would be an embarrassing understatement. The next thing I knew, a bunch of people were squaring off, pushing and shoving. I felt that strange hollowing in my gut, that nervous feeling you get when real punches are about to get thrown. The guy who was shouting at me went back into his motor home and locked the door. But his son came out—a guy named John Paul Jr.—and he and I talked everything out. Everyone calmed down and went about their business. That's how I first met John Paul Jr. and John Paul Sr., two guys who would cross my path again soon. John Paul Sr. was known as "the Old Pirate," because he looked like one; but he was also a Harvard-trained businessman. His son Jr. was the hottest up-and-coming talent in the business.

All these people—the Whittington brothers, Marty Hinze, John Paul Jr., and John Paul Sr.—were already or were soon to become legends in both the motor-racing and the weed-smuggling worlds. I didn't yet realize how strange it was that these two worlds were becoming so entangled.

In my national championship race, I faced the best amateur racers in the country. I believed I was every bit as fast as them, faster even, but I couldn't get the car to be a winning car. During the race, however, I suffered engine failure early on. That's the thing about motor racing. You can have the goods, but if the car doesn't cooperate, it doesn't matter. You can practice and work on the car all night long. But sometimes, you can't get the car dialed in, or a ten-dollar part can end your day. Happens all the time.

That's how my 1980 season ended—with a full letdown, followed by full commitment to build on the foundation I'd created. I wanted to become a professional. Nothing or nobody was going to stop me.

I was making more money than God smuggling weed. I bought my dad his first thoroughbred racehorse in 1980, and my father started breeding racehorses. Soon he had a stable of thoroughbreds, and the first horse he bred he named after my daughter, Brandie Boodle Doodles. I was also taking care of my mom in style. My wife lived in a mansion and drove a convertible Mercedes SL. I was living the American dream, South Florida style.

Early that year, I got a phone call from Ben Kramer. Ben had gotten himself arrested for smuggling cannabis in a job I had nothing to do with. He got nabbed after a high-speed boat chase off the shore of Miami, a chase that made the newspapers and TV news. He'd done some prison time, and now he was out. He needed to get back on his feet. I didn't let anybody outside my family know where my new house was. But I'd known Ben since we were kids, and I invited him out to my place in Davie.

When he arrived, he looked a little different than I remembered. I hadn't seen him in four years. He looked a little older, but that wasn't it. Looking back, I realize that prison had done something to him.

"I got some ideas," he told me. "I can get a crew together. All I need is a boat to get started, and right now, I don't have the money."

I looked at him closely. Ben had eyes like deep black holes, eyes that clued you into the fact that he was a bit of an evil genius. You didn't want to be on his bad side, and I never was. I'd known him for so long, I trusted him like a brother.

"Ayyyight," I said. "You find the boat, and I'll cover the expenses. I have some business I can cut you in on, to get you going."

That's how we came to buy the *Ursa Major*, a sixty-five-foot wooden, stunningly beautiful vessel built in Holland. It was already named before we bought it (after a constellation of stars shaped like a large bear). It had a massive diesel engine, a full captain's bridge, a captain's state room, and crew quarters below. The ship was big enough for a family of six to live comfortably for weeks at a time, along with a professional boat crew. It had radar equipment on top and a back deck perfect for lounging and smoking in the sun. I bought that boat for about $220,000, and Ben and his guys brought it to a boatyard called Merrill Stevens in Miami. Our plan was to have it rebuilt and refitted, and I wanted a large secret compartment built into it. The work was going to take a year.

Meanwhile, I had several deals in the works, and per my promise, I found ways to cut Ben in on some business. Time and again, however, things kept going wrong.

On one run, I took my thirty-six-foot Cigarette out of Fort Lauderdale to meet a mother ship, fifteen miles north of Bimini. I made contact with the ship in the middle of the night. When we pulled up alongside it, the boat captain came out of the salon door of his vessel with a shotgun, and a buddy of his came out with an AR-15. They were panicking.

"We gotta go now!" he was shouting. "We gotta go now!"

Turns out, the Bahamian police had spotted them. A police vessel had approached the mother ship wanting to board. This captain came out with his shotgun and fired off a shot. The cops had taken off, but surely a whole army was now on the way. We had to get out of there fast.

The captain of the mother ship went down into the bilge to cut the intake hose to sink his vessel. As it was going down, we loaded as much weed as we could, about a thousand pounds, onto my boat. The rest was going down with the ship. That ship's crew got onto my Cigarette too, which meant that my boat was now exceedingly crowded with people and bales of weed. One of this crew was a Colombian guy who had no identification papers. He had not intended on trying to enter the United States, but now he had no choice. He was going to have to enter illegally, aboard my boat.

From the Cigarette, I watched their ship slowly go down. I'd never seen anything like that before—a boat sinking under the moonlight, making death gurgles as air pockets found their way out the top. I couldn't help but imagine what it would feel like to be so helpless, to be on that boat, in that moment. That thought didn't last long; we had to get the hell out of there.

Another time, I got a knock on my door in the middle of the night. It was Ben and Slick, and they were covered in mud.

"What the fuck happened to you guys?" I asked.

I knew that Ben was supposed to be coming into South Florida with a load of several hundred pounds of weed on a small aircraft, along with a pilot named Nathan (who later was killed in a plane crash into the ocean while flying a weed run). As it turned out, they were fueling up the plane on a potholed airstrip in the Bahamas when a police vehicle came speeding onto the runway. So they had to take off before the plane was fully fueled. They ran out of gas and lost the first engine just off the coast of Miami.

They had a personal stash of coke on board, and believing they were about to die, they started snorting large amounts. They ended up belly-flopping on the edge of Biscayne Bay near a federal nuclear power facility called Turkey Point. All of this area was off limits, big-time. They had to leave the crashed airplane in some mangroves on the edge of the bay.

I got dressed, and we were out the door in less than a minute. We towed my seventeen-foot ski boat out to a launch spot on Key Biscayne. We had to find the aircraft, and it was not going to be easy in the middle of the night.

We entered those waters under the cover of darkness and split up, wading on foot through the shallow salt water and mud, pushing aside the thick mangrove brush. "Hey!" yelled Slick. He started whistling, and we made our way through the darkness to where he was. He'd found the plane, plunged into bushes and mud and salt water. I went and got my boat, and we had to transfer the weed. The water was so shallow and the weed so heavy, I had to raise the engine prop and then we all had to push the vessel into deeper water. The sun was starting to rise, and we were knee-deep in sand and mud.

When we got the load back to the boat launch on Key Biscayne, the sun had come up, and there were fishermen launching their own boats from the parking lot. All these bales of weed were just sitting there in my ski boat for the world to see, and I was worried someone might call the police. But amazingly, we got the load safely to a stash house.

That nobody called the cops on us? Purely a stroke of luck. Which is another thing about racing and smuggling: sometimes you have no control over how things are going to turn out.

The worst episode—the one that forced me to change my business model entirely—occurred soon after when I was contacted by a horse jockey friend who introduced me to the Smith brothers. This wasn't their real name, but they were known as the Smith brothers because they resembled the guys on the Smith Brothers cough drops package. Basically, two old white guys with long beards.

We all met at the docks behind the Signature boat factory at Thunderboat Alley, right next to the Cigarette boat factory, and we talked over the deal in privacy aboard a seventy-foot trawler. They wanted to know if I had a couple of boats they could use to help off-load a mother ship. We agreed upon my commission. I wasn't going to sell any of this haul; my job would just be to bring it in, deliver it to a stash house, and get paid.

I got a crew together, and we took off in two boats headed for Bimini. We had my thirty-six-foot Cigarette and a forty-foot Bertram that we borrowed. Both boats had engine trouble before we even got to Bimini, caused partly by bad luck and partly by heavy seas. Now I was screwed. We managed to get back to Miami, but I still had a job to do.

Through some networking, I contacted a Cuban smuggler out of Miami that everyone in the business called Felix the Cat. He owned a shrimp boat, which I paid him to use to do the job that night. Bad move.

The next day, I got a ping on my beeper. I went to a pay phone, and one of my contacts told me that the weed was in an industrial van parked in the local Kmart parking lot, with the keys on top of the driver's side front tire. I called the Smith brothers, and they gave me a delivery address. One of my drivers and I picked up the van and then headed to this house in Hollywood. When I reached the house, a huge Irish boat captain opened the door. He was a giant, probably six foot six and over three hundred pounds. I'd never seen someone so sunburned. We did our business, and the Irishman said, "Where's the rest of it?"

"What do you mean?" I said. "This is it. This is the load."

The Irishman picked me up by my neck, right off the ground. Dangling in the air, I was face-to-face with this dude, and the look in his eyes told me he wouldn't think twice about breaking my neck. "Motherfucker," he growled, "there was 250 bales on that boat. And all I'm getting from you is 100 bales. Where's the rest of the weed!?"

He put me down, and I tried to explain to him that I didn't know anything about any 250 bales. I was just the middleman.

"I am going to give you until tonight," he said, "to find those bales. That's all the time you got, motherfucker."

Now I had to go find out what happened and quickly. I called the guy that connected me to Felix the Cat. Felix was now claiming that he bottomed out his shrimp boat on a reef, and during this exigency, his shrimp boat had sunk. In his telling, he managed to get about half the load off before it went down. I had no way of knowing if Felix was telling the truth, or if he was ripping me off. Either way, now this hulking Irishman wanted to kill me.

From a pay phone, I explained to the Smith brothers what happened. They were not having it. I had to call my connection to Felix the Cat, again. I asked for coordinates of where Felix's shrimp boat had gone down. If it had truly hit a reef, that's shallow water and there'd be evidence of a sunken boat. Felix gave up the coordinates, and the Smith brothers went out to look for the boat. They found nothing. Some contacts vouched for me, so the Smith brothers concluded that I was a decent guy. But now it was clear: Felix the Cat was ripping them off. So they went to a warehouse Felix owned where they thought they'd find the weed.

It didn't take long for the whole situation to spiral out of control. That night, I got a phone call. Felix the Cat and the Smith brothers had a gun battle in a warehouse in Miami. Several shots fired, nobody killed. But somehow the warehouse had gone up in flames, and firetrucks with sirens showed up. It was a disaster.

These were the people I was dealing with. They were killers. Once you make the leap that far out outside the law, especially in a place like South Florida, you encounter people who do not weigh risk or value life the same way that you do. Even if you're careful, you can end up a cog in their violent machine. You can end up buried in cement.

That was a breaking point. I was going to change my strategy. The *Ursa Major* was ready to go. From here on out, there would be no more meeting up with any mother ship on the high seas. *The* Ursa Major *was going to be the mother ship*. And I was no longer going to be any kind of middleman. I was going to be *the* man. We needed to control our operations and our destinies and to be in control of who we were dealing with.

In a meeting with Ben at my house in the fall of 1980—right around the time Ronald Reagan was sworn in—we decided we needed to go directly to the source itself, the farms. "I'm talking about Colombia," I said. "That's where the best weed is at now. It ain't Jamaica anymore." The Colombian farmers were dominating the market of high-end smoke. They were growing the best in the world, probably the best in all of history. We began to lay plans to take the *Ursa Major* to South America—the new mecca for the international cannabis trade.

7

Turning Pro

January 1982

One winter day in Florida—another balmy, beautiful, blue-sky morning—Pam and I packed some beer and clothes and all our baby gear into the motor home and headed north with Brandie. We were going to the 24 Hours of Daytona, the biggest sports car endurance race in America.

Teams from all over the world come to the Daytona International Speedway with their machinery every January for the kick-off race of the year. There are production GT cars (showroom sports cars like Corvettes and Porsche 911s, with performance and safety gear added) and prototype purpose-built race cars (which looked like spaceships with wheels). The prototype cars at that time topped out around 190 mph—three times the speed limit of the fastest highways in the country.

In endurance racing, a team of three to four drivers is assigned to one car, with one driver in it at a time, and the car that makes the most laps over the time period (in this case, twenty-four hours) wins. The Triple Crown of endurance racing is Daytona, Sebring, and, of course, Le Mans.

The 24 Hours of Daytona is run on the famed racetrack's road course, which combined the banked oval that you see in NASCAR racing, along with a twisty course in the middle of the infield with lefts and rights and hyperfast straightaways. That's the point of sports car racing: to challenge not just the driver's speed and skill but also every part of the car—the front and rear suspension, the electricals, the engine, the windshield wipers (it rains sometimes at Daytona), and even the headlights (as you're racing all night long). The car has to be bulletproof under absolutely brutal driving conditions to win, which makes endurance racing a team effort. The mechanics have to be as quick and smart as the driver. Meanwhile, the grandstands fill up with thousands of spectators and the TV cameras roll.

I was just a spectator that year at Daytona, though I hoped to come back soon as a driver. We took friends along with us, and we aimed to turn it into a party weekend. A few other friends met us there in their motor homes. I had a buddy who worked for the Preston Henn North American Racing Team. The day before the race start, during practice, I was hanging around the team's garage. The team was running a Ferrari BB 512, racing in the GTO class with engines over 3.0 liters (the second-fastest class). The car was painted red with sponsorship decals all over it. It had a wide stance and a big wing on the back, a pure badass blood-red Ferrari race car. The team had three world-class pilots—Bob Wollek and Edgar Doren, both from France, and Janet Guthrie of the United States, who was at that time the only woman ever to compete in both the Indy 500 and the Daytona 500.

I overheard people talking in the garage that morning, and I could tell something was wrong. Janet Guthrie had gotten sick. They were going to need a replacement driver. I went up to my buddy who worked for the team.

"Hey," I said, "can you tell Preston about me?"

That would be Preston Henn, who was in charge. Preston was a character, and he was there in the garage wearing cowboy boots and a cowboy hat, sporting a trimmed gray beard. He was a South Florida guy like me who'd made a fortune owning drive-in theaters. He held huge swap meets during the day and then showed movies at night. When my buddy introduced us, I told Preston that I was a friend of the Whittington brothers and that I'd won the SCCA Southeastern E Production championship with my Porsche speedster a year and a half earlier.

"Are you comfortable on this track?" Preston asked me.

"Yes, indeed I am! Daytona is one of my home tracks. Ayyyight? I live three hours away, in Davie. Listen, man, I can get the job done."

I could tell he was skeptical. He asked, "Can you get any sponsorship?" This was a normal question. Drivers were often chosen not just for their speed but their ability to bring sponsorship money to the team.

"Damn skippy," I said. I told him that I ran a jet ski rental company out of Fort Lauderdale called Sun Coast Jet Ski Rental and that it could be a team sponsor. "I have $5,000 in cash in my motor home. I'll give it to you right now."

Preston stood a solid foot taller than me. He ran his eyes up and down, sizing me up. "Go get your helmet," he said. "I'll give you four laps. Let's see what you can do."

It is said that success occurs when preparation meets opportunity. I sensed that this was a moment that could change my life. If, that is, I didn't fuck it up.

Because I used the motor home for my own racing, I had all my gear on board—helmet, race suit, and, of course, cash. When I got back to the Preston Henn team garage, I could tell that there was some friction. Wollek, the French endurance racer, wasn't keen on giving me a tryout. I could hear him yelling at Preston. "Brilliant Bob" Wolleck was a star endurance athlete. I was a nobody. I wasn't even a professional. But the race was set to start the next day, and they needed a driver.

We had to mold a seat for me because I was shorter than Wollek and Doren. The team mechanics got out a regular kitchen garbage bag and filled it with some chemicals. Then they put the bag on the race car seat and sat me on top of it. The bag molded to my body, and the chemicals turned into a hard foam so that I could sit comfortably and my feet could reach the pedals.

While we were making the foam seat, I tried to hide how nervous I was. I'd never driven a Ferrari, let alone a full-on Ferrari race car. Out on the track, other teams were practicing, the cars ripping by with engines thundering. This track was about serious speed, hard braking, and precise cornering. One mistake and you could take out another car or hit a cement wall.

If I crashed the team's car the day before the race? It would be a disaster. I'd be humiliated, my reputation permanently ruined.

I hit the ignition and dabbed the accelerator with my toe. There is no sound like a Ferrari race engine—angry, high-pitched, twelve cylinders, superhigh compression, the most exotic engine on earth. The power was so extreme, I felt like I could blow a hole in the atmosphere from the cockpit of that car. The gear shifter came through a gate that was unlike anything I'd seen, and I wasn't comfortable. I motored out of the pits onto the track and decided to take my first two laps easy, to get a feel for the car. Slowly, I built my speed.

By the time I came around at the end of my second lap, down the pit straight past the grandstands, I'd settled down. It was go time. I hammered the throttle, and the car responded. I was motoring over 175 mph—the fastest I'd ever traveled—before braking hard into the left-hand turn one, through the fast kink on turn two, to the heavy g-forces of the turn-three switchback. I was in the zone: shifting up, shifting down, brake, clutch, throttle, the steering wheel light in my fingers. When I got up onto Daytona's thirty-three-degree banked turn, I floored the throttle, and the g-force acted like a slingshot, hurling me around the bend.

When I came back into the pits after my four laps, Preston was standing there, his eyes shaded under his cowboy hat. I unclipped my five-point harness, pulled myself from the car, and took off my helmet. The team crew chief, a guy named Al Roberts, showed me my lap times on a clipboard. On my last two laps, I was about one second off the pace of Wollek, one of the best endurance racers in the world.

Preston said, "Get yourself ready, Randy. You're on the team."

Pam couldn't believe it. We'd come to *watch* the biggest endurance sports car race in America, but now, I was going to be in it. We stood in our motor home hugging each other. It was an awesome moment but also scary as all hell. People die racing at Daytona. Less than a year earlier, a stock car driver named Don Williams had been killed on this same track. I thought of my little brother Glen—how psyched he'd be if he were with me but, also, how his passion for motoring had ended his life.

The next day, I arrived early at the garage in my fireproof driving suit with my helmet under my arm. Each of the three drivers were to do three-hour stints, and I would go last. So, by the time I got in the car and fastened myself in tight, the race was already six hours old. We were somewhere in the middle of the pack. The grandstands were full of race fans, draining the Daytona International Speedway of its beer. When I pulled the Ferrari out of the pit straight and into that swift left-hand turn one, I was no longer Randy Lanier, club racer. I was a professional athlete.

I put myself in the zone. My meditation training served me well again. Gear shifts happened automatically as if I were part of the machine. I hit the corner apexes time and again. The view from inside the cockpit became something like tunnel vision—total focus through every revolution of the engine, every spin of all four wheels. In a race car you can come to feel like you're superhuman. The great Sir Stirling Moss once put it this way: "I believe that if a man wanted to walk on water, and was prepared to give up everything else in life, he could do it. He could walk on water. I'm serious." When you reach that level of commitment, you feel that you can't possibly make a mistake. That confidence ignites more speed on the track but also more risk. Even if you don't make a mistake, someone else on the track could. And just like that: light's out.

You're hyperaware of everything around you, cars at speed sometimes inches away, but at the same time, you're hyperaware of what's happening in the distance, in the next turn and the one after that.

Never mind the searing heat in the cockpit.

Never mind the furious noise and the spine-wrenching vibration.

None of that exists. You are in a flow state.

No two laps are ever the same. The car changes its behavior according to the track conditions or how much fuel is weighing you down. There's so much going on, and you cannot let your focus slip. The race wears you down. It wears down your car. You see broken machinery around the track, where somebody made a mistake. Not going to be you! Not this time!

Midway through my stint, I started to feel that the car was not shifting gears as smoothly as it had earlier. The more laps I drove, the more sure I was: something was wrong with the car. But I kept pushing. At the end of my three-hour drive, I pulled the car into the pit feeling very, very relieved. As I was getting out, Wollek was getting in. I yelled to him, "Watch the gearshift!" I don't know if my words even registered. I was so exhausted it was all I could do to drag my body back to my motor home and lie down in a quiet place.

It was pitch dark when I had to report back to the pit for my second stint. We were doing well: I believe we were running fourth, so if we picked up one spot, we would make it to the podium. When Edgar Doren pulled into the pit, I took some quick deep breaths. Then I got in the cockpit. After a few laps—racing in the darkness, with the headlights trying to knife through fog—I was convinced the car wasn't shifting gears well. I was flooring the throttle on the back straight, preparing to enter turn three of the embankment, when the gear box let go. I couldn't get the car in any gear. It was stuck in neutral, totally undrivable.

I had enough speed to coast down to the entrance of pit road. When I pulled into our pit, even before I got out of the car, I made a hand motion, slicing my neck, to show the team that the car was dead. The crew chief came sprinting over, and I explained myself to him.

Immediately, I saw Wollek jump over the pit wall. He started screaming at me with that French accent. "You took the car off the track!" he was yelling. "You took the car off the track!" Meaning, I had busted the Ferrari, that it was my fault.

"Bullshit! The gearbox let go! I just happened to be the guy in the car when it blew."

I climbed out of the cockpit. He was up in my face.

"You broke the car!"

"Shut the fuck up, man!"

Preston was there, watching so see if any punches were about to get thrown. I walked away, Wollek still screaming at me over the sound of revving engines from out on the track. That was the end of my first pro race.

JLP Racing's Porsche 935 took the checkered flag at the 1982 24 Hours of Daytona. The father-son duo John Paul Sr. and John Paul Jr. won, along with Rolf Stommelen, a German ace who would die a year later in a crash at the Los Angeles Grand Prix.

That Sunday night, as the teams were packing up their cars and gear, I went to Preston Henn's motor home to thank him for the drive and tell him I was sorry for the way things turned out. He invited me in, and the next thing I knew, we were snorting cocaine, and although I never was a big drinker, we were moving quickly through a bottle of whiskey. Preston was a wild guy, turns out. He said something about John Paul Sr. and Jr., and I told him about the time, eighteen months earlier, when I'd nearly come to blows with John Paul Sr. at the SCCA runoffs at Road Atlanta.

Preston shot me a look that I didn't quite understand. He said, "You know what? There's somebody I'd like you to meet."

"Not right now," I said. "We're sitting here snorting cocaine!"

"Don't worry," he said, "you'll like this guy."

He left and minutes later, when the door swung open, Preston had John Paul Sr. following him into the motor home. I jumped out of my seat because I knew that this man did not like me at all.

The two of them burst out in laughter, pointing at me and cackling. "Calm down, Randy," Preston said. "John Paul here is my good friend."

I felt the tension ease. I slid over and John Paul sat down. We started talking racing. We snorted some coke. We partied all night long. John Paul Sr. had just won the 24 Hours of Daytona, and let me tell you, that will put you in a good mood. Our friendship was sealed that night.

I was becoming part of this fraternity of South Florida professional sports car racers—Preston, John Paul and his son, the Whittingtons, Marty Hinze. We were all living for adrenaline, and we all had money. Crazy to think, in retrospect, every one of us except Preston Henn would end up in prison, on the front line of the War on Drugs. John Paul Sr., it would turn out, was a man fully capable of actual murder. He was a killer. At the time, I didn't know any of that; we were just partying together, as we did after a hard-fought race.

In the morning, Pam and I packed up the baby and headed south for home, feeling happy and excited about our future together.

"Someday," I told Pam, "I'm going to win the 24 Hours of Daytona."

"Sure, Randy," she said. "Maybe someday you will."

That's my philosophy: believe and you will achieve.

8

Welcome to the Jungle

Spring 1982

*T*he *Ursa Major* was ready to go. Ben and I were amped to take our business international, to risk our necks and our freedom to bring a massive load of the finest sticky weed on the planet into South Florida. In March 1982—two months after the 24 Hours of Daytona—we took off from Miami airport on a commercial flight bound for Colombia. When the jet plane's wheels lifted off the pavement, I felt the cold hand of destiny gripping the back of my neck.

This was to be our first full-scale smuggling operation, using our own source we hoped to cultivate in the jungle. We were full of hope and determination. I carried a healthy bit of fear in my gut. Ben perhaps not so much. He wasn't afraid of anything, or at least that was how he acted.

We landed in Barranquilla. We had tourist visas, and we flew into this specific airport because we didn't want anyone to know where we were really going: Santa Marta, a port city on the Caribbean Sea. Ben had a potential source there that he had found through someone he'd met during his prison term. I also had a potential source, which I had found through South Florida networking. But we really had no idea what we were getting into.

The whole marijuana scene was changing in 1982. When I'd started out bringing in loads of weed from mother ships in the Bahamas in the late '70s, South Florida felt wide open, like there were no consequences. Sure, the Coast Guard monitored the seas. But think about it like this: I was one of countless small-time smugglers bringing in a plant that damn near everyone wanted in the 1970s. I didn't know anybody who got long prison time for cannabis offenses. Ben did four years, the most of anyone I knew. In 1976, Jimmy Carter ran a presidential campaign promising to decriminalize weed, and he got rid of federal criminal penalties for possession under an ounce.

Everyone was smoking in the late '70s. Even, it seemed to me, a lot of cops.

But now, a few years later in the early '80s, times couldn't be more different. So much cocaine was coming into South Florida, it was everywhere. Snowbanks of the stuff. Most of that coke was coming from Colombia. Cartels had formed around Medellín and Cartagena, and gangs and kingpins were rising up on the streets of Miami, Los Angeles, Chicago, and New York. There was a noticeable increase in violence in Miami, and weed got lumped in with cocaine as an evil presence. Ronald Reagan's incoming administration in 1980 made a sharp turn in federal policy concerning not only cocaine importation but also the whole drug universe, which included pot.

The way the feds saw it, and the message they were sending out into the communities, was that weed was a gateway drug.

A schedule I narcotic. You smoked the stuff, and the next thing you know, you're hooked on LSD and cocaine, howling at the moon and jumping off buildings. From my point of view, it was all bullshit. This plant heals the planet and its people in so many ways.

In 1981, Reagan signed a bilateral extradition treaty with Colombia. In October 1982, not long after Ben and I flew down to Colombia, Reagan officially declared America's War on Drugs. That meant, among other things, a war on the outlaws in Colombia, exactly where Ben and I were now headed. Meanwhile, in Colombia, Pablo Escobar was elected to Congress.

In Barranquilla, as we expected, customs detained us at the airport because we were American. There weren't a lot of American tourists going to Colombia in 1982; it was thought of as a dangerous place because it was. The officers took Ben into one office, and me into another, and as they searched my suitcase, they were talking to each other about a pair of headphones they found in my bag. I didn't speak the language, but I got the hint. I gave them my headphones and they let me go.

When you first step out of an airport in Colombia, you walk into a wall of heat and humidity. To get from Barranquilla to Santa Marta, Ben and I hired a driver at the airport, and we traveled for hours in a creaky old car down half-ass roads that had more potholes than pavement, roads that hugged the coastline. We'd pass nothing but jungle and a few one-room shanties, for miles, then in the middle of nowhere, we saw little settlements with thatched-roof homes up on stilts. These people had nothing. They were completely impoverished.

At one point, we came up to a stop sign at this dirt road intersection in the jungle, miles from any building of any kind, and we saw this kid—he must've been ten years old—come out of nowhere carrying a stick with fish tied to it. He was trying to sell us fish.

"Damn, man!" I said to Ben. "Where the hell did that kid come from?"

We drove along the coast and finally made it to our hotel, Port de Galleon, right on the Caribbean, outside the city of Santa Marta. The hotel had a restaurant that resembled an antique galleon ship. The entire hotel was surrounded by chain-link fence and patrolled by what looked like military but were in fact private security guards. We checked in and made some calls from the pay phone in the bar. Ben called his connection, and I called mine. No luck yet, on either side.

There was a lot of waiting. The beer in the hotel bar was room temperature, and a TV in the corner showed soccer games and the news in Spanish. Ben and I had known each other by this point for over a decade, and we were used to each other, so we didn't talk much. We had very different temperaments, like hot and cold water. I was a hippy. Ben was more gangster. He was on the phone constantly, and I could tell he was pissed off that things weren't happening fast enough. We'd come all this way, and we weren't sure either of our connections was going to show up.

Finally, one night, this dude appeared at the bar. He was about five foot six with stained teeth, a well-trimmed moustache, and dark chocolate–colored eyes. It was Ben's guy. He couldn't speak English, but Ben spoke decent Spanish— something he'd picked up from his Colombian cellmate in the joint. In between drags on a cigarette, the guy told us we were going out in the morning to look at product. We were to meet a boat at a place called El Rodadero Beach. He said he would come by to pick us up and take us there.

That night I lay awake in my hot hotel room staring up at a creaky ceiling fan. I felt like Captain Benjamin Willard in *Apocalypse Now*, as he was about to go on his mission. Scared. A little drunk. Wondering what was in store for us. For all I knew, this Colombian was going to take us out into the jungle, rob us, and leave us for dead.

In the morning, we made it to El Rodadero Beach at sunrise, and these Colombians showed up with what they called a *cayuca*. It was a forty-foot-long canoe hacked out of a tree, with a little diesel engine MacGyver'd onto the back and a seat for a driver to steer the thing by rudder. We got in there—Ben and I and a couple Colombians—and headed north into the ocean. The whole time, the guy in the back steered the boat with one hand while bailing water out with the other using a coffee can. The water was up over my ankles.

"Ben," I said, "this guy ain't bailing fast enough. We're going to freakin' drown out here."

Ben didn't say anything. He rarely showed any emotion unless he was angry.

We kept motoring, and El Rodadero Beach disappeared from behind us. The cayuca trip took about four hours. All we could see were empty beaches with huge mountains rising up behind them, all covered in jungle. The ocean water wasn't like in Florida; it was brown and murky. By the time we arrived at our destination—a quiet cove with a little horse-shoe beach set in the jungle—it was already noon, and I was worn out from the heat and the sun.

We jumped out into shallow water and pulled the cayuca up onto the beach. Nobody else was there. Then the Colombian who'd steered the boat made a loud whistling noise, and suddenly, all these Colombians came out of the jungle with rifles and machetes. They were dressed in camouflage, like revolutionaries. Ben talked to them in Spanish, and they told us to follow them. We started hiking up a mountain.

There was no trail. A Colombian in front hacked a pathway through the jungle with a machete, and I later learned that these guys didn't want to use any pathway that somebody might find, so every time they hiked up this mountain, they had to hack a new path. The ground was wet, and my shoes were caked in mud. Bugs. Heat. Thirst. Unfamiliar animals shrieking.

Every now and then we stopped, and the Colombians made that whistle sound again. Each time, more guys came out of the jungle with rifles. I realized we were being watched. We couldn't see them, but they sure as hell could see us.

After hours of hiking, we got to a campsite. The Colombians had hacked tree branches down and built a level platform on a mountainside. Their ingenuity impressed me, that they could do that on this crazy steep pitch without any modern construction equipment. A guy brought out some raw vegetables and some pieces of chicken. I didn't eat the chicken; this was not a place I wanted to come down with food poisoning. Again, the whistling sound, and again, more guys showed up. One of them had a burlap sack full of weed, and I was thinking, finally, we get to see some product. They gave me a knife so I could cut open the bag.

I took a look. I took a sniff. We'd heard about this weed. It was called Santa Marta gold. It was the gooiest, gummiest, stickiest weed I'd ever seen, beautiful buds of yellow-gold flecked with silver-white crystals and small blond hairs. I motioned to them to ask if we could smoke some of it, and one of the guys produced matches and a pipe that had been whittled out of wood. I sucked that delicious smoke into my lungs and breathed dragon smoke.

"This is gooooood," I said, inspecting a bud in my hand. "This weed is the *reeeeeaaaal deal*." I considered for a second and asked, "Where's the rest of it?"

Turns out, they'd brought five hundred pounds of it down from the mountain, which was bagged up ready to go. There was some confusion. The Colombians started talking to one another, and one of them kept looking at me and laughing. I asked Ben what they were saying.

"They didn't expect us to want more than five hundred pounds," he said.

One of the Colombians left us and headed up the mountain by himself, and we were told to wait. After about an hour, he came back and told us that it was OK, we could keep going. We started hiking again, and finally, we got to the top of the ridge. That's when I saw it: a whole mountainside covered in cannabis, basking in the sun. It was a beautiful sight. It smelled like money. There were a dozen Colombians hanging around, and one came forward. He was the only guy that didn't have a rifle over his shoulder. He said something in Spanish.

"What did he say?" I asked Ben.

"He wants to know how much we want."

I moved my eyes toward that sunny ridge, covered in Santa Marta gold.

"Tell him we want all of it," I said. "The whole goddamn mountain."

We stayed up in the jungle that night and hiked down the next morning, back to the oceanside. Sure enough, when we reached the beach, we had to make that same trip again, four long hours in a cayuca back to El Rodadero Beach, bailing seawater all the way.

"If we ever come here again," I told Ben, "we're gonna make sure they have an open fisherman," meaning a center-console motorboat. "I don't like this at all. This shit worries me."

Ben and I made a deal with his connection for fifteen thousand pounds. We agreed to pay a fair price—$60 a pound—and they agreed to front us the product, with a $50,000 downstroke. We'd pay off the rest of the roughly million bucks we'd owe for the load after we'd sold it. The price was good money to them, and at that price, we could make what felt at the time like a killing—if everything went as planned. That was a big if! Everything had to go right, from the transportation to the distribution to the many exchanges of money—and all of that without getting busted by the federally funded antidrug warriors.

I had no idea what the consequences would be for getting busted for fifteen thousand pounds. Never even thought about it.

It was going to take a couple weeks to get all that weed harvested, trimmed, cured, and packaged, so we flew out of Barranquilla to an island six hundred miles off the coast called Bon Aire. This became a routine. Every time I left Colombia, I flew to some other spot to clear customs, so when I came back to the United States, I looked more like a tourist on a Caribbean vacation than a smuggler.

We had what are called sideband radios, these huge radios with big antennas. We set one up in Ben's house, and the connection in Colombia had one, so we had a schedule to check in at a particular time, on a particular frequency. That way we could talk to them without using telephones. When they told us they were ready to go with the fifteen thousand pounds, we sent word through our sideband radio to the *Ursa Major*, which was docked in the Bahamas. I had hired Slick to be my boat captain because he could fix anything—diesel engines, hydraulic pumps, AC units—and he was trustworthy. We also hired two other crewmembers, and we outfitted the three of them in nice khaki boat uniforms to make the operation look like a charter yacht for rich vacationers in the Caribbean.

The *Ursa Major* left the Bahamas for Aruba, an island a half day's ride from Santa Marta. That would become our spot for staging our operations. A couple days later, Ben and I boarded a flight bound for Colombia. It was on.

9

Becoming an
International Smuggler

Summer 1982

*T*he streets of Santa Marta can humble you. It has these whitewashed colonial buildings, and mountain vistas all around. The old cathedral, the Catedral Basílica de Santa Marta, is so beautiful when it's lit up at night, it could make any skeptic believe in God. At the same time, the poverty is extreme. A lot of shanties. A lot of people without shoes. Meanwhile, I'd just purchased for Pam her second Mercedes. Still, this trip to Santa Marta was about to crystalize a wonderful relationship with the family in charge of the mountain farms and the whole tight-knit community around them.

On the outskirts of town, we reached the compound where we would be staying—with the family in charge. Let's call them the Family with a capital F, from here on out. The Family lived in this compound, which consisted of a few houses surrounded entirely by a tall wall painted blue, with shards of glass from broken bottles of all different colors cemented onto the top of the wall, sort of like barbed wire. Some guys opened a big wooden gate, and our driver took us inside.

The Family consisted of a couple, in their forties, with two kids, ages eleven and fourteen. Other houses were for workers and other family members, all of it enclosed in the compound. The Family's house had a roof built out of wooden trellises covered in grapevines, and there was this big patio with stacks of cages filled with all kinds of birds. Some of the birds could speak Spanish. I stood there listening to them as they shouted at me in a language I didn't understand. It was bizarre. Felt like the *Twilight Zone*.

Ben and I introduced ourselves. They spoke no English, so I had to rely on Ben to roughly translate. While the matriarch and her help cooked dinner—I could smell that we were going to have some kind of seafood—their daughter got my attention. She brought out a vinyl record and showed it to me. Surprisingly, it was the Kenny Rogers album *The Gambler*.

"Hey Ben," I joked, "it's your favorite singer."

He rolled his eyes. The girl put the record on the player in the house. She could sort of sing the words in English, and she wanted to know what the words meant. Ben tried to translate for her. Over and over, she played that song until her father told her to stop.

We all sat down at a long table outside, and big bowls of fish soup came out of the kitchen, with chunks of bread. I looked down at the soup and I saw a fish eyeball staring back at me. There was fish skin and fish scales and bones along with some corn and potatoes floating in there. As we ate, they told us about the political situation in Colombia and about the rise of Pablo Escobar as a kind of revolutionary folk hero. We

talked about motor racing. We talked about everything, seemingly, except weed. The Family had a strict rule: no business
at the dinner table.

The patriarch had a warm smile and looked into my eyes
when he spoke. He was inviting trust, and I communicated it
back to him. We were forming a partnership. In my mind, we
were going to make history by creating an empire together.
The Family stood to gain from this as much as Ben and I did,
perhaps more.

On the day of the load, Ben, myself, and some Colombians
went out to a small bay surrounded by jungle and mountains.
This was the location where we had instructed Slick to meet
us. We motored around in a cayuca, searching for the *Ursa
Major*. All day we hunted for it along the coastline, until finally we saw the ship appear on the horizon.

"That's it!" I said, looking through binoculars. "I see it!"
With all that work we'd done, she was a true beauty, freshly
painted crystal white, as clean as the white of a wedding
dress, with navy-blue trim and brown wooden accents. The
name *Ursa Major* was painted in small, elegant black letters on
the bow. The sight of it made me proud and more than a little
exhilarated. I loved that boat!

We made contact and motioned for the *Ursa Major* to follow
us. When we got to the bay where we would load the ship,
all these Colombians came out of the jungle, many of them
pulling cayucas onto the beach. After a little huddle and some
logistical discussion, the Colombians went to work. These
deeply tanned shirtless men started loading the cayucas with

bales of weed. Meanwhile, we took our cayuca onto the water, up alongside the *Ursa Major*. Slick's face was sunburned, leathered, and creased. We made eye contact, but there was no time for polite conversation.

The cayucas were now coming our way. If you saw this scene in a movie, it would blow your mind—all of these cayucas filled with men and weed, surrounding the *Ursa Major*, which was aglow against the setting sun. Slick threw ropes down so the Colombians could hold the cayucas in place while they handed these heavy bales up to guys on the deck, one bale at a time. Other Colombians stood on the deck of the ship, carrying the bales down into the belly of the hull. It was strangely silent.

Right as the last rays of sun were disappearing, I saw a ship pull up along the coastline on the edge of the horizon. I stood up in the cayuca, ready to panic.

"Fuck!" I yelled. "Right there!"

Ben turned and saw the ship. It was about a quarter mile away.

"*Amigo*," yelled the Colombian at the helm of our cayuca. "*No te preocupes. Esa es la policia. Ellas estan aqui para protegernos.*"

He smiled.

"What the fuck did he say?" I asked Ben.

"That's the police," Ben responded. "They're here to protect us."

Goddamn, I was thinking. *Only in Colombia.*

It took hours to load all fifteen thousand pounds. This was enough grass to fill an eighteen-wheeler to the ceiling. And we were just getting started. Let me tell you: it was fucking amazing.

When we had it done, Slick fired up the engines and steered the *Ursa Major* for the open ocean doing twelve knots, full speed ahead. Ben and I went back to the compound in Santa Marta, arriving after midnight. We stayed up all night listening to the birds sing to us in Spanish. Then we flew out that day. We were partly there but had a long way to go.

Days later, I stood on the beach in Fort Lauderdale, staring out at the horizon, knowing that the *Ursa Major* was making its way toward me with a load that amounted to millions in cash. I was a millionaire already, but this kind of cash would double my net worth. I stood there for hours staring, listening to the crashing waves, thinking about what that money could do for Pam and me, for Brandie, and for my motor racing. I felt as nervous as I did before my first professional race, as expectant as I did the night before I got married, and almost as excited as I did the day Brandie was born.

With that kind of cash, I could build my own professional team from the ground up, with top-level machinery. That was the plan.

I'd rented a house right on the A-1-A road, its back facing out on a bluff on the beach near the Sebastian Inlet, eighty miles north of Fort Lauderdale. This is where we'd unload. There were only two houses on this beach bluff, and weeks in advance, I'd mailed paperwork to the only neighbors for an all-expenses paid trip to Disney World. They took the bait, so I gave this family of strangers a fully paid vacation, and the week of the landing, they were gone. We had the whole beach to ourselves, for about a mile in either direction.

Ben and I were in touch with Captain Slick via sideband radio. I was expecting the *Ursa Major* to appear off the beach at night, and on the morning before, I had a friend who owned a twin-engine Cessna take me up on a flight to monitor the coast. I was in the front passenger seat with binoculars when I saw it—a one-hundred-foot Coast Guard cutter sitting right at the mouth of the Sebastian Inlet, its nose pointed toward the Bahamas, and a huge rotating radar unit on the bridge.

"Goddamnit!" I yelled. "Look at that, right there!"

"What?" said the Cessna captain.

"That Coast Guard cutter! Right there!"

We turned the aircraft around. When we landed, I rushed to Ben's house because he had the sideband radio. I got a message out to Slick. "It ain't gonna be tonight," I said. But the next day, the same thing happened. I went up in the plane, and there was that Coast Guard cutter again. It hadn't moved. I radioed Slick again, but this time, he wasn't hearing it. He had no choice; he was going to have to risk motoring right past that cutter.

"I'm low on fuel, Randy," Slick said. "Running out of gas. I have no choice. I'm coming in tonight."

That evening, as Slick motored on low throttle toward the Florida coast, the Coast Guard cutter contacted him directly on the radio: "This is the US Coast Guard. Please leave this area. We will be conducting firing practice." He had to change his course while trying not to use up fuel. And the Coast Guard had him on their radar.

I had a massive operation ready to go. I named it the Beach Assault. I wanted everything to run smoothly, safely, and quickly.

Inflatable Zodiacs, the same kind used by the Navy Seals, lay on the sand by the water ready to go—six of them with 25-horsepower motors.

A fleet of vans sat in a nearby motel parking lot, and I had rented rooms for the drivers, who were now waiting by their phones for my go signal.

I had two men stationed on the beach a half mile away on either side of the house, armed with guns; if these look-out guys saw any lovers strolling on this beach, they were instructed to flash the guns and tell these people to sit down on the beach and remain quiet. If anybody came upon this beach and was told to leave, they'd go to a pay phone and call the cops, so I told my guys to say, "You're not going to get hurt. Something's going on. I need you to sit here on the beach and not move. We're not here to rob you, not here to hurt you."

I had night vision goggles strapped to my head, and I paced the porch on the back of the rented house, awaiting the ship.

Meanwhile, a dozen guys waited on the beach, enough manpower to carry the fifteen thousand pounds, everyone dressed in black so they wouldn't be seen by a helicopter or airplane overhead.

After midnight, I spotted the *Ursa Major* a half mile off-shore—an orange light beaming in the moonlight.

"Alright," I yelled. "Go time! Let's go! Let's go!"

Slick had one Zodiac on board the *Ursa Major*, and this was to be the first boat in. He sent one man from his crew motoring to the beach with the first bales. Now, as if I'd flipped a switch, my guys sprang into action and the operation began. They fired up their Zodiacs and started motoring out into the ocean. From the house, I could hear the engines buzzing against the sound of crashing waves. Two men stayed on the beach, ready to wade into the surf to help pull the Zodiacs onto the sand when they arrived fully loaded. I thought to myself: *I can't believe it. It is really happening.*

It was grueling work. The beach bluff rose eight feet high, and the men had to throw these fifty-pound bales up that bluff to the next guy, who was going to carry it into the house—fifteen thousand pounds in total—with the sand shifting under their feet. The Zodiacs came in through the surf loaded down with weight. But after unloading, when they headed back out to sea, they were lighter and the waves pummeled them.

At one point, I heard screaming. "Help! Help!" One of the Zodiacs had flipped in the surf, and I had a man in distress. I couldn't see him, even with the night vision goggles. It was pitch black out there and the waves were three to five feet high. All I could see was the faint orange light aboard the *Ursa*, a half mile out. I ran off the wooden deck behind the house all the way to the edge of the sea, searching for this guy. I could hear him yelling, "Help!" But my eyes couldn't find him.

"Swim, you motherfucker!" I screamed. "Swim!"

The last thing I wanted was for anyone to get hurt. I ran down the beach, figuring the guy got caught in a riptide. Finally, I saw him swimming his way in and clawing up onto the sand. When he made it, he lay on the beach on his back in all his clothes, breathing so hard he looked like he was having a coronary. That he was alive was good news, but the Zodiac he was on was gone. Now we were down a boat.

I turned and sprinted back up to the house so I could get on the phone and start summoning the vans. The first one pulled up, and I began loading the bales as fast as I could. Then came the next van and the next. Drivers screeched off as soon as the vans were loaded, heading for the stash house, where Charles Podesta was waiting to log in each bale and keep track of everything.

All night long, the Beach Assault moved like clockwork, and the last van took off minutes before sunrise. When that sun came up, all my guys were lying on the beach exhausted from the longest night of manual labor of their lives. We'd moved fifteen thousand pounds in one night—and we still weren't entirely done yet. I sent Zodiacs out to the *Ursa Major* full of cleaning products, a vacuum cleaner, and fuel. I told Slick and his crew to clean and sterilize the fuck out of that boat. I didn't want even a hint of cannabis residue anywhere on it.

Sure enough, the following day, that same Coast Guard cutter I'd seen earlier approached the *Ursa*, and the Coast Guard officers asked to come aboard. By that time, the boat was clean and clear, and the inspectors found nothing. Slick followed my orders to take the ship to Freeport in the Bahamas and wait there for word from me.

At the same time, the distributors started showing up at the stash house in their vehicles, and Charles supervised loading in the stash house garage behind closed doors. Within twenty-four hours of landing this weed, it was all gone, on highways bound for New York, Michigan, Pennsylvania, and elsewhere. The distributors brought it to their own stash houses, and from there, they sold bales to smaller distributors, who busted open the bales and packed up pounds and ounces for fun-loving customers. Everything was compartmentalized. The smoker who bought it knew nothing and no one, except the guy who sold it to him. The middle man knew nothing and no one, except the guy who sold it to him. Etc.

Meanwhile, the money made its way up the food chain. I was at the top.

And at the top, it was time to party. I rented out a private room at my favorite French restaurant in Fort Lauderdale. There was champagne. There was cocaine. Mountains of caviar. We had a big team of men, maybe twenty of us total. It was an unforgettable night. Just unreal.

When you run an operation like this, it takes time for all the accounts to settle up. I had Charles keeping a ledger of who owed whom and how much. A couple weeks passed before we were all paid out. Since the Colombians had fronted us the product (aside from the down payment), I had to pay them. They had connections that owned small businesses in Miami. A little bar-restaurant. A small travel agency. They told us where to go, and we delivered cash, driving up in unassuming cars and pulling huge suitcases full of money out of the trunks.

I was twenty-seven years old and a rich man. A score like that should have been a once-in-a-lifetime event, but I was already planning the next Beach Assault—an even bigger load, an even greater rush. We'd just pulled in the biggest beach smuggle operation Florida had probably ever seen. But we were just getting started.

10

Le Mans

1982

By the end of 1982, I'd brought in two more loads aboard the *Ursa Major*—one Beach Assault and one into the Florida canals. Each was bigger than the one before. Which meant multimillions in cash. Over the course of many desperately dark years in the future, while living behind bars in prison, I asked myself countless times: Why didn't I stop there? I could've lived out the rest of my years in style. So why didn't I?

The basic answer is this: I wanted to drive race cars. And when it came to racing, I wanted to up the ante, to get more experience, to invest in world-class equipment, and to hire the best personnel. I was thinking: How does a South Florida guy with a little jet ski rental business get to the Indy 500? With no backing from Marlboro cigarettes or Coca-Cola? No help from anybody? I wanted to get to the top—to be a champion.

Isn't that what every kid dreams of? To be the best?

I believed in myself. All I needed was money—a lot of it.

There were other reasons, too. I'm not trying to rationalize my choices, but a lot of people were depending on me. A lot of people were looking to me to help them put food on the table. All the off-loaders, the drivers, the distributors, the stash house sitters. Most of these people were childhood friends, people I'd known for most of my life. There were bonds of trust that went both ways: I trusted them to get the job done and keep their mouths shut, and they trusted me to keep the work coming. We all came from nothing, and they were becoming financially stable because of my exploits, at an age when many of them were starting to have children.

Then there was the whole culture of South Florida. There was something in the ethos of the place that made it unlike any other. There were so many characters—the Muscle Billys and the Ben Kramers—who looked to the sea and to boats as a way to make money and a way to compete and who were comfortable taking extraordinary risks.

I was a product of that ethos. It was in my blood.

Anytime the threat of getting caught entered my mind, I was able to whitewash it. When you're in a race car, you can come out of a turn at extraordinary speed, and you know this cement wall is there and if you fuck up, or even if there's an equipment failure that's out of your control, you could hit that wall and it's going to hurt. You could die. If you let yourself think about it—if you let that doubt and fear creep into your consciousness—you won't be able to get on the throttle. So you push those thoughts out. In my mind, the threat of getting caught did not, could not, exist.

Somebody may crash today or die tomorrow. Ain't gonna be me.

Still, there was another reason I continued building my empire. I have to admit: the lifestyle got ahold of me. Being able to *provide* my family with the best things in life—there's a pride that comes with that. Pam grew up the daughter of an alcoholic butcher. I grew up working construction. We wanted Brandie to have a different life, and we were getting used to the lifestyle. Living in a mansion. Having a maid. Drinking the best champagne. I loved being able to give those gifts to my wife, the love of my life.

And when you start making millions of dollars, actually holding all that cash in your hands, feeling the invigoration of success and achievement—you want to feel that feeling again and again. The exhilaration can be addictive.

In the winter of 1982, I bought my first house in Colorado in a town called Nederland in the Rockies. Pam and I brought a babysitter out there, and we'd ski for days on end at Vail, Copper Mountain, and Breckenridge. We played with the baby in this winter wonderland, feeding wild elk from our hands and hot tubbing while the snowflakes collected in our hair. These were magical times.

We started going to Europe regularly, with a whole entourage. I brought my brother Bobby to Paris, Geneva, and Venice. Charles Podesta—always the elegant gentleman—brought along his girlfriend. Charles was like our guide because he could speak Italian and could get by in Spanish and French. We went to London, Amsterdam, Milan, Florence. I loved to go running through Rome and Venice at sunrise, when the streets were empty except for the shop owners who were sweeping the sidewalks with homemade brooms.

These trips weren't just vacations though. I hired a lawyer in Europe who was teaching me how to set up offshore accounts in Panama and trust accounts in Switzerland and

Liechtenstein. After the Beach Assault loads, I started flying over on the Concorde with hundreds of thousands of dollars hidden in my suitcases each time to hide in these offshore accounts.

One day, back in Florida, I was driving down Sunrise Boulevard in Fort Lauderdale when I passed an auto dealership called Prestige Motor Cars. I turned around and pulled into the parking lot, and through the glass window, I saw a Ferrari BB 512. This was the flagship production Ferrari that came out after the 308, the famous *Magnum P.I.* car. It was also the consumer version of the BB 512 Ferrari race car that I'd driven in my pro debut at Daytona. This particular model on the showroom floor was a strange color—raspberry. I bought it for $82,000 on the spot, and let me tell you, when people saw that raspberry Ferrari roll down the streets under the South Florida sun, they stopped in their tracks. They'd gawk from the sidewalks, wondering who the beautiful woman was riding in the passenger seat.

The cars, the houses, the vacations, the responsibilities—it all got to me, plunged me in deeper and deeper. Most of all, though, it was about winning. It's a mind-set. Smuggling was going to get me there.

In the spring of 1982, I was in my race shop one day working on my Porsche when the phone rang. It was Preston Henn, who'd given me my shot at the 24 Hours of Daytona.

"Randy," he said, "I'm putting together a team to go to Le Mans. I want to know if you wanna come."

"What," I said, "you mean to hang out and party?"

Preston chuckled. "No, Randy. I want you to be a driver on the team."

I damn near dropped the phone. Le Mans? To my mind, this was the most important race in the world outside of the Indy 500. It's an international phenomenon, a historic event where the world's best sports car racing teams, some backed by the big factories like Porsche and Jaguar, clash in a world war of speed.

"Hell yeah, Preston!" I said. "Damn skippy! I won't let you down, man!"

"Good," he said. "Get your things in order. We leave in six weeks."

I was a busy man. At this time, I was just putting together my third Beach Assault. My plan was to get it done before heading to Le Mans. So I gathered the team—about eight guys—in a private room at a French restaurant in Fort Lauderdale. My right-hand man, Charles, was there, as was Slick with his crew. We ordered a whole mess of food—stewed fish and duck and escargots—and when the waiters had brought it all to the table, I shut the door so no one in the restaurant could hear us.

"What do we need to do," I asked the team, "to make this operation run more smoothly this time? How can we innovate? What can be done better and faster?"

One of the guys brought up the issue of weight. Carrying all that weight up a ten-foot beachhead, with your feet in the soft sand, was no joke. During the last Beach Assault, the guys were complaining of fatigue and aching calves.

I said, "What if I got, like, an AstroTurf carpet that we could roll out from the edge of the water where the Zodiacs are landing on the beach, all the way to the back of the house?"

"That'll work."

I added, "I can also arrange to have the bags weigh forty pounds rather than fifty."

Another one of my guys said, "We still have to carry all that weight and load it into the vans."

"OK . . . ayyyight . . . ," I was thinking. "What if we got some kind of conveyor belt that can run from the bottom of the sand dune to the top. There would be no heaving the bales up."

"Yeah, that'll work."

"That sounds good."

I was able to find a collapsible electric conveyor belt at a construction equipment store, and it plugged right into a wall outlet. I found AstroTurf carpet at a hardware store, and I rolled it out to make a perfect pathway that led from the surf, up the beach bluff, and all the way into the house. On the night of the third Beach Assault, I still felt those same nerves, that same rush. We had the Zodiacs fueled up and in position, and the van drivers waiting in their nearby motel rooms. When I saw the *Ursa Major* appear—like clockwork, an orange light flashing a half mile out at sea—I set the operation in motion.

"Go! Go! Go!"

A few months earlier, it had taken us all night to unload fifteen thousand pounds. Now, we brought in twenty thousand in half the time on this integrated transportation system. Henry Ford would've been proud. I know I was.

I had distributors ready to roll, and within forty-eight hours, all the weed was gone from the stash houses. Slick and his crew scrubbed the *Ursa Major* clean with bleach and were headed for Freeport on the island of Grand Bahama. Charles Podesta was counting money in one of the stash houses.

Two weeks later, I packed my bags and headed to the airport for a flight to France to compete at the oldest, still-running endurance racing event in the world.

The weeks leading up to Le Mans in 1982 were eerily bloody in the field of motorsport. The Canadian Gilles Villeneuve was killed at the Belgian Grand Prix on May 8. Two weeks later, Gordon Smiley died in one of the most horrific crashes in Indy 500 history, when he hit a wall pretty much straight on at 200 mph during his qualifying runs. "He couldn't hit the wall no harder," A. J. Foyt said. "Car just exploded. There was nothing left of him." On the very day we were scheduled to leave for France, the Italian Riccardo Paletti was killed in the Canadian Grand Prix.

Meanwhile, Le Mans was probably the most dangerous race in the world, the most dangerous sporting event of any kind. It was here in 1955 that the French driver Pierre Levegh launched a Mercedes-Benz 300 SLR racing car off the track and into the crowd, killing around eighty-five people; this was the deadliest incident in sports history. Not even that could stop Le Mans from happening. It was a race so important to win that drivers were willing to risk everything.

Our team of three drivers at Le Mans was supposed to be Preston, John Paul Jr., and me, but when we boarded the flight, John Paul Sr.—who was coming with us in a supporting role—told us that his son had missed the flight.

"What the fuck, man!" Preston said. "Where is he?"

"I don't know," John Paul Sr. answered. Turns out, he was lying.

We took off on our overnight flight from Miami to Paris. I had a whole entourage. Pam was with me (we'd left Brandie at home with Pam's best friend), along with Charles and his girlfriend, Margaret, and my brother Bobby. Preston and John Paul Sr. both had their own entourages. The team (meaning Preston, mainly) was paying for us to stay in an incredible chateau. It was huge—fifty-six rooms, just for us. When we pulled into this dramatic circular driveway in the rolling hills of the Loire wine region, the maids and the chef came out all dressed in clean white and lined up to greet us and help us bring our luggage inside.

There was drama right off the bat. John Paul Sr. waited until we were in our chateau to tell us his son wasn't coming at all. If I remember correctly, John Paul Jr. had gotten some kind of offer with NASCAR. So we were down a driver.

"I'll fill in for him," John Paul Sr. said.

"Hell no, you won't," Preston came back. "Not happening."

I could tell John Paul Sr. had assumed that Preston would let him drive. Preston had sponsorship money for the car, but otherwise, he was paying for everything himself, so he was calling the shots. This was not a factory team from Porsche or Ferrari. We were a privateer team, our own little outfit, which meant money was always an issue, no matter how rich we all were. The team had to rent out a place to stay, had to ship the car and a spare engine and thousands and thousands of dollars' worth of spare parts and tires, from Florida to France and back. Preston had lined all this up, and there was no way he was going to let John Paul Sr. drive on our team. Preston felt that Sr. should have alerted us that Jr. wasn't coming, in advance. Besides, while Sr. was fast, I believe that Preston felt that Jr. was the real talent of the two.

The next morning, we all met in a dining room that had a walk-in fireplace for roasting hogs and a wooden table that easily sat twenty people. Everyone showed up for breakfast except John Paul Sr. After breakfast, we went to the track for the sign-in day. At Le Mans, the sign-in day is a giant ceremony with swarms of people, where every driver comes up onto a stage, has his name and nationality announced to the fans, and then signs his name into the register book. There were no fewer than fifty-five teams racing at Le Mans that year with three to four drivers each, and every one of the drivers got a hero's welcome at that ceremony. It's a surreal experience.

I'd competed in my first race less than three years earlier, and now I was at Le Mans surrounded by my heroes. Mario Andretti was set to compete. Bobby Rahal. Jacky Ickx. Hurley Haywood. Derek Bell. Bill Whittington was there, too, and an army of the best endurance racing drivers from Japan, Germany, Britain, and France. Swarms of media approached our team. I even signed my first autographs.

When it was our turn to sign in at the ceremony, the officials told Preston that one of our team drivers had already signed in. A look of confusion came over Preston's face. I heard him say, "Who would that be?" The official took us to the register book and showed us. There was John Paul Sr.'s signature. Smoke started coming out of Preston's ears. He went hunting for John Paul, and I was sure these two were headed for a brawl. As in, actual fisticuffs.

Meanwhile, I stuck with our Ferrari racing car. Scrutineers studied every one of the cars to make sure it met the gazillions of Le Mans rules.

When I got back to the chateau that night, John Paul Sr. was gone. Preston had kicked him out and hired a third driver—a French guy named Denis Morin, who promised sponsorship money from a French company called Chemises Playboy (*Playboy*-branded clothing for the French market). This guy didn't speak a lick of English. Not one word. We spoke no French. So getting him acclimated to the car during practice was going to be tricky. To me, this felt like an ominous way to go into this race. I was feeling the nerves, big-time.

On race day, 250,000 fans were at the track. That's the equivalent of packing Yankee Stadium four times over. There was a lot of partying, a lit-up Ferris wheel spinning, and a drunken, carnival atmosphere. TV cameras were ready to roll, relaying footage to all corners of the globe. While Le Mans fanfare didn't approach that of the Indy 500, it was the most watched motor race in the rest of the world.

Finally, after all the anticipation, the time came to get in the car and drive. This was the same BB 512 Ferrari I drove at Daytona. Lightning fast. Explosively loud. Just an all-around badass car. Europe's most famous race was held on an 8.467-mile course made of cordoned-off public roads that run through the countryside outside the old city. Like the 24 Hours of Daytona, at Le Mans, teams of drivers race this course for a full twenty-four hours, with one guy in the car at a time, and the car that travels the farthest during that time wins.

In practice, my lap times were solid. I felt comfortable in the car, and I felt comfortable on the track. When the race started at 3 p.m. on June 19, 1982, Preston took the first stint, and I stood in the pit, watching the action and listening to the French announcer screaming into the loudspeaker system. The whole place thundered with the sound of engines and speed. After a few laps, you could close your eyes and identify a specific race car motoring past you just by its exhaust note. There was certainly no mistaking the wail of our Ferrari's twelve cylinders.

After an hour, Preston pulled into the pit. He stepped out of the cockpit, and I jumped in. Here we go. Time to shine.

Pulling out of the pits at Le Mans, you accelerate up a hill, under a big bridge, then down a hill that leads to an uphill left-hand turn. Imagine the most powerful roller coaster on earth, with g-forces that cannot be believed until you experience them. That's the sensation, and this is only the first few turns of this long track. A fast right-hand corner leads you onto the Mulsanne Straight, the most famous and fastest straightaway in all of international racing—3.7 miles of throttle-pinned speed. At any other track, you'd be hard-pressed to find a spot where you're flooring the pedal for more than ten seconds. At Le Mans, you're doing it for roughly a minute—straight line top speed.

At the end of the straight, you have about two seconds to brake from top speed, which was about 190 mph for us, into a 35-mph right-hander. Dumping that amount of velocity that fast makes you feel like your brain is going to liquefy and spill out your nose.

Then it's back down hard on the throttle, into a left-hand corner called Indianapolis (after the Indy Motor Speedway), and then you jerk the car into a right-hand turn called Arnage. A handful more turns, and you end up hurling yourself back down the front straightaway with the grandstands on either side, so you feel like you're motoring at top speed on a straight road through a sold-out football stadium.

All around you, the world's most exotic racing sports cars are doing what they were made to do. Porsche 956s and 935s. Other Ferrari BB 512s like ours. BMW M1s and Ford-powered Rondeaus.

I got myself into a flow state. Something was happening inside me. Five years of racing experience had led me to this moment. I could demand all that this car could give, while aiming it with acute precision. All my senses were raised to their limits. Time ceased to exist. "To become one with the machine" is an oft-used cliché, but it can be an actual reality on the track. The thing that gets you is exhaustion. You become so mentally and physically depleted, so drenched in your own fluids, you can lose sight of your braking point so easily.

After my one-hour stint, I pulled into the pits. I felt immensely relieved. No bent metal, no drama. I got out and handed the car to our French teammate, Morin, who looked tremendously nervous to me.

I yelled, "The car is running beautifully. Ayyyight?"

He didn't make eye contact, and I realized he had no idea what I'd just said.

Preston was stalking the pit in his cowboy hat and fire-proof coveralls. I mentioned to him that the Frenchman was going to have to come in for fuel at some point. When the time came, we started signaling to him. A member of the crew leaned over the pit wall with a sign that the driver could see when he passed the pits. PIT 5 meant pit in five laps. Then PIT 4, PIT 3, etc. Well, we flashed the pit signal, and this Frenchman drove right by. He just kept going. We tried to reach him over the radio, but the guy didn't respond.

Standing in the pit, I turned to Preston. "What the fuckkkkk?"

Preston shook his head. We had no idea what to do. The tension was unbearable. We had to reach this guy before it was too late.

Just under four minutes later, when he came down the pit straight again after another lap, we signaled to him: time to pit for fuel. Again, he kept on going. There was a big orange light that flashed on the Ferrari's instrument panel when fuel was low, but the Frenchman didn't know what it meant. We'd tried to explain to him what that light signified during practice before the race, but apparently he didn't understand.

And then it happened. This guy ran out of fuel on the track. He pulled over, parked the car, and our race was over, after just forty-three laps. When we got word in our pit, Preston picked up his helmet and threw it against a wall. We'd come all this way, lugged a car plus all that equipment, just so this guy we'd never met before could run the car dry. Pam was in our garage in the pits, and when I explained to her what happened, she couldn't believe her ears.

"You got to be fucking kidding me!" she said.

All I could answer with was, "Well, honey, that's racing."

The 1982 24 Hours of Le Mans was won by the team of Jacky Ickx and Derek Bell, in a Rothman's Porsche 956. Porsche racing cars took the top five spots. Even if we didn't do as well as I'd hoped, I now had Le Mans on my résumé, which put me among the top rank of sports car racers in the US. We headed back to the States to finish our racing season in America. I was ready for the next step, to drive into the limelight of American sports car racing.

11

Cocaine

1982

*I*t seemed like every time I turned on the TV in 1982, Ronald Reagan was staring back at me. The president's anti-drug campaign dominated the news. A lot was happening in 1982. Argentina and Britain were at war over the Falkland Islands. Michael Jackson released *Thriller*. But above all that was this unprecedented and relentless campaign by the Reagan administration to warn the nation about this perceived threat—that weed and cocaine were going to fry the brains of the next generation of American kids and destroy humanity in the process.

In October, Reagan announced the hiring of twelve hundred new federal agents to fight organized drug crime. He announced that the United States was going to spend millions of dollars to build new prisons to house all these drug crooks. He also announced a plan to create a new drug task force headed by his vice president, George Bush, with its headquarters located in the heart of the American drug frenzy—South Florida. The Associated Press reported:

The Administration has claimed that, with the help of military technology, it has reduced the smuggling of drugs into Florida. The government used planes equipped with sophisticated radar devices to detect illegal entries along the South Florida coast. Officials said the drive caused a drop in the wholesale prices of marijuana and cocaine in Colombia, the main source of the drugs.

That same month, Reagan told Americans, "We're making no excuses for drugs—hard, soft, or otherwise. Drugs are bad and we're going after them. . . . And we're going to win the War on Drugs." He never mentioned that this was a war on our own citizens. Prohibition didn't work back in the 1920s, and it wasn't going to work this time.

Days after making this statement, Reagan flew to Bogota for talks with Colombia's new president on the country's cocaine and marijuana export business. The newspapers were estimating that Colombia was supplying 80 percent of the world's cocaine and 70 percent of the weed. Reagan wanted it stopped, and he was prepared to negotiate.

The effects of the War on Drugs were far reaching in so many ways. Although I certainly didn't think about it at the time, the War on Drugs had disastrous effects on the poor and on minorities. I was a white guy living in a white world, but what was happening to Black and brown communities was devastating. The War on Drugs overflowed the prison system with people of color.

I saw nothing morally wrong with what we had been doing in the weed smuggling business. Sure, we were breaking the law. But nobody should be locked up for a plant. I believed in the healing properties of marijuana, and I still do. To me, smuggling weed was certainly no more villainous than what R. J. Reynolds—one of the biggest companies in the US—was doing, providing cancer-causing nicotine to millions.

Meanwhile, Coast Guard and customs ships began patrolling the coast of South Florida, big vessels with every kind of technology available and smaller speedy vessels with US customs logos on the side. The guys running these boats marked their hulls with a crossed-out marijuana leaf for each bust, like notches in a gun fighter's holster. You'd see these boats on the water with their long blue hulls, agents wearing sunglasses in the cockpit, out hunting for guys like me. We were not afraid of them, although we should've been. With the War on Drugs raging, we were preparing to scale up again.

One day early in the summer of 1982, I got a call from Slick with bad news. We had the *Ursa Major* anchored in Curaçao, a Caribbean island off the coast of Colombia. The ship's hynautic lines had broken, so now I had to ship barrels of hynautic fluid plus some parts and more equipment down to Curaçao. It was going to take a while to fix.

Then, several days later, my beeper went off. I didn't recognize the number. I called it back from a pay phone on a street corner in Fort Lauderdale. A crewmember of the *Ursa Major* answered the phone, from down in Curaçao.

"Holy fuck, Randy," he said. "I got bad news. Slick was working on the outboard engine of a Zodiac, and he fell into the flywheel. It ripped off half his bicep and threw him in the bay."

Turns out, Slick was using the Zodiac to go onto the island to drink whiskey and see prostitutes.

"Man!" I said. "I told him not to be doing that shit!"

"It was a bloody mess, man. I heard him screaming and ran out to the stern of the vessel. I found him in the water freaking out, man. Blood was everywhere. All over the Zodiac, all over the water. I dove in and got him out. Slick may lose his whole arm, man."

Naturally, my first concern was Slick's health. We found doctors on the island to take care of him. But I also needed a ship captain. He wasn't going to be ready, it sounded like, by the time I was going to need him. Then Slick made not only a dumb move but a disappointing one. He called me to complain about money. He told me that even though he wasn't going to be able to captain the ship for the next load, he was insisting he get paid in full anyway.

"If I'm not getting paid," Slick said, "nobody's getting paid."

I damn near lost it. What he meant was, if we didn't pay him his full amount for the next haul (even though he wasn't going to be the captain), he would drop a dime on all of us. He was threatening to go to the police. I was dumbfounded. Slick and I had been friends since we were kids.

I met up with Ben. It wasn't looking good for Slick. "We gotta get control of this situation," I said. "We gotta make sure Slick's mouth remains shut."

"I got the right guy to send down there," Ben answered. "I'll have it taken care of."

This made me nervous. Let's just say Ben didn't always play nice.

"Ayyyight," I said. "But I don't want Slick getting hurt. You understand?"

Ben sent someone down to Curaçao. This guy put a gun to Slick's head and told him to go to the *Ursa Major*'s captain's quarters. Slick was going to get locked in there until we had this whole thing straightened out. The room had a bed and a toilet in there, and they'd bring him meals. I imagine Slick was petrified, thinking they were going to take him way out to sea and chuck him overboard to die because the guy Ben sent down was the kind of guy who would do something like that.

Meanwhile, Slick's mutiny—if you can call it that—put us up against it. We were lining up the next load, and we needed a replacement. Finding a boat captain willing to bring in a load, during the drug war? Not easy to do. You can't just start taking résumés from strangers. The whole situation—Slick, the Reagan crackdown—was giving me insomnia.

"It's too friggin' dangerous," I told Ben one night while we were smoking a joint at his house in Hollywood. "We don't even have a captain now. The government is setting up navy blockades. The Coast Guard is stopping every vessel it can, and the Florida Marine Patrol is running all up and down the Florida coast. It's a fucking war out there, man. We're putting our crew in danger. People's lives are at stake here, man."

We were worried about logistics. Weed took up so much cargo space. You could smell it. The bales were so big, it was hard to move. Ben and I talked and talked, and at some point the conversation came around to: You know what takes up less cargo space? You know what's easier to hide? You know what doesn't smell?

Cocaine.

This was one of the most regretful decisions I ever made. Ben and I decided to work our contacts in Santa Marta for a cocaine connection. Thanks to Escobar and the whole scene in Colombia, cocaine importation into the United States in 1982 was exploding. Everybody else was getting in on it. Why not us?

Our contacts in Santa Marta recommended some guys in Bogota. We flew down there in the summer of 1982. Some guys picked us up at the airport and took us outside the city to a restaurant in a remote spot, with windows looking out at the jungle and the mountains. The view was incredible. We met our contacts there, and they spoke enough English that we could talk freely. We told them what we wanted and how we intended to carry our cargo aboard secret compartments in the *Ursa Major*.

The whole time, I felt it in my gut: I was crossing a line. Nobody should go to jail for a plant. But cocaine is not a plant. It's a drug made out of plants mixed with all kinds of nasty shit, and it's highly addictive. I had a gut instinct from the get-go that this was a bad idea, but I didn't listen.

These Colombians weren't like the Family. They were slick. They wore sport jackets, gold chains, and smoked a lot of cigarettes. When we were buying weed in Santa Marta, our source fronted us the product, and we paid them when we got the money. These guys weren't having it. They wanted to be paid up front, and they wanted us to carry more than we could hide in the ship's secret compartments. We couldn't make a deal, so the whole thing was a waste of time.

We flew back to Florida empty-handed.

But Ben had a connection in Miami, and he ended up working out a deal with a lady who had a badass reputation. She was from Colombia but lived in Miami. She would later go on to become a highly famous and powerful kingpin in the South Florida cocaine scene, a woman responsible, reportedly, for a lot of dead people. At that time, she was just getting started, but she was already a dangerous woman. Let's call her the Spider.

Ben and the Spider met in Miami without me. She arranged for us to pick up a load in her home country and to have it fronted to us, so we could pay later, after we moved it. We'd smuggle it in, sell it, and pay her $20,000 per kilo. At the time, a kilo of high-quality powder was going for $50,000 in South Florida.

"That is not a bad deal," I told Ben. "We'll sell it for $50,000 a kilo and profit thirty grand per key."

We decided to go ahead with this deal.

We brought in a load of one hundred kilos of coke, planning on a $3 million profit. This would be the last time we used the *Ursa Major* because, from here on out, a sixty-five-foot boat wouldn't be big enough. Not even close. The entire time the *Ursa Major* was motoring west through the Caribbean Sea from Colombia with all that coke on board, Slick was still locked in the state room. Ben had brought in a new captain, a guy I didn't know.

I arranged for a twenty-eight-foot open fisherman to meet the *Ursa Major* off of Freeport, in the Bahamas. We arranged a set of coordinates and a meet-up time to transfer the load. This twenty-eight-footer was faster and nimbler than the *Ursa Major*, and the secret compartment was better. The whole center console of this boat, with the throttle and steer-ing wheel and all the gauges, was on secret hinges so it could lift up on one side, right off the floor. Under it was the secret compartment. That's some ingenious shit.

The day that this cocaine-laden twenty-eight-footer was set to pull through Haulover Inlet into the Port of Miami, I went out there in my thirty-six-foot Cigarette. We chose a weekend day when we knew there'd be a lot of boats on the water. I went out to Haulover Inlet, taking it easy. When I got out into the ocean, I spotted the open fisherman. I kept myself within sight of it but at a distance, and I hammered the Cigarette's engines, tearing up the water as aggressively as I could, think-ing that if the Coast Guard was going to pull anyone over, it'd be me. Those Cigarette boats had so much power, it was in-sane, and I made sure I was the biggest idiot out there. I never did get pulled over though.

While I was racing around in my Cigarette, the twenty-eight-foot open fisherman slid quietly into Haulover Inlet in North Miami. We had a friend of mine waiting at the first boat ramp north of the inlet with a trailer and truck to pull the open fish-erman out of the water. He trailered the boat behind his truck to his house, where it stayed overnight, with the whole load still inside. The next day, I showed up at his house. We quietly unloaded the cocaine into a van and took it to a stash house.

Each kilo was the size of a football, and the coke was stun-ningly good. It was a product we called mirror flake, and when you busted some out, it looked like fish scales. I went through the kilos and picked out the choicest one. That was going to be my personal stash. Now that was a mistake right there—the first of many.

At that time in 1982, seemingly overnight and despite the War on Drugs, South Florida suddenly got flooded with cocaine, and from there, it went everywhere. Everyone had it. It seemed like at any club, any party—from the small-town discotheques to the toilet stalls of Wall Street—there were lines of cocaine spread out on a makeup mirror, and some dude bent over hoovering them up. I later learned that, in Colombia, Pablo Escobar had established a new route through the Caribbean into South Florida, and the Medellín cartel was smuggling in so much cocaine that the bottom dropped out of the market. I'd agreed to sell our coke for $50,000 per kilo, but in reality, I would be lucky to get half that.

On top of that, I was no coke dealer. I didn't have any network—no distributors, no buyers, nothing—and I was not about to go out and pedal this shit on the street myself. Over the phone, I pleaded with the Spider, but she wouldn't budge. She wanted $20,000 per kilo.

Now I was screwed. I couldn't get rid of the stuff. It seemed the only coke I was moving was going up my nose.

"Ben, I can't sell this shit," I told Kramer over the phone. "I don't have this lady's money. I just want to give all this coke back to her and put all this behind us."

"If you want to do that, Randy, then we have to call a sit-down," Ben said. "You need to tell her that to her face."

Talk about an uncomfortable silence. Finally, I said, "OK. If that's what we gotta do to get us out of this mess, then let's get it over with."

This was the only time I saw the Spider in person. We met at the Aventura Mall in Miami, right near Thunder Boat Alley. She was a small woman from Cartagena with jowls that belied her young age, and eyes as mean and cold as you ever will see. We talked quietly at a restaurant—she, Ben, and I—while her bodyguards sat at the next table.

"Listen," I said, "I can't sell this shit. The bottom of the market has dropped out. This is a disaster. We need to negotiate and figure out a fair deal."

She was adamant about how much money she wanted. There was no way I was going to sway her. There was tension through the whole meeting.

At the end of it, I told her: "The bottom line is, I can't sell it. It's been months since we've had all this coke. It's not the market I'm in. I don't know any coke distributors."

I ended up giving her the coke back and taking a massive loss. I still had to pay my boat captains and all my crew who had worked on the load, thus far. I also paid off Slick—$150,000 if I remember correctly—and settled that matter. I promised myself I would never do anything again that went against my gut instincts.

I was partying too much, and the coke was making me paranoid. I moved my family out of our house and into a town house I purchased in Fort Lauderdale, on the Intracoastal Waterway. I didn't tell anyone where it was, not even my brothers and my sister. I didn't want anyone knowing where we were living. For the first time, I felt real fear of the law, and once that fear gets under your skin, it never leaves.

12

Blue Thunder

1983

Early in 1983—while the whole cocaine fiasco was playing out—I was in my race shop in Fort Lauderdale when I heard the phone ring.

"Hey, this is Randy speaking."

A guy was calling from Orlando. He said he owned a race team, and he planned on fielding a car for the 1983 24 Hours of Daytona, which was coming up fast. He had a March 83G GTP racing car. He had a major sponsor in Executone Communications, a phone company. And he wanted local South Florida drivers for his team. Notably, Marty Hinze, another guy named Terry Wolters, and myself. Was I interested?

"Damn skippy!"

I knew Marty Hinze through the Whittingtons. Marty had made a lot of money in the same business I was in, and he also lived in Davie. He was also a very accomplished driver. This dude could get the job done in a race car.

When I first set my eyes on that March 83G, my heart revved up. It was a slick machine, with a wide stance, a nose just inches off the ground, and a big Chevy V-8 mounted behind the cockpit—the rear engine position having been in vogue in racing since the 1960s. The car was painted white with blue, yellow, and black stripes, and it had a wing on the back as big as a surfboard. The word *Executone* was printed across the nose.

March may not mean much to race fans today, but back then, it was badass—a small but highly accomplished builder of racing chassis out of England (the company didn't build its own powerplants, thus the Chevy engine in the Executone car). The name was an anagram for its four founders: Max Mosely (a lawyer and driver who would go on to become one of the most powerful impresarios in the racing world), Alan Rees, Graham Coaker, and Robin Herd. March also had a young engineer working for them who'd go on to become one of the most accomplished race car designers ever—Adrian Newey, who, at the time, was just an up-and-comer.

While the March brand didn't have the glamour of Italian Ferrari, the 83G looked like it could be just as quick. I couldn't wait to get this thing on the track.

From my first practice lap in our March racing car, I was loving it. It had so much power, so much flat-out speed. Its center of gravity was so low to the ground, it cornered beautifully. Marty Hinze felt the same way as I did—that this car could be a winner. It would have to be good; the competition at Daytona was serious. Preston Henn was there, and he'd recruited A. J. Foyt with a bunch of money to join his team. My old friend Dale Whittington was there too, as was John Paul Jr., both racing Porsche 935s.

On race day at Daytona—February 7, 1983—we went out and ran hard. When it rains in sports car racing, the show goes on, and there's a delicate art to going fast on a wet track. Marty and I both squeezed all the speed out of that race car we could, and when the sun set, we were leading the field by far. In the middle of the night, I was awakened in my motor home to take over the car for another stint. I took off in the pounding rain, and after one lap, the car started sputtering on a few cylinders. I brought it back to the pit.

"Hey!" I screamed at my chief mechanic. "We need to either fix it or park it."

The team went to work. Water had gotten into the distributor. Meanwhile, the conditions worsened. A tropical depression had parked right over the track, and the stands had completely emptied out. By the time our car was ready, I charged back out in second but laps behind the A. J. Foyt and Preston Henn Porsche. I was clicking off the fastest laps I'd ever driven in the rain, as the Florida sun came up. I was lapping the field, gaining on the leader. I knew I had the fastest car out there, and if I kept on going, I would recapture first place.

Suddenly, I saw track stewards waving red flags. Game over. I punched the wheel in frustration. The officials were ending the race due to safety reasons. It was heartbreaking. If the race had run the full twenty-four hours, I would have won. But we finished in second—behind Preston and A. J. Foyt. And if I was only one place behind my hero now, close enough to touch greatness, it showed the rest of the world what I already knew: that I could hang with the best.

What followed early in 1983 was to set the stage for the launch of my own professional team. Marty had acquired his own March GTP race car, and he and I took it to the first-ever Budweiser Miami Grand Prix in February 1983. For the first time, Miami was going to host a professional sports car race on a road course mapped out on the city streets, right in my backyard, in the Bayfront neighborhood. All the best endurance drivers in America were flying into Miami. Fans turned out in droves. It was a wild scene.

I rented the biggest suite at the Everglades Hotel, which overlooked the racetrack. I also rented a pavilion next to the track, where I threw a big catered party. Pam and Brandie were with me, the Whittington brothers, Mary Hinze, John Paul Jr. and Sr. My brothers and all my friends came to party and watch us compete.

We qualified well, but in the morning practice session—the day of the race—our gearbox broke, and we didn't have the parts to fix it. It was a massive letdown. Pam was shocked; I was humiliated. Even Brandie was ornery. This was the biggest race on my home turf, and we didn't even make it to the starting line!

Three weeks later, we raced in the Coca-Cola Classic 12 Hours of Sebring, one of the biggest sports car events in North America. Our March car bit the dust after 128 laps, with engine problems. Again, we didn't have the right parts to fix it. My frustration was so extreme, I ended up in my hotel room pacing, just thinking over and over: *This shit can't keep happening.*

The Executone phone company team didn't have the right personnel. Marty Hinze didn't have enough funding. The

reasons why I needed to approach racing from a different an-
gle were piling up. I made up my mind: I was not going to rely
on others anymore. I was going to create my own team. I was
going to have the right equipment, the right manpower, and
I was going to be the leadership. My goal: to buy new March
racing cars and win the 1984 International Motor Sport Association (IMSA) Camel GT series, America's elite professional
sports car racing league.

The two things that mattered were time and money. One
of them I didn't have to spare, but the other—I knew how to
get it.

Days after making that decision, I drove my raspberry Ferrari
to General RV to meet with Bill Whittington. We went to Les-
ter's Diner on Marina Boulevard in Fort Lauderdale, a spot
known for its huge cup of coffee. I wanted to convince Bill
to team up with me. He was a bona fide Le Mans champion.
He'd been in the game longer than me, and he knew more
people. I told him I would take care of all the expenses for this
team and that I wanted him to be my codriver. We could get
Ben to come in also, as a sponsor.

Bill was game, right off the bat.

"We need to hire the best talent," I said. "No matter what
it costs."

"Do you know Keith Leighton?" Bill asked. "He's one of
the best crew chiefs in the business."

"Ayyyight," I said. "Can you hire him?"

"I'll find out."

Keith Leighton was a Brit who had started working for Cosworth race engines at age fifteen. He'd worked on the build of the first Cosworth DFV motor, which won its first race back in the '60s with the legendary Jimmy Clark driving. Keith had worked in Formula 1 with Ronnie Peterson, Niki Lauda, and Jacky Ickx—the biggest names in European racing. This guy was the real deal, and Bill convinced him to come on board as our crew chief and head mechanic. When I first met him, I told him, "You hire whomever you want to work under you. You have carte blanche. Whatever it costs— spend it! Put together the best crew you can."

Meanwhile, I went to work buying equipment. I flew to England and went straight to the March factory. I paid $150,000 for a chassis. Then I found another March car that I bought for the same amount, one that'd been used for one season by the Leon brothers, twins from Texas who had their own racing team. I spent and I spent. I ordered ten fuel-injected Chevrolet V-8 race engines—$75,000 a pop. I spent $250,000 just on transmission parts and tens of thousands of dollars on tires.

I leased a bigger shop in Fort Lauderdale. I set up a contract with an engine builder to do all our rebuilds because race engines are in a constant state of death and rebirth. I ordered a custom Kenworth eighteen-wheeler transporter to move the cars, engines, and tires from track to track around the country.

As the old saying goes, if you want to make a million dollars in auto racing, start with two.

It took months to get all our gear situated and the cars ready to go, and I couldn't wait to get out for our first practice session. Our eighteen-wheel transporter wasn't ready yet, so our new crew chief Keith Leighton borrowed one from a buddy who managed a famous collection of vintage cars in South Florida. He was kind enough to let me use it to take the March cars to Palm Beach International Raceway for the first shakedown. His truck was painted blue, and it had a big tag on the front that read Blue Thunder. I liked the sound of it right away, so out of respect for this friend who had lent me his tractor trailer, I named our new team Blue Thunder.

Now, all of this team launch business happened during and just after my debacle with the Spider and those kilos of cocaine. Which meant that I was spending almost incalculable amounts of money at the same time my smuggling business was taking a hit, losing hundreds of thousands of dollars. I needed money, badly and quickly. I was launching a team that was going to be competing against the Porsche factory of Germany and the Jaguar factory of Britain. And if I was going to race against Porsche and Jaguar, I needed to have as much money as Porsche and Jaguar. So as Blue Thunder was coming together, I laid the foundation to level up my smuggling business—on an exponentially bigger scale.

If the *Ursa Major* was only capable of hauling a twenty-thousand-pound load, what would it take to bring in twice that much in a single shot? There had to be a way.

13

Score of a Lifetime

1983

The idea to rethink my business model came to me during a breakfast meeting at a bagel shop in North Miami called the Rascal House. Real busy place. Ben was there. I worked with a distributor named Billy, who'd told me he wanted to introduce me to these two guys named Gene and George. Billy was probably my best distributor, had been for years— always on time, always trustworthy, never any drama. We once shared a house together in the '70s. Billy was the real deal. If he told me this meeting would be a good fit, I trusted him. So I was sitting there in this bagel shop and in walk these two pudgy dudes. I got a good vibe right away.

George was a New Yorker with a thick accent. Six feet tall, dark hair. He was businesslike, straightforward, but he also had a sense of humor and a taste for fun. I could tell right way: this was a guy who liked to snort cocaine and drink whiskey. We were about the same age.

Gene was more reserved and intellectual. He'd spent a year working for the State Department, stationed in Nicaragua.

He was older than George and me by about a decade. Thinning hair, starting to go gray, glasses, very courteous, and soft spoken.

Neither of them fit central casting for marijuana outlaws. They looked like guys you'd be standing next to at the hardware store on a Saturday morning.

Gene owned a tugboat and ship salvage company in Santo Domingo in the Caribbean. It was a legit company with a lot of equipment—ships, cranes, barges—and George worked for Gene. They shipped products mainly from South America to the US. They also did salvage operations on old boats headed for the scrap metal pile. Both Gene and George split their time between New York, Miami, and Santo Domingo.

After shaking hands, I said, "My buddy Billy tells me you guys can be trusted and you're interested in discussing business."

Gene did the talking. "That's right, Randy. We know Billy. Billy vouches for us, and Billy vouches for you. To me that means we can talk candidly."

"Agreed," I said. "So, what is it you're interested in?" I was keen on letting them bring up the topic of smuggling, not me.

"Randy, I've been told you're a smart guy. I can tell just by sitting here with you that you're not a bullshitter so lemme cut to the chase." He glanced at George, then his eyes moved back to mine. "What do you know about our business?"

"I know you guys run a marine salvage and shipping operation in the Caribbean."

"That's right. We're looking to expand. You have a lot of expertise," Gene said. "More importantly, you have the contacts in South America. We have a lot of equipment and a lot of logistics experience. We've been shipping coffee beans and whatever else all over the Caribbean and Florida and Texas for years. Seems like our skills could fit together nicely."

I liked what I was hearing.

Over several meetings over the next few days, we came up with exactly the kind of bigger, bolder plan I'd been looking for: we would send one of their salvage operation's 150-foot tugboats down to Colombia to load thirty-five thousand pounds of weed, using their crew. A tugboat would appear less suspicious than, say, a trawler or a shrimp boat, which a lot of smugglers were using at the time. To avoid the drug war battles of South Florida, we would bring the boat up through New York Harbor, right under Lady Liberty's nose.

For an unloading spot, George found an abandoned gas station surrounded by chain-link fencing in a crime-ridden neighborhood in Bridgeport, Connecticut. "It's perfect," he told me. To get the tug there, we'd have to bring the boat through New York Harbor past the Statue of Liberty, into Long Island Sound, and into this industrial river port in Bridgeport. The abandoned gas station—located on a street called South Avenue—backed up to the river, and there was a beat-up dock right there where we could tie up the boat.

I flew up to New York and rented a car so I could check it all out. When I got to the abandoned gas station, I cut the engine and sat there for hours, observing the neighborhood. Gene was right. It seemed like a perfect unloading spot. There was only one thing about it that I didn't like; it was across the street from a Sikorsky Helicopter factory, which meant there'd be a lot of security across the street and some air traffic overhead.

Now, creating this operation from scratch was like launching an entire corporation. It required tremendous attention to detail, to see where problems might arise and head them off early on. I rented a four-bedroom place on Bleecker Street in Greenwich Village, where I could meet with George and Gene and where my men could sleep when we needed to be in the Northeast. We leased the old gas station in the name of a shell company I had in Panama. George flew down to Santo Domingo to get the tugboat ready and recruit a boat crew.

Meanwhile, Ben communicated with the Family down in Santa Marta, to set them moving on harvesting and curing the thirty-five thousand pounds. I also scouted out three stash houses in the New York area. And we'd have to hire manpower.

A few months after our first meeting with Gene and George, Ben and I flew down to Colombia to load the tugboat, which was coming in straight from Santo Domingo.

By this time, we had a center-console open fisherman waiting for us at the compound. In smuggling, like in racing, speed equals survival. I wasn't spending one more minute in any cayuca. On the day of the load, Ben and I jumped into this boat with a couple Colombians and fired up those big-ass outboard engines. Ben manned the helm while I stood by with binoculars.

I scoured the secluded bay where we were supposed to meet the tugboat. Sure enough, I spotted the tug coming in on the horizon, just before sunset. Up until this point, I hadn't seen it yet. I couldn't believe my eyes. I don't know what I was expecting, but this thing was huge! I was thinking: thirty-five thousand pounds? We could load twice that much on that damn tug.

Once again, here came the Colombians, out of the jungle with their cayucas. That night, while the Colombians were loading the weed onto the tugboat, I got asked to board the tug and go up to the flybridge, where the captain and his mate manned the boat. I was so hot, so sunburned, and so tired from lack of sleep, I looked like a crazed pirate. I had my shirt wrapped around my head because my hat had blown off. I climbed the ladder to the bridge, and there was the captain, along with this two-hundred-pound dude, well over six feet tall. He looked at me and said, "Is that you, Randy?"

I looked at the guy. "Damn! Johnny Ringo! What the fuck are you doing here?"

It was a guy I knew from Miami. What were the chances of that? The world of smugglers and South Florida outlaws was a small one. He told me they were going to pilot this tugboat all the way to New York without stopping. They needed a bag of cocaine because they were going to take twenty-four-hour shifts, and they'd need to stay alert. Would I ask the Colombians? I said I'd take care of it for him.

"Make it a big bag, Randy!"

I was about to leave the flybridge when I looked out the window and saw a Colombian Coast Guard boat coming into the bay under the moonlight. We all looked at each other.

"What the fuck is that?!" I asked.

I ran down the flybridge ladder and jumped onto the open fisherman. Ben was there with one of the Colombians, who started explaining in Spanish. That Coast Guard boat was there to protect us. We'd seen this happen before, with local police, so it wasn't all that surprising. Since the first time I'd come down here, Colombia had become a full-on narco nation. Still, it was unnerving to see that big Coast Guard ship sitting there on the water. The kicker: the Coast Guard captain wanted Ben and me to come aboard to say hello.

"Are you fucking kidding me?" I said. "No fucking way."

Ben and I took off on the open fisherman, got ourselves to the airport, and flew home.

Back in New York, I assembled a crew of about a dozen guys to unload the weed. The boat wasn't going to come in for a few days, so they slept in my Greenwich Village apartment. To keep morale high, I took everyone out to an Italian restaurant one night in Little Italy. This was a mobbed-up joint, owned by a friend of one of my partners.

We pulled up in a limousine, and I told the driver to keep it parked right out front. When I walked through the door, it was like walking through a time warp onto the set of *The Godfather*. The maître-d' wore a full tuxedo, and there was a dessert tray by the door with all these beautiful Italian cakes and desserts in all different colors.

My brother-in-law Ronnie was there that night, and he'd asked if he could bring his driver with him. I was hesitant, but I trusted Ronnie, so I said sure. There were a dozen of us, and we had a table in a private room so we could talk business. We'd only been there a few minutes when Ronnie's driver whispered something in his ear. Ronnie nodded his head and said, "Yeah. Go ahead." So the guy got up and walked out of the room.

"What's up with him?" I asked. He was making me nervous.

"He's not feeling good," Ronnie said. "He's gotta go to the bathroom."

The next thing I knew, I heard a crash. We all shut up and listened. The maître-d' came running into our room completely covered in cake and chocolate sauce and tiramisu. He had whipped cream in his hair, and he was screaming at us in Italian. This man was not happy! I went out and what I saw blew my mind.

On his way to the bathroom, Ronnie's driver had apparently passed out right on the dessert tray. He was still unconscious, and two waiters in tuxedos were dragging him by his armpits through the dining room and out the front door. My limo was out there, and the waiters were yelling at the driver to put this unconscious guy in the back seat.

Turned out, the guy had a heart issue and needed a pacemaker. My driver took him to the hospital. We stuck around and had quite a dinner. The food was excellent, but we decided not to order dessert.

A couple days later, my beeper went off. One of my guys told me that the tugboat was crossing New York Harbor at that moment, so we assembled and headed to our abandoned gas station in a bunch of rented cars. Everyone was in dark jeans and black sweatshirts, so they'd be hard to see at night.

When we got there, the tugboat was already tied up at the dock. We'd rented six thirty-foot U-Haul trucks, and they were parked on the property. Chain-link fence surrounded the place, but there were no lights, so even if you were looking through the chain-link fence, it'd be hard to see what was going on. The ship captain and my old buddy Johnny Ringo stepped off the tugboat onto our dock, and I greeted them there.

"Go time!" I shouted. "Let's go, let's go!"

We started a bucket brigade operation, bringing bale after bale out of the tugboat's bowels and up into these thirty-foot U-Haul trucks. The bales just kept coming. Let me tell you, when you see thirty-five thousand pounds of weed all in one place, you won't ever forget it. Anybody walking by the property would've smelled it, but in this neighborhood, after midnight, with no streetlights or lights of any kind, nobody was around. One by one, my crewmembers fired up the engines and took off with these trucks full of weed, heading to one of three different stash houses—two farmhouses in Pennsylvania and one warehouse in Manhattan.

Back down in Florida, Charles Podesta began his work of counting all the money as it came in. He had money counters, the same kind bank tellers used. Man, I loved the sound of that little machine. Beautiful music. Charles was a busy man. We're talking about swimming pools full of money. Managing it was about managing space, so I stopped accepting five dollar bills from my distributors. I only dealt in tens, twenties, fifties, and hundreds now.

We kept the money in organized stacks with no mixed bills. If it was a ten-thousand-dollar stack, we'd use only hundreds. If it was five thousand, we'd use only fifties. That way you could tell what you were looking at just by glancing at the pile and what bill was on top. You have to understand how much space this amount of money can take up. A seven-foot-by-four-foot safe will only hold about $7 million in hundred dollar bills.

When it was all said and done, Charles gave me my cut of that score—about $3 million—in a suitcase. Ben was using a wealthy guy in California named Sam to manage his money, so Charles had to fly suitcases of cash aboard a private jet to the West Coast.

I was now twenty-nine years old and as rich as any CEO, making as much as an NBA player or a high-profile entrepreneur. The only difference was it was all in cash. I realized I'd reached the point where I had to put a lot more time and resources into figuring out how to hide all this money from the IRS. That would be an adventure all its own.

Once all the accounts were settled, I met with Gene, George, and Ben at my apartment in New York. Our first operation together had been highly successful, and so there was no reason not to try it again. Only bigger.

"A tugboat is a great idea because nobody would suspect it," I said. "That's good. But you know what a tugboat is really good at doing?"

I paused to see if anyone would catch on. Gene did. He flashed a shit-eating grin. "Yeah," he said. "Tugging things."

"What do you mean?" asked George.

Gene said, "If we can do thirty-five thousand pounds with a tugboat, why don't we put a barge behind the tugboat and do a bigger load?"

"That's right," I responded. "Damn skippy. We can bring in the biggest load in all of history."

14

A Barge the Size of a Football Field

Fall 1983

We were ambitious, audacious—you might even say, out of our minds. Sitting in my Manhattan apartment with Gene and George, we came up with a new idea, one with the potential to make everything we'd done before look like a tiny mom-and-pop operation.

"A cargo barge," Gene said. "The tug can pull a cargo barge."

"A barge?" I responded.

"Yes. A barge. As in, a barge the size of a football field."

"Huh." I thought about it. "Do you know how much motherfucking weed we could put in a barge?"

Gene and George owned an industrial barge as part of their marine salvage business in Santo Domingo. It was three hundred feet long—exactly the length of a football field—and it stood six stories from top to bottom, they told me. The barge carried cargo in the center of its hull, and it had ballast tanks running the whole length of the vessel, on either side and from top to bottom.

When the barge was carrying, say, a million pounds of coffee beans, it had enough weight to steady itself through twenty-foot seas. When it was empty, with no manifest, the ballast tanks could fill with seawater to keep the barge heavy and stable on the water.

"We can put the weed in secret compartments inside the ballasts," Gene said. "And then fill the ballasts with seawater. There's no way we could get caught."

"It's fucking genius," I said. "Genius!"

Our plan was to put 130,000 pounds of weed in the bottom of the ballast tanks. We could create three-story-high compartments inside these ballast tanks, and each could hold around 20,000 pounds. Then we'd weld a three-quarter-inch steel ceiling over the secret compartments to hide the product. We could pump salt water into the tanks, on top of the closed-off hidden compartments, so even if someone tried to look in there, all they'd see is salt water—routine.

Literally, just days after our last successful score, we were launching a new one almost four times as large.

Gene and George ordered their guys down in Santo Domingo to ready the tug and the barge. We agreed we could use the same abandoned gas station in Connecticut as the unloading spot and the same three stash houses. I made the arrangements with the Colombians. I was busy as all hell getting the Blue Thunder racing team off the ground, and I knew it would take the Colombians time to get the 130,000 pounds ready. They had to pick, trim, and cure all that cannabis and bring it down the mountain. All the while, we could communicate with them via sideband radio. After a few weeks, they were nearly ready, so Ben and I flew to Colombia.

When we arrived, we were in for a major surprise.

By this time, the compound where the Family lived in Santa Marta felt a bit like home. Our Colombian partners had come up in the world over the past couple years because of the business we were doing together. We'd also come up in the world because of the business we were doing together. So there was a bond there. Their kids treated me like an uncle.

Ben and I stayed at the main house in the compound behind those big walls. Every morning, I would wake up in this room on the second floor of the two-story house, and I'd go downstairs into the courtyard. The kids would make fresh watermelon juice for me, and I'd smoke a joint, sipping my fresh juice as I listened to all those birds in their cages, singing in Spanish.

Because this next load was going to be so mammoth, the Family had to create a new process to get it down the mountain. In the past, they moved all the weed on the backs of donkeys. Now they were using donkeys and several flatbed trucks, with canvas coverings over the top of the flatbeds. Think about it: 130,000 pounds. Sixty-five tons. That's a *lot* of weed! The workers kept the trucks parked in their own driveways, right in Santa Marta. The Family had paid off the police, the Coast Guard, and a judge who had a lot of local influence. Walking through the neighborhood where these trucks were parked, the stink of buds was overwhelming. There was no secret about what was going on.

Now on this morning, right before our barge was scheduled to arrive, I was drinking my watermelon juice and hanging out with the birds when several people I didn't know showed up at the compound. They were all carrying rifles. They were yelling in Spanish, and they were very emotional. It did not sound good. Something had gone wrong, but I couldn't figure out what.

It didn't take long to realize that the police had come at night and confiscated all the weed. Meanwhile, more and more people were showing up at the compound. There were guns everywhere. These people were assembling an army, apparently preparing for a gun battle with the cops. Ben and I tried to reason with them. He and I were two gringos in Santa Marta. If a war was going down, there was a good chance we were not going to make it out alive.

Ben got the facts. The Family had apparently told the police that 25,000 pounds of weed were coming down from the mountains. The police, wanting their share for protecting the load, started patrolling the streets and they saw all these trucks. They figured out that we intended to export exponentially more than they'd been told. So, in the night, they came and confiscated the trucks.

"Listen," I told the Family, as Ben translated. We were sitting at their table, gun-toting guys all around us. "You have to pay these cops off," I yelled. "Having a gun battle is not going to get the weed back. It's not going to help anybody with anything!" I turned to Ben. "Maybe we should just go to the airport now and get the hell out of here," I said, "before the bullets start flying."

This shit was out of control. The amount of artillery was terrifying. People were screaming in Spanish. Even the birds were flapping their wings and freaking out. "I don't want to lose this load," I said to Ben. "But I don't want to die, either."

It took hours to bring these people to their senses. That night, money changed hands, and everything got worked out. The police brought back the trucks with the weed. The barge appeared in the bay the next day. When I saw that thing, holy shit, I couldn't believe the size of it. It was like a skyscraper tipped on its side, floating on the water. Just fucking mammoth.

We were ready to load, and the Colombians went to work, lifting bales of weed from a flotilla of cayucas, using ropes to lower them into the bottom of the barge's ballasts. We'd arranged for the welders to then come on board after everything was loaded and seal the secret compartments shut with the three-quarter-inch steel plate. Then, from the deck of the barge, our crew filled the ballasts with salt water.

We sent the loaded barge via tugboat to Gene's salvage company in Santo Domingo. There, we hired an unsuspecting crew to bring in the barge loaded with weed. This crew had no idea that the barge was carrying this contraband. And they were going to pull it right past the Statue of Liberty. Nothing to see here!

I spent the whole next week—while the barge was at sea—in the Blue Thunder race shop with my team. By this time, our new shop was full of men. Bill Whittington and I had nearly a dozen guys working for us. The two March cars were in pieces in the shop—we inspected and cleaned everything down to the screws. Brand-new Chevrolet race engines worth $75,000 were stacked in huge crates, from the floor to the ceiling.

We were hoping to be ready for the 1984 24 Hours of Daytona, but it was going to come down to a game-time decision. My guys were moving as fast as they could to prepare the race cars. Meanwhile, I was torn in two directions. The smuggling operation was demanding all my time. We couldn't allow any mistakes. The stakes were getting so high, the race team had to play second fiddle, for me at least. It was agonizing to have to prioritize one over the other.

Making matters more complicated, there was more news on America's War on Drugs. Vice President Bush had set up new regional headquarters for his drug-fighting operations. Up to that time, all the focus had been on South Florida. But the feds knew what we knew: if the government put all its resources in South Florida, then smugglers were going to take their business elsewhere. Bush set up new task force headquarters in Texas, California, Illinois, Louisiana—and, of course, New York, right where our 130,000 pounds of weed were headed.

The vice president told the press just weeks before we loaded the barge how "we have witnessed an increase in drug smuggling up and down the Atlantic Coast." The feds were going to be in New York, looking for bad guys.

Anxiety doesn't quite capture the essence of what I was feeling while that barge was out to sea. Even when I found time to attempt to sleep, I couldn't. On nights when I wasn't running around yelling into street corner pay phones or working in the Blue Thunder shop, I'd lie awake staring at the ceiling, promising myself that all this was going to pay off with checkered flags. One of my guys had hats and T-shirts made for all the Blue Thunder guys with a logo that read, "Whatever It Takes."

When the barge arrived in Bridgeport, at the dock behind the abandoned gas station, I set my side of the operation in motion. I had guys working all kinds of jobs, and everything was fully compartmentalized: nobody knew what any of the other guys were doing, for security reasons.

That first night, I sent in a rental tractor trailer just for a dummy run to see if we had any heat. The instructions to the driver were to load up two empty fifty-five-gallon drums and then exit the premises. At the same time, I sent out two drivers in rental cars to patrol the neighborhood, with Bearcat 250 scanners preprogrammed to listen in on channels carrying local police, customs, DEA, marine patrol, and so on.

After the sun had set, I had the eighteen-wheeler pull into the gas station through a gate in the chain-link fence. But my beeper went off soon after it arrived. It was one of my guys, who was keeping track of the two drivers patrolling with the Bearcat 250 scanners. I called him from a pay phone on the street in this empty neighborhood. It was freezing cold that night, and as I spoke into the phone, I was shivering like mad.

"Hey," he said, "you have two guys patrolling the neighborhood with the Bearcats, right? Neither of them knows of the other, right? Both of them, Randy—*both of them*—independently called in at 8:18 p.m. saying that they heard over the scanner the words 'suspect entering compound.'"

"Fuck!" I said. That time—8:18 p.m.—was exactly when that tractor trailer pulled into the gas station.

I dialed George from the pay phone. "We have a problem. We cannot use the gas station to unload. We got heat! We have to shut everything down and get that fucking barge out of there right now."

George thought for a moment. I could hear him breathing heavily over the phone. He said, "OK, I know of a spot where we can put the barge temporarily."

The next morning, we had the tugboat captain pull the barge out of Bridgeport and into the Long Island Sound, past Riker's Island and into the East River between Brooklyn and Manhattan. George had set up a contract with an industrial marina he'd used before in New Jersey to pull this huge barge out of the water with giant marine cranes and clean off the barnacles from the hull. It seemed like a normal maintenance procedure, from a marine point of view. But really, we were just stalling for time until we could figure out a place to unload.

Up to that point, almost all our communication was by beeper and pay phone, but now we had to get the team together. Gene, George, Ben, and me. We met at the apartment I'd rented in Greenwich Village. George told us he might have a spot where we could unload. "But we have to involve some people that manage this spot," he added.

"Who?" I asked.

"The Italians," he said. Meaning the Mafia.

"Fuck, man."

George—a real New Yorker—knew about some abandoned wharfs that had once been a part of the Brooklyn Navy Yard. There were big, long docks and empty warehouses, and we could pull trucks right up to the wharfs. He made some calls and reported back to us.

"I think the unloading spot is perfect," George said. "They want $500,000 up front to let us use the spot."

"First of all," I told George, "I'm not meeting anybody face-to-face. I'm not even talking to nobody on the phone. If you know these people, and you trust 'em, then *you* set it up. Secondly, there's no way we are handing over $500,000 to these guys. Ayyyight? What if we give them the $500,000 and then we bring in the barge? They could rob us right there. What are we gonna do, call the cops on them? You tell them we'll pay half up front and the other half once we get all the weed out of there."

Everyone agreed, and George went off to cement the deal. Meanwhile, I drove down there to take a look. The whole place was blocked off with fencing, and there was a kiosk out front manned by a guard, who presumably would do whatever his bosses told him to do. George was right. The spot was perfect.

We were going to need a lot of guys for unloading because we were going to have to do it much faster than I'd planned. Once again: speed meant survival. So I flew in more people from South Florida. My place in Greenwich Village turned into a crash pad, with people lying all over the couches and all four bedrooms and lots of empty beer cans filled with spent cigarette butts. We worked at night. I had my distributors supply tractor trailers. The first night of unloading brought pounding rain. I sat in a parked car a quarter mile from the kiosk where the guard manned the entrance to the abandoned docks. I didn't feel comfortable at all. I had a Bearcat 250 scanner switched on. I never felt the need to carry a weapon, but Ben and a couple of his guys were well armed. We all had walkie-talkies.

The street where I was parked was empty and dark—no foot traffic, no streetlights. I watched as the first tractor trailer pulled up to the kiosk. The driver had a word with the guard—who'd been paid off by the mob. There was a long pause, and I couldn't tell what was going on. But then the guard lifted the arm and waved the driver through. Hours went by. I waited and waited, feeling so tense that in moments I forgot to breathe. Turned out, the guys were having trouble getting the weed out of the bottom of the ballasts and up to the deck of the barge, six stories high. It took the guys all night to load a single truck. At that rate, it was going to take a whole week to off-load. Way too much time for something to go wrong.

They later told me that, when that first tractor trailer pulled out of the loading zone toward the kiosk, Ben was standing on the truck's running board, holding onto the driver's side door with a machine gun strapped over him. This was apparently a signal to anyone thinking of trying to rob us.

We had another meeting at my apartment at the end of the first night and decided to try a cherry picker, one of those cranes on wheels that telephone repairmen use to get to the tops of telephone poles. We could lower a cherry picker into the hull of the barge and use it to pull the weed bales out of the secret compartments. George found us a machine, and I flew in five more guys from South Florida.

The next night, I sat in my rented car near the same spot, a quarter mile from the kiosk. Again, pouring rain. The water pounding on my car was so loud I had to turn up the volume on the Bearcat. The first eighteen-wheeler pulled past the kiosk. Suddenly, I saw headlights in my rearview mirror—a car pulling down the dark street, headed my way. I pulled my body down onto the floorboard of my car and peeked out the window as the car went past.

It was a cop.

The cop car passed the kiosk and continued to the end of the street, and then the driver did a fast one-eighty. Now he was driving back toward me again in the rain. I feared that he'd seen me. I pushed myself back down on the floorboard and pulled the Bearcat scanner down with me. I whispered into the walkie-talkie: "We may have company."

My heart was pounding. Pure adrenaline. Everyone had instructions: if there was a raid, everyone was supposed to drop everything and motherfucking run.

The cop drove past me again, and once again, at the end of the street, he did a one-eighty. This time he drove by me and kept on going. Now it made sense. The guy was practicing one-eighty turns because the street was wet and there was nobody around.

I called into my walkie-talkie: "All clear."

It took us three nights to unload all 130,000 pounds. We got it all to the three stash houses safely. Within a week, we'd moved out all the product and had gotten paid. I think my cut on the first barge operation was $10 million cash, in 1983 dollars.

Gene and George couldn't have been happier. Ben couldn't have been happier. But all I could think about was racing. I was spending too much time doing business, and not enough in a car. There was no celebrating our score. The War on Drugs was getting crazier. Within days of our operation, Nancy Reagan went on ABC's *Good Morning America* for an entire news program dedicated to drugs. On this show she introduced the world to the phrase "Just Say No."

Right after we had cleared all the money from our last load, Gene called me up. He said, "Randy, I got the perfect spot. The iron is still hot. Let's strike it." I couldn't say no.

"Ayyyight."

We met at a little restaurant on the water on the Intracoastal Waterway in Fort Lauderdale. The place was called Gold Coast, and it had a gorgeous view. We had a bite to eat, and then we sat in Gene's car in the parking lot.

"This unloading spot is perfect," he said. "I want you to go see it."

"Where is it?"

"It's in a place called Redwood City, California. The Golden State, Randy. I have a buddy who leases a rock quarry right on the water. There's a dock big enough for the barge."

I flew out there with Ben to take a look. Gene was right: it was perfect. The tugboat could pull the barge right under the Golden Gate Bridge and into San Francisco Bay, and the quarry was perched on a quiet estuary in the bay's southern basin. I could use my same distributors. They'd bring their big rigs to the left coast. There was less of a drug war spotlight on the California coast, too. So, we set the gears in motion.

15

The Golden Gate

Spring 1984

*I*n January, Ben and I flew down to Colombia to negotiate the deal. We were chartering private jets for these flights now, with our own pilot and copilot. This meant when we flew into Santa Marta, we no longer bothered with customs. Guys met us at the gate and escorted us around customs and right out the front door. Usually, there'd be two cars and drivers waiting for us, but this time there were three. We noticed something unusual right away. All three cars had drivers dressed in nice suits and ties. That was not how they usually appeared.

One of the drivers started speaking Spanish. I asked Ben, "What the fuck is he saying?"

Ben grimaced. "He's saying there's been a tragedy."

The farmers had brought a lot of weed down from the mountain, and they were storing it in a cave outside Santa Marta. The cave had apparently collapsed with two people inside. One of the guys made it out, but the other didn't. The day of the funeral happened to be the day we arrived in town.

I was floored. Ben was too.

Off we went in this caravan, three cars through the bustling streets. Ben and I weren't dressed for a funeral, but we were going anyway. I remember honking horns, humidity, and flies buzzing around my face. When we got near the church, the streets clogged. There were cars and trucks parked everywhere, and I was thinking it must have been raining a lot because so many of the vehicles were splattered with mud.

Our driver maneuvered right to the front door of this little white steeple church. All these people were milling around outside. Some were dressed in suits and dresses, while others were laborers wearing the only kinds of clothes they owned. Our drivers escorted us into the crowded church. Every seat was taken. There was no air-conditioning, and it was sweltering. Many of the women were fanning themselves with cardboard fans decorated with religious images.

I felt so little, so ashamed, because we were mixed up in something that had gotten a young man killed. We walked to the church's front row, and I could tell that this was where the family of the deceased was sitting—this young guy's parents, his sisters and brothers. The drivers who brought us walked up to these people and bent down, eye level with the family. I could see the family members listening and glancing in our direction. I thought: *These people are going to blame us for their son's death. They are going to spit at us, maybe worse, right here in a house of worship. And they'd be right.*

We were told to approach this grieving family, so we did. Every muscle in my body tensed up. They spoke to us in Spanish in melancholy voices, and our guides translated. To my surprise, the family members wanted to shake our hands and thank us. These bereaved people wanted to shower us with kindness because of all the good they believed we had done. Our smuggling operations had pulled this entire community out of poverty. We had given them work. We had given them dignity. And they wanted to thank us for it.

I'd never felt so stunned in my life. I felt responsible for this young man's death, at least to some degree. They didn't see it that way. To them, any other line of work their son could be in would be just as dangerous.

We sat in the church and paid our respects, the only two gringos there. I prayed that day for God to show me ways that I could redeem myself and be of service. After the funeral, we went to the compound and stayed a few days with the Family. I needed to decompress, and this was a place I could do it.

When we were ready, we made all the arrangements for our next score—once again, our biggest yet. The biggest, perhaps, in all of history. The Family told us 155,000 pounds of high-quality sticky weed called *punto rojo* would be ready by the end of March.

Blue Thunder debuted at the 1984 12 Hours of Sebring, not far from my home in Davie. We rolled in at night a few days before the race, showing off our new eighteen-wheel transporter, the side of the big rig freshly painted with our Blue Thunder logo. Talk about a proud moment: watching my team of guys rolling our two March racing cars out of the back of that transporter and seeing the way those cars—emblazoned with our Blue Thunder logos—looked under the stars.

The 12 Hours of Sebring was second only to the 24 Hours of Daytona in the American sports car scene. Porsches and

Ferraris, race-prepped Mazda RX-7s and Jaguar XJSs and BMW M1s—about eighty teams were set to face off in combat on the track for twelve straight hours. Whichever car completed the most laps on Sebring's twisty 4.86-mile circuit would win.

We didn't have Blue Thunder ready for the first two races of 1984, so this was actually the third race of the season in the IMSA GT championship sponsored by Camel cigarettes. This sanctioning body's Camel GT series was the premier sports car-racing series in North America. In the entire Western Hemisphere, in fact.

Top flight. Best of the best.

Nobody had heard of Blue Thunder, and no one took us seriously. But Bill Whittington and I were there to win.

Our March racing car carried the number 57, which had been my number ever since the 1957 Porsche. I named the car Sweet Pea, after my daughter. We had three drivers assigned to the number 57 car, one man in the car at a time. Bill Whittington was a Le Mans champion, and Marty Hinze had been around for many years. Even though I'd raced at Daytona and Le Mans, I was still the new kid.

This sport, like no other, is all about quantification. Hundredths of a second in a lap time can have a huge impact. I knew I had to be fast. I had everything to prove, literally down to the split second.

It was a wild time in American racing history. When I looked around the pits at Sebring, I saw all my friends—guys who were in the same business as I was. The Whittington brothers, Marty Hinze, John Paul Sr. and Jr.—we were all deep into the marijuana smuggling trade. And we were all funneling our money into these race teams. Rumor had it—though I didn't know if it was true or not—that the Whittington brothers landed airplanes full of weed at night on the straightaway of Road Atlanta, the racetrack they owned. The whole thing almost felt like an open secret. It would later become a joke that IMSA—the International Motor Sports Association—really stood for the International Marijuana Smuggling Association.

What we were doing was dangerous, and we knew it. We were flaunting our millions in the form of shiny racing equipment in front of television cameras. That year of 1984, *Miami Vice* came on the air. It was all about cops and bad guys, boats, Ferraris, and speed, all of it in South Florida. We were living the real-life version.

The Sebring International Raceway was built on a World War II airfield—even incorporating the old runways into the course. It was unique in that it was as flat as could be. The 12-Hour classic had been held every year going back to 1950, including the infamous 1966 race when a crash killed the driver and four spectators. It was a historic annual battle and a hell of a place to debut a new team. When our cars thundered past the start on that opening straightaway, it was like a war zone—the sound, the smoke, the crackle of gear shifts.

Sebring features some of the fastest sports car racing in the world. (The track layout is different today than it was then.) Turn six and turn nine were these bends that you took with throttle pinned, so fast you could feel the rubber desperately clinging to the pavement. Same with turns fourteen, fifteen, and sixteen. Left hook, right hook, left and right again, sometimes three cars abreast fighting for position. Then you get to turn seventeen, widely considered one of the hardest turns to get right, in all of motorsports. It's a place where the heat can be extreme, and the pavement insanely bumpy, where the vibration in the car can literally rattle your brain.

For long hours, we fought hard, and as the race wore on and the sun went down, we pulled into the lead. Bill was driving, and he kept stretching that lead. Watching from the pit, I was fully charged with adrenaline because I believed we were going to win a major international race on our debut. This would make headlines in every sports page in the country.

With two hours to go, in the dark of night, Bill pulled into the pit for a driver change. It was my time. I was going to go out and bring the victory home. I strapped in. I waited for the pit crew to finish changing my tires so I could go out on fresh rubber. Deep breaths. No mistakes. Don't fuck this up, Randy!

"Go! Go! Go!"

I tore out of the pit and headed into my first lap. Hammering down the front straightaway, I entered turn one. Quick dab on the brake. Settle the car. Then back smooth on the throttle. Back on the brake. Hit the apex on turn two. Back on the throttle. Sebring's asphalt was the roughest and bumpiest I'd ever experienced, and with my five-point harness strapped tightly across my body, that translated to extreme vibration. On the straights, I was moving so fast it was hard to see because the car was trying to outrun the headlights. Smoke from the hundreds of fires from people camping out at the track—plus the wrecked cars parked on the sides of the tarmac—made the place feel like a scene in *Mad Max*.

I could smell victory. I wanted that podium so bad. I charged through my laps, one after the other, hoping the time would drain off faster than the clock hands could move.

Then, coming into turn one late in the race, I carried too much speed. I dropped my right front wheel off the pavement into the dirt. It was a mistake of mere inches, with catastrophic consequences. The bodywork of this car was so low to the ground, it caught some earth going over 100 mph. In an instant, the front end tore apart and the car's radiator got dislodged and thrown into the windshield.

Bang!

The windshield spiderwebbed, so I couldn't see. Now I was at over 100 mph on a track full of speeding cars at night with no vision. I had to slow down and limp back to the pit with whatever vision I could manage.

In the pit, the team jumped into action, rebuilding the car as we watched our lead evaporate. I sat in the car, waiting and waiting, knowing that all this was my fault. Almost forty years later, I can still feel the heartbreak. When I finally got the car back on track, we had lost the lead. I motored very carefully through the final laps and brought the car in, in second place.

In Blue Thunder's first race, we made the podium, beating the Porsche team of A. J. Foyt, Bob Wollek, and Derek Bell. We also beat Preston Henn's Ferrari team. None of that changed the fact that it was the most frustrating moment of my life. I needed to get back on track to prove to myself and to the rest of the team that I was no rich gentleman driver, some guy who'd bought his way into pro racing. On top of that, the bumpy pavement left me so sore I had bone-deep bruises all over my body that took a week to heal.

But there was no rest. Not for me. Right after Sebring, I flew out to California. I had rented an apartment across from Opera Plaza in San Francisco as a home base for my operations. Our tugboat and barge were making their way up the coast of California. While the Blue Thunder team was headed to the Road Atlanta 500, I had to attend to business. Bill Whittington would drive the whole race at Road Atlanta for Blue Thunder. I was needed, as they say, at the office.

I spent a lot of time over the next few days at the rock quarry in Redwood City, wandering around those huge piles of crushed stone. I wanted to know everything that happened there and exactly when it happened. The rock quarry was a simple business, nothing special about it. Which is exactly what made it a good unloading spot.

The quarry was on the water on an estuary, a few miles north of Palo Alto, in an industrial neighborhood. The owner of the quarry had a contract to dredge parts of San Francisco Bay, so he had huge piles of crushed oyster shells that he'd pulled off the bottom, plus mountainous piles of different kinds of crushed rocks that his workers hauled around in trucks with open tops. It was a thirty-minute drive from downtown San Francisco, and on a clear day you could see the Oakland skyline across the bay.

The only downside to the spot was that a security guard patrolled the waterfront, independent of the rock quarry. Using my watch, I sat there all day and night long, timing the guard's rounds, noting them in a ledger. He would drive by, take a look around, and keep going. One time, he'd be gone for forty-two minutes, the next time, forty minutes, the next, forty-five.

The way I figured it, we had to wait for this dude to pass by, and then we would have a window of time to drive our trucks in through the gate and secure it closed behind, under the cover of darkness. During loading, we could keep the gate closed and the guard wouldn't be able to see anything. The dock was additionally hidden behind huge mountains of rocks and oyster shells. Then we would have to time the exit of these big trucks, again in this window when the guard would be gone on his rounds.

The estuary had an inlet called Redwood Creek, which was big enough for a tug pulling a football-field-sized barge through. Across from the dock was nothing but salty swamp, so there was privacy. The plan was for the tug to pull the barge under the Golden Gate, clear customs, then go sixty miles up the Sacramento River Deep Water Canal. At the public docks in Sacramento, we would have the legit tugboat crew—who had no idea they were carrying weed—replaced with our own crew. Then the tug and barge would come back down the Sacramento River to the rock quarry in Redwood City on the other side of San Francisco Bay.

There was no room for error, and I gave my distributors meticulous instructions from start to finish. First, we needed to use the same kinds of trucks that the quarry used, otherwise it would look suspicious. I instructed the distributors to obtain big industrial trucks with steel cargo bays in back, with no top, so an industrial crane could put stone (or, in this case, weed) into them. I also told them to rent warehouses in rural places but not far from the quarry. No farther than thirty minutes. Time on the highway equated to time these open-top trucks could be pulled over and busted. Inside these warehouses, the distributors could transfer the weed from the quarry trucks to cross-country eighteen-wheeler big rigs.

Each eighteen-wheeler would hold around twenty-five thousand pounds, pushed as far into the trailer as possible.

I instructed the distributors to build a false wooden wall to cover it up. After that, they were to get themselves manifests, so if the drivers were pulled over, they could open the back of the eighteen-wheelers and reveal actual shipping product.

One guy planned to fill a refrigerated tractor trailer with boxes of lettuce piled all the way to the ceiling. Another was going to fill his truck with hot tubs, which I thought was ingenious because they were big heavy things packed inside wooden crates; you couldn't possibly unload the hot tubs without heavy equipment and a serious reason to go digging in there.

Then I instructed the distributors to have a guy with a typewriter assigned to each warehouse, whose job it would be to create manifest paperwork for each truck. Everything had to look perfectly legit. Each distributor had to have a truck-size scale so that the fully loaded truck would weigh the amount on the manifest paperwork in case the trucks got stopped at weigh stations on the highways.

For a final touch, I created counterfeit customs seals. These looked like big industrial bobby pins that got hooked onto the doors on the back of the big rigs and signified to anyone who saw it that this truck had been weighed and cleared by customs, locked at that point, and had not been opened since.

When the tugboat pulled the barge under the Golden Gate bridge on a cold April afternoon, I was standing on a pier in San Francisco with binoculars. I could see it—a 150-foot tugboat, fronting a 300-foot barge that stood four stories high (with another two underwater). Every minute that barge sat there at the customs house shaved a year off my life.

I watched and waited. When customs finally cleared the barge on the second day, I got no notification. I came down to the pier one morning with my binoculars and could see across the bay that the tugboat and barge were gone. The legit crew was towing it up the Sacramento Deep Water Canal to the state capital. Our crew then took over and steered back down the Sac River into San Francisco Bay. When it reached the rock quarry, I was there. I will never forget the sight of that magnificent barge, lit up in the moonlight at the quarry dock.

That same night, I got a buzz on my beeper from Bill Whittington. Bill had scored a second place for Blue Thunder at Road Atlanta. In our first two races, Blue Thunder had two second-place finishes. Things were starting to roll.

On the first night of unloading, I was on the quarry site, and when I saw the security guard go by the gate, I jumped in my Hertz rental car and drove to the nearest pay phone, which was in the parking lot of a Malibu Grand Prix indoor go-kart racing facility. I beeped Ronnie, my brother-in-law and one of my distributors, and he called the pay phone.

"Send your driver," I said. "The security guard is gone. We got a short window. Do it now."

"OK."

I sped back to the quarry. I waited. And waited. Per my instructions, his truck was supposed to be waiting five minutes from the quarry. Every minute that passed, I got angrier. Where was the fucking truck? Finally, I drove back to the Malibu Grand Prix parking lot and beeped Ronnie again. "Man," I said, "what's going on? I gave you very specific instructions!"

"I called my driver. He said he went to get a haircut."

"Ronnie, are you fucking serious?"

"I'm calling him, but now he's not answering."

We had some words on the phone. To say I was bent out of shape would be a gross understatement. "Meet me at the fucking Malibu Grand Prix," I said.

While I waited for him to show up in the parking lot, I went to the trunk of my rental car and pulled out the tire iron, just in case. Ronnie was a large, muscular, hotheaded man. An ex-football player. For all I knew, Ronnie was going to come after me because I'd called him every name in the book, and I felt I might need to protect myself. When he drove up, I had the tire iron in my grip.

"What are you going to do with that, Randy?"

"I can't have this, Ronnie! You fucked this up, man!"

He shook his head and apologized. I put the tire iron back in the trunk and drove away, all the way back to my apartment in San Francisco. I decided to wait until the next night to unload into the first truck because I had to calm down and because the timing and the schedule had gotten out of sequence.

The next night, we went through the process again, only now I was using a different driver. I put Ronnie on the back of the line. I waited for the security guard to pass, and then hauled ass over to the Malibu Grand Prix parking lot. I beeped the distributor. He beeped his driver. I raced back to the quarry, waited two minutes, and this driver pulled his truck in. I shut the gate behind him. Already, the incompetence on the part of my distributors was glaring. Walking over to the front of the truck, I said to the driver, "What the fuck is this?"

"A truck," he said.

"This is not the kind of truck I asked for."

It was a regular tractor trailer with a flatbed on the back. All around the outside of this flatbed, these guys had built sides out of plywood. The top was open. They were planning on placing the weed onto the back of the flatbed truck, inside this area created by the plywood walls all around the edges. They tried to save some money by showing up with this joke of a truck. I expected professionals, and this was some *Beverly Hillbillies* shit.

"Fuck it," I said. We couldn't wait any longer. "Let's do this."

The driver drove the truck to the dock. I had men in the barge, and they'd prepared the first pallet of weed bales. The crane operator picked up the first pallet and swung it over to the truck, but when he went to set it down, the pallet tipped and dumped about a dozen bales of weed all over the back of the truck and onto the ground. A couple of the bags ripped and spilled product. Now I had a mess on my hands. I set some of the guys to work on cleaning it up, and we kept on going. When the truck held all it could, we put a tarp over the back, and I sent it off, timing the exit when I knew the security guard would be gone. The truck headed for this distributor's warehouse, and I went back to my San Francisco apartment to rest my head. The nerves were getting to me, and I had to cool off.

My beeper went off at 2 a.m. It was my distributor Jeff, who was in charge of the truck we'd just loaded. I went down to a pay phone on the street and called him.

"We got a problem," he said.

"Yeah, you got a problem for that bogus truck your guy showed up with. That's not what I asked for. It was a piece of shit. Now what's the problem?"

"The truck."

"What about it?"

"The driver was going around a turn and the pallets on the back shifted, so the plywood buckled and weed started coming out the side."

"Where's the fucking truck now?"

"At a truck stop."

"You took a truck with thousands of pounds of weed busting out of the side to a place where cops hang out?"

I heard Jeff take some heavy breaths. He was stressed out, and so was I. Then he said, "I'm going to bring another tractor trailer to the truck stop and do the transfer there."

"You're going to get yourself arrested is what you're going to do!"

"Randy—"

"Don't Randy me shit. This is what you're going to do. You're going to go get some type of come-along hoists. You know what those are?" Come-alongs are hoists with canvas straps that moving and trucking companies use to secure whatever they are hauling. "Get some come-alongs and use them to tighten down the plywood surrounding the weed," I directed him.

He did what I told him and managed to save the load.

On the third night of unloading, we worked until dawn, a whole mess of guys, and finished the job. The process took longer than I'd expected. But it worked. The distributors moved their trucks from the quarries to the warehouses, where the men unloaded the bales into the cross-country big rigs. In each warehouse, I had one of my guys with a click counter, keeping track of how many bales each distributor had. The operation was moving, but it was never done until all the money was in hand. All it took was for one driver to get pulled over and busted, and the whole thing could come crashing down like a house of cards.

At sunrise the next day, I headed for the airport. I flew down to LA from San Francisco on Bill Whittington's private Lear-jet. I had already missed practice for the Los Angeles Times Grand Prix at Riverside International Raceway. I had never been to Riverside, and I was going to have almost no time on the track before qualifying. I felt a tinge of anxiety when I arrived in LA; at the previous year's race, a driver named Rolf Stommelen had been killed in a fiery crash. But I had to keep my cool.

It was time to bring my A game.

16

Thunder Beats Lightning

Summer 1984

The day after we finished unloading in Redwood City, I woke up in my motel near Riverside International Raceway, one of America's most iconic old racetracks, just north of Los Angeles. Pam was with me, and we went down to the restaurant for breakfast, where we met Bill. I had a leather bag with me carrying a bunch of beepers, a ledger cataloging who owed me what from the Redwood City haul, and $50,000 cash. Bill knew exactly where I'd been and what I'd been doing, but he knew better than to ask about it. Over breakfast, he updated me on how the car was performing in practice, on lap times, and track conditions.

It was a Saturday, qualifying day for the six-hour race on Sunday. Pam had some friends with her and wanted to go shopping on Rodeo Drive in the city. So Bill flipped her the keys to the Mercedes 500 SEL he was driving. Then he and I drove to the track in my rental car.

When I got into the March for my short practice stint, I had a lot of work to do very quickly, to learn the ins and outs of ·

this high-speed circuit. Nine turns, 3.25 miles, with a blistering mile-long straightaway and a famously tricky set of S-turns. Out on the track in the Blue Thunder car, I was finding the apexes, getting a feel for the pavement. There's always a fastest route around a track, what they call the racing line, and it can change constantly according to the conditions or how the car is behaving. Because a car is like an animate object with a personality all its own. I was working to find that racing line and to tease out how the car was handling.

Then something bizarre occurred. I was on the mile-long straightaway, flat out around 180 mph, when a thought entered my head. I shouted, "Fuck!"

I came around, pulled the car into the pit, and motioned frantically for Bill, who was sitting on the pit wall. He ran to the car and opened the door.

"What's wrong?" he asked me.

"I forgot the bag at the hotel! The bag has all my money in it! I set it down under the table at breakfast!" I didn't mention that it also had beepers and a potentially incriminating ledger in it too. "You gotta go back to the hotel to find my bag!"

Bill rolled his eyes. I got back on the track, and he headed to the parking lot. When he returned to the track from the hotel, practice was over. "The manager says he has your bag," Bill said, standing in our pit. "But he wouldn't give it to me. He asked me what was in it. I didn't know."

"Shit, man!"

When I got back to the hotel, I found the manager. He did indeed have my bag. At the front desk, he asked me, "Can you tell me what's in the bag, Mr. Lanier?"

"Fifty thousand dollars cash and some beepers," I said.

Without pause, he handed it over. When I looked inside, it was all there. I was stunned, as I'd figured whoever had found this bag would take the money. I asked who had found it, and he gave me the name of a waitress. When I found her the next morning, I tried to give her two grand as a tip. But she wouldn't take it. So I gave the manager five grand in cash and told him to tip out the whole wait staff.

Now I could go back to focusing on racing. Over fifty teams qualified for the LA Times Grand Prix. Ford Motor Company brought three Mustang GTP race cars. Toyota came with a new turbocharged 2.0 liter. Porsche's factory-backed 962 was a beast, and there were several other privateer Porsche 935 teams. But the big story was Blue Thunder. Bill's lap times were considerably faster than mine, and he'd qualified second. So we were set to start right on the front row.

On race day morning, TV announcers Ed Ruse and Brock Yates welcomed viewers nationwide to the broadcast of the six-hour-long LA Times Grand Prix at Riverside.

"At three and a quarter miles," Ruse said, holding a microphone and staring into the camera, "it's one of the largest and most impressive courses in the country. This course offers a real challenge to the drivers and the crews who tackle it. You'll be seeing some of the best international teams in the world competing in some of the fastest racing machines in the world."

Bobby Rahal set a lap record to qualify on pole in a Ford Mustang prototype—a purpose-built, fast-as-all-hell, front-engine race car designed by Ford with the help of space

From left: My mother Elise Maude Elliott Lanier, Pam (pregnant with Brandie), me, and my brother Steve, in 1979.

One of the best days of my life: my wedding to Pam on Valentine's Day in 1976, at the Little Flower Church in Hollywood, Florida.

The #57 Porsche Speedster, my first race car, on the track at Road Atlanta in 1980.

With Pam and baby Brandie in Colorado in 1983.

The 1957 Porsche 356 Speedster, ready to roll at Palm Beach International Raceway, in the late 1970s. I'm in the car. My father Noel Lanier Jr. is standing to the left.

The Executone-sponsored March GTP at the 1983 24 Hours of Daytona. We finished second overall.

Five-time Le Mans champion Derek Bell tugging on my moustache before a race in 1984.

Hanging with racing phenom John Paul Jr., twice the winner of the 24 Hours of Daytona, in 1984.

The Ferrari BB 512 I raced at Le Mans in 1982 with codrivers Preston Henn and Frenchman Denis Morin.

The #57 Blue Thunder March racing car that I drove to win the 1984 IMSA Camel GT championship (*photo by Marshall Pruett*).

On the way to the winners' circle after a triumphant 1984 Los Angeles Grand Prix, hanging out of the side of the car (*photo by Marshall Pruett*).

Accepting the 1984 Camel GT national championship trophy at the IMSA awards banquet in Daytona.

Celebrating with Bill Whittington at the 1984 Los Angeles Grand Prix, on the road to Blue Thunder's IMSA Camel GT national championship.

Debuting as an IndyCar rookie at the Toyota Grand Prix at Long Beach, in 1985. Notice Ben Kramer's Apache Power Boats logo on the car.

The 1984 IMSA Camel GT series saw a rivalry between Blue Thunder (an American team) and the Porsches of Germany and Jaguars of Britain. Here, the Blue Thunder car rocks the Stars and Stripes.

Inspecting our Lola IndyCar in 1985. Notice how the car has almost no sponsorship logos; the racing campaign was funded almost entirely through weed smuggling.

Chatting with Bill (center) and Dale Whittington at the Indianapolis Motor Speedway in 1986.

Posing with Pam at the 1986 Indianapolis 500, ready to make my Brickyard dreams come true.

Qualifying day for the 1986 Indy 500, where I set the fastest rookie lap time in history (*IMS Photo Archive*).

Bill Whittington and me in Gasoline Alley at the Indianapolis Motor Speedway, in 1986 (*IMS Photo Archive*).

Signing autographs for the fans at Indy (*IMS Photo Archive*).

The Indy 500 Rookie of the Year ceremony. Behind me is the Borg-Warner Trophy (*IMS Photo Archive*).

Fifty years old, at Leavenworth penitentiary, in 2004.

Glen, Pam, and Brandie taking a selfie minutes before my release from prison after twenty-seven years, at United States Penitentiary Coleman in Florida, in 2014.

In the visiting room at Federal Corrections Institution Oxford in Wisconsin, with Pam, Glen, and Brandie, in 1991.

A 2021 vigil outside of the White House, asking President Biden to pardon nonviolent cannabis prisoners.

With my daughter Brandie at her wedding in Telluride, Colorado, in 2021.

engineers. Stiff competition was a gross understatement. Judging by the qualifying speeds, this was going to be the fastest LA Times Grand Prix ever. We'd qualified second behind Rahal. I was set to drive the first stint in the number 57 March. I wore a fireproof Blue Thunder racing suit and a white helmet with a full jaw guard. A cameraman aimed his lens at my car, and a TV commentator said I was in "the water sports equipment business down in Florida." When the cameraman leaned into the cockpit, all you could see of my face was my eyes, peering out of the helmet. The announcer Brock Yates approached me.

"On the outside of the front row," Yates said into his microphone, "the Randy Lanier–Bill Whittington car. Randy . . . uh . . . you got a fast car right beside you [referring to Bobby Rahal in the Ford]. Are you going to try to take the lead early or are you going to hang back a bit?"

"We're going to just stay back, play it by ear for the first hour, see what falls out," I said. "Then go ahead and run a little bit on it then."

"OK, well good luck."

"Thank you very much."

I revved the engine. A pace car led the whole field out onto the track for a warm-up lap. I moved the car left and right, grinding some heat into my tires to make them stickier. The pace car pulled off, the green flag waved, and we hammered forward. My first lap was lousy, and I dropped two spots to fourth. But then I settled in. Got myself in the zone. I began to peel off good laps, charging hard and fast.

What unfolded was one of the most exciting IMSA Camel GT races ever held. We battled for hours, and it all came down

to a sprint race in the final minutes between Bill in our Blue
Thunder March and the great Al Holbert in the factory-backed
Porsche 962. Bill was leading, but Holbert was gaining fast. I
was in the pit watching, trying to keep myself from pissing
my pants.

On lap 172, we were 13 seconds in front. On lap 173, we
were 9.6 seconds ahead. By lap 177, our lead had melted to
7.3 seconds. Then 6.4 seconds, then 5.8 seconds, then 4.3 seconds, then 2.3 seconds, until Bill and Al Holbert were nose
to tail.

Announcer Brock Yates was screaming at the TV audience:
"It could go right down to the wire! We could have a photo
finish! This is absolutely the best finish in any endurance contest I have ever had the privilege of watching!"

When Bill motored past the checked flag, just inches
ahead of the Porsche, the fans went mad and so did I. We
had won. We'd beaten the best in the business, which meant
we *were* the best in the business. We'd also set a track record for highest average speed in a six-hour race. The team
came together in the pit, and we were jumping up and down
and punching at the sky as the television cameras filmed us.
Brock Yates put his arm around me and thrust the microphone in my face.

"Randy," he said, "let me get you first! Kind of tense at the
end, huh?"

"Oh, it was like waiting for a baby! Most exciting race for a
six-hour race I've ever seen!"

"Congratulations," Yates said. "Super race, Randy."

And it was! As one racing journalist put it: "Thunder Beat
Lightning."

That night, all the teams loaded their big-rig transporters and headed north to Laguna Seca for the Red Lobster Monterey Grand Prix, a forty-five-minute sprint race set to take place one week after the LA Times Grand Prix. The wife of one of my mechanics was looking after Brandie, back in Florida. Pam, Bill, and I drove to Monterey early so we could squeeze in a couple of vacation days. I had so much adrenaline pumping, I was a little out of control.

At that moment, I had seven eighteen-wheelers hauling weed across the country to Michigan, Pennsylvania, Kentucky, Louisiana, and New York. Blue Thunder had just won its first team victory. I was driving a rental car up the coast with the speedometer pinned, hitting speeds so high that when we made it to Monterey, both Bill and Pam got out of the car, dropped to their knees, and kissed the ground. In town, the party was on. One bottle of Moët followed another. I handed out hundred dollar bills to homeless guys.

But as much fun as we were having, I was feeling manic. I had these jolts of paranoia. Like, maybe the FBI was watching me. I'd be walking down the street and there'd be a guy in sunglasses and a suit staring at me. Or I'd be in a crowded restaurant and get this feeling that some of the other diners were undercover agents. I couldn't tell if I was being overly sensitive or if this was the real deal.

One day we were having lunch at the Hog's Breath, this great bar in Carmel just south of Monterey. The place was owned by Clint Eastwood (who would be elected mayor of Carmel two years later). Carmel was so quaint it looked almost cartoonish. It was full of fancy art galleries, and after lunch, I strolled into one of them. My eye immediately fell on this painting of a tugboat going under the Golden Gate Bridge. This was just uncanny. It was like a scene out of my actual life. I bought it on the spot, and it still hangs on my wall today.

On race day at Laguna Seca, the pit was crowded with mechanics, fans, and a few reporters buzzing around, because suddenly Blue Thunder was a story worth covering. Since it was a solo sprint race, I entered two Blue Thunder cars: the number 57 car for me and number 56 for Bill.

Laguna Seca was one of the most thrilling, intimidating, and beautiful racetracks in America, with plenty of hard-throttle cornering, flat-out straights, and major elevation changes. It's famous for its corkscrew, in which you approach a high-speed section into hard braking, followed by hard acceleration down a steep hill that's also a right-hand bend. The hill is so steep, and the acceleration so hard, you feel like you're in an elevator in a skyscraper when the cable breaks and sends you into free fall. All the weight of the car lifts until you get to the bottom, where the hard g-forces pin you to the back of your seat.

You screw up this corner, and it could be the last turn you ever take. But if you get it right, you can carry tremendous speed and pass other cars because you can count on some drivers to lift their foot off the pedal purely out of fear.

Bill blew out his engine early in the race, but I fought all the way. Nearing the end, I came down the pit straight in second place, into the last lap, trailing nose to tail the Red Lobster March 83G, this white car with a big red lobster painted on it. Up to this point, it was the best race of my life. I was ahead of all the Porsches, all the Lolas and Fords, just one car length away from first place. When I passed the start-finish line, the track steward waved the white flag. Last lap! On the pit wall, I saw my whole crew jumping up and down and screaming.

Go! Go! Go!

I knew my best shot to pass the Red Lobster car was at the entrance to the corkscrew. I'd practiced it many times. If I planned in advance, I could set myself up to dive for the inside racing line upon entering this turn. Then I could leverage that position to make the Red Lobster car go wide. It was a dangerous move, but I was prepared to take the risk.

A fast, uphill straight leads to the sharp left-hander into the corkscrew. This is where I made my move. Approaching the turn, at the top of the corkscrew, I poked my nose into the inside line and forced the Red Lobster car wide.

We were side by side, wheels to wheels. In that split second, it was a contest of wills and courage. I kept my foot down all the way. I knew he was going to lift his foot off the throttle, and he did. We both flew into the corkscrew with me on the inside line, and I came out of the corkscrew in front as the new race leader. It was the best pass of my life.

Over the next two corners, I gained another half second on him. I felt like the hand of fate had reached down and given me that extra boost of speed. When I saw the checkered flag waving, I screamed so loud I felt like I could smash my windows. This was my moment: my first professional victory, all on my own. As I took my victory lap, looking out at thousands of fans cheering me on, with the television cameras rolling, I wanted time to stop forever. I wanted to hold onto this feeling.

Throughout the season, the TV announcers had been calling me a "gentleman driver," a rich team owner, saying that Bill Whittington was the real talent on our team. But at Laguna Seca, I won on my own. I'd proven to the competition, my team, the fans, everyone—Randy Lanier was the real deal. The podium, the ceremony, the look on Pam's face—it was indescribable. I found a new level of belief in myself, and I was determined to become the IMSA Camel GT series national champion.

17

Launching the Louisiana Load

Summer 1984

*A*fter Laguna Seca, Pam flew home to Florida on a commercial flight. I had the Blue Thunder crew on Bill's private jet, taking off out of Oakland. The champagne was flowing. A few minutes after takeoff, I said, "Hey, who wants to go to Vegas!?" I heard an explosion in response.

Vegas! Vegas! Vegas!

I told our pilot Nick to radio Las Vegas airport, announcing our arrival, and I asked him to make sure we had a limo waiting. I'd spent a lot of time in Vegas and always traveled under the name Ray Lane when I was there. I gambled huge amounts of money—sometimes $50,000 in a single night— and I didn't want people to know who I really was for IRS reasons.

When Ray Lane came to Vegas, Caesars Palace comped him the special Fantasy Suite, and that's where we were going. When we landed, the limo driver pulled right up to the Learjet on the tarmac. He had a sign reading "Ray Lane."

The driver was throwing our luggage in the trunk while looking at me. He said, "Excuse me, sir, aren't you Randy Lanier, the race car driver?" Turned out, he was a race fan.

"Yessir," I said. "Damn skippy."

It was the first time a stranger recognized me after seeing me on TV. From that day on, anytime I went to Vegas, this guy was my driver. And I always paid him well.

The Fantasy Suite at Caesars was something to behold. It had two floors, with two golden spiral staircases and huge two-story windows looking out on the Vegas strip. You could push a button and the hot tub turned on. Push another button and the shades on the two-story windows opened. Real 007 shit. I told the team, "Whatever you want, just call the concierge and tell 'em to bring it up. I'm going downstairs to play some blackjack."

I was gone two hours, and when I got back, the party in the Fantasy Suite was off the rails. They had girls everywhere. There were empty champagne bottles floating in the hot tub and clothes scattered all over. They were having the time of their lives. Meanwhile, I was thinking about the next race.

When I got back to Florida, I met with Gene, George, and Ben at Joe Sonken's Gold Coast Restaurant in Hollywood. Ben and I loved this place. It was on the Intracoastal Waterway with beautiful views of big yachts going by. Great stone crabs. Frank Sinatra and Cary Grant hung out here. Joe Sonken himself was such a classic South Florida character. He had two bulldogs that went everywhere with him, and they looked exactly like him—short, squat, chubby—except the dogs didn't always have a cigar in their mouths. Joe knew us, and he knew to keep waiters from hovering over our table so we could eat well and talk business.

Our team was ready to bring in another load. We were ready to scale up again and to improve our operational methods. We were always thinking bigger, always evolving to improve our profits and stay ahead of the law. My personal motivation? I wanted to spend more money on Blue Thunder. If we were winning now with the resources we had, more millions could make us unstoppable. I imagined a dynasty. We could destroy the competition for the entire 1980s. There was another thing: since I was a kid, I'd never stopped thinking about the Indy 500. For the first time in my life, I felt like it was within reach, and it was going to cost money.

"I got a new spot," Gene told us. "It's in Louisiana, right near New Orleans. It's ideal for us, I'm telling you. Perfect."

Gene had recently bought a boat business on the coast of Louisiana, and while he was doing business down there, he'd come across this spot on a waterway called the Industrial Canal. It was a short drive from Bourbon Street. We all agreed it was a good idea not to return to the Redwood City quarry right away. Better to switch it up, keep things changing. Gene's idea was to load the barge in Santa Marta, and then swing it around to Venezuela.

"In Venezuela," he said in between bites of stone crab, "we can put a million pounds of cement in the barge, as manifest, so if anyone goes snooping around in there, the barge will appear totally legit, moving real cargo. Then, from Venezuela, we'll send the barge to my salvage operation in Santo Domingo. There, we will switch crews, so we'll have a legit crew on the tugboat, who'll have no idea they are hauling a large load of weed. This way, customs won't pick up on anybody being nervous. If anything goes wrong, we can keep our guys from getting arrested."

I thought a major improvement would be to start the un-loading process inside the barge so that no weed could ever be seen coming off the vessel. I suggested that we use a crane to place empty shipping containers into the hull of the barge. Then, during off-loading, workers could move the weed from the secret compartments in the ballasts into the shipping con-tainers, then the crane could haul those out of the barge's hull and put them on the back of tractor trailers.

Constantly evolving, baby!

I flew to New Orleans and drove out to the Industrial Canal to check it out. Gene was right. It was perfect. The canal connected Lake Pontchartrain to the Mississippi River. To access it, the tug could pull the barge from the Caribbean Sea, through an inlet into Lake Pontchartrain, and right up to the mouth of the canal. There was an airport at the opening of the canal, and from there on, it was all industrial. We leased a piece of property with a long concrete dock, a little front office, and a storage facility behind the office—all of it in the name of a fake importing company.

I started scouting for warehouses and found an area full of them on Tchoupitoulas Street on the outskirts of New Orleans. This was where all the big companies had their warehouses, including Coca-Cola. My plan was to get a crane that could move CTIs—containerized trailers, the kind that fit right onto the back of a flatbed eighteen-wheeler. With the crane, we could load two CTIs on a truck, with the doors to the two

CTIs facing each other so you wouldn't be able to access the interior of either. I was also going to use fewer distributors this time—just three of them, the best of the best, because I thought it was safer to have fewer people involved. But each of those three would be responsible for a significantly bigger cut of the total load.

It blew my mind when I stopped to think about it: just two years earlier, we'd brought in 15,000 pounds on my first Beach Assault. Now we were planning a score of 155,000.

During these days, I was so busy and running on so much adrenaline, I barely ever slept. On top of racing and smuggling, I was launching a bunch of legitimate businesses as a way to clean money. I was driving a raspberry-colored Ferrari around, but on paper, I wasn't making much. So I had to create an identity that would smell OK to the IRS.

Welcome to Hunky Dory's, my new restaurant on the water in Hollywood, Florida. Hunky Dory's was a burger and seafood joint with an outdoor bar that smelled of salty air and suntan lotion. The restaurant already existed under a different name; I bought it, and then rebranded and renamed it. I had the Blue Thunder team bring one of our race cars and roll it out in the parking lot for the grand opening. T-shirt giveaways. Women in bikinis. Badass Cigarette boats docked along the 1,800 feet of dock space. Reggae bands on weekends. It was a happening spot and an almost entirely cash business.

I was also working another deal with Ben. His father had a contact who said he could get us a casino license in Southern California, so Ben and I flew out to Los Angeles for a meeting.

This gentleman, Sam, was a well-known business figure who handled all Ben's money, and his office was in the Wells Fargo building in LA.

"There is going to be a casino license coming up," Sam said. "I can help you secure it." The cost for the license would be $500,000. We talked through the possibilities for hours. This would be an excellent revenue stream, but more importantly, a casino was also a cash business—an ideal place to launder money.

"I think we go should forward," I decided. "This seems like a great deal."

Ben agreed. Our cut between the three of us (me, Ben, and Gene) would be 30 percent of the casino, with other partners in on the rest. We scouted out property, finding what we thought was a beautiful spot just off the highway in Gardena near LA. Our plan was to start building as soon as possible.

It did not occur to me that it might not be the best idea to get myself deeper into business with Ben at this time, to weave our destinies more tightly together. He had been my business partner from the start. Why change now? Turns out, there was a good reason, but I couldn't see it at the time.

In 1984, Ben was making a name for himself in the offshore racing world, big-time. He'd cofounded a racing boat company called Apache, which he intended to build into a direct rival to Don Aronow's Cigarette. Ben built the Apache boat factory and marina at 302 NE 188 Street in North Miami, right next door to Cigarette at Thunder Boat Alley. He called his new home base Fort Apache.

That same year, the Offshore Racing Commission— basically the NFL of speedboat racing—was expanding its national series and a tremendous flood of sponsorship money was pouring in. Just as I had launched Blue Thunder to race cars in the IMSA Camel GT series, Ben had created his own Apache racing team and was kicking ass in national powerboat racing, which was centered around South Florida.

On occasion, I'd go to one of Ben's races. I'd lease a helicopter, and we'd chase after his Apache boat. The offshore racing scene was incredible. When you watched these big boats race, they'd move across the water like skipping stones, with the ocean off the coast of Florida sparkling in the sun. The engines had so much power that the boat would spend as much time over the water as in it. All above were helicopters chasing these boats, including TV camera crews.

Ben was creating an empire of his own to rival Aronow's, both in the salesroom and in offshore racing. The *New York Times* later referred to Ben as Don Aronow's protégé.

In 1984, Ben and Aronow got tied up in a deal that went sour, and Ben apparently lost money. He never talked to me about it. This was all to come out later. Point is the relationship between Ben and Aronow was becoming strained.

Don Aronow had built Thunder Boat Alley in the 1970s, and everybody admired Don. He was "the millionaire guru of the powerboat set," as one South Florida reporter wrote of him. He'd built boats for all kinds of famous people, from the Shah of Iran to Vice President George Bush himself. From the

Sultan of Oman to Haitian dictator Jean-Claude "Baby Doc" Duvalier. Aronow had it all: good looks, charisma. Ben didn't have those things, but he did have something Aronow didn't: a gangster persona. Ben was intimidating, he was feared, and he was loaded with guns and money.

Ben was out to eclipse Aronow as the king of Thunder Boat Alley. How it was all going to play out, we didn't know. The competition was fierce, and Ben always played to win.

One day, apropos of nothing, I got a chilling phone call from Ben. "Randy," Ben said, "your buddy Gene is up to something."

"What are you talking about? That's crazy."

I drove down to meet Ben in his office at Fort Apache. The smell of resin and fiberglass was thick in the air, and the shells of boat hulls were all over the place.

"I heard through one of my guys that Gene was down in Colombia," Ben said, "at the compound. He went down there to meet with the Family without us. Did you know that?"

"I didn't."

"This fucking guy. . . . He's up to something. He's being disrespectful. Set up a meeting, Randy. Get Gene's ass here asap."

I didn't like this at all. Ben believed that Gene was trying to cut us out of our operations. I tried to convince him that this was ridiculous. "Listen," I told him, "Gene is not a weed salesman or a distributor. If he cuts us out, how's he going to move any weed? He can't sell shit. He can't distribute shit. He doesn't know anybody. He's never sold an ounce of weed in his life. Gene is a kind man, Ben. He's not capable of treachery. You're looking for something that doesn't exist."

Ben didn't have Gene's direct contact. I kept it that way, on purpose. But Ben was insisting on a sit-down, and I was scared that he might hurt Gene. Darth Vader was capable of anything, it seemed to me. So I set up this meeting, hoping we could straighten it all out.

I picked up Gene on a Miami street corner in my Ferrari at night and took him to Fort Apache. Ben's office was in back. I was feeling uncomfortable; if some dude jumped out of a closet with a sawed-off shotgun, it would not have surprised me. When I pulled my Ferrari in, it was dark around the factory and marina. No lights on. I parked the car facing the exit in case we had to get out of there fast, and right away, I spotted a guy lurking in the darkness inside one of the buildings that had racks of boats in storage.

I recognized this guy right away. I called him No Neck, because he was a heavy, thick, football player kind of guy with big shoulders and no neck, like his head was attached right to the shoulders. There was a little light from the moon, and I could see that No Neck was holding a gun.

"Stay in the car," I said to Gene.

I got out right as Ben was walking up to the driver's side. We shook hands.

"What the fuck's he doing here?" I asked, pointing with my chin over at No Neck.

"He's here because I asked him to be here."

"Well, why's he holding a piece?"

"We're going to settle this right now."

I felt that I had one shot here to save Gene's life. "Listen, Ben," I said, "you've got this all wrong. Gene's a stand-up guy. He's like a brother to me, and I trust him. He is married to a Venezuelan. He does business in Venezuela and Colombia. Legit business, cargo hauling with his barges. That's why he contacted the Family in Santa Marta. It was just legit business."

Ben and I talked at length. Gene remained in the car, and I had no idea if he understood just how much danger he was in. I had a feeling I was getting through to Ben, but I couldn't be sure.

"Tell him to get out of the car," Ben said.

"I'll do that under one condition," I responded. "You have to give me your word that you're not going to hurt him."

Ben nodded. "OK. Now tell him to get out of the car."

I walked over and opened the Ferrari's passenger side door. Gene climbed out and shook Ben's hand. The three of us talked for about ten minutes, and in the end, Gene promised he would never contact the Family again. That's how it ended. When I pulled out of Fort Apache with Gene, it was past midnight. I could see No Neck in my rearview, standing in the darkness. I never saw him again; soon after, No Neck caught his girlfriend in bed with a guy and bludgeoned him to death. He was caught by the cops, trying to dump the body.

My partnership with Ben remained intact for the time being. But it did occur to me just how dangerous of a man he was becoming.

18

A Crowning Moment

Spring, summer, and fall 1984

Blue Thunder rolled into North Carolina in mid-April for the 500 Kilometers of Charlotte at the Charlotte Motor Speedway, a mecca for American racing fans. I'd seen plenty of big races, but I couldn't believe what I was seeing. These crowds! There were people everywhere, swarms and swarms of fans. It was like Woodstock for gearheads.

"Look at this, man!" I said to Bill Whittington on the morning of the event. "They've come to see *us!*"

The story of Blue Thunder—this upstart, come-out-of-nowhere, underdog team gunning for the national series title—was making headlines. The Charlotte race drew the largest crowd in the history of IMSA—eighty-five thousand people. Countless others were watching on TV.

On the grid that morning, revving that March's engine, I knew a win at Charlotte would give our team enough points to put us in first place on the season's leaderboard. We were fighting factory-backed cars with major sponsorships, notably the number 14 Lowenbrau beer–sponsored Porsche 962 driven by aces Al Holbert and Derek Bell, whom everyone believed to be the team to beat.

Blue Thunder had no sponsor like Lowenbrau or Red Lobster. We had Ben Kramer's Apache boats for our main sponsor, and Ben paid us zero dollars. We just put his logo on the car as a favor to him. With my smuggling, we didn't even need corporate backing. We were as big as the corporations!

We went out and won at Charlotte. It was our third straight victory. Blue Thunder was now in first place, ahead of Porsche, and I was leading the driver's championship. The writer Jonathan Ingram put this moment in perspective for us in his recap in *On Track* magazine:

> The Blue Thunder race team ought to consider changing its name: *Rolling* Blue Thunder may be more appropriate. For the young, five-race-old team is, without a doubt, on a roll. . . . At Charlotte Motor Speedway, before the largest crowd ever to witness an IMSA event, the Blue Thunder privateers have come out on top.

When our big rig pulled out of Charlotte, the spirit of the team members was so high we couldn't wait for the next race. We had full tanks of attitude. All eyes were on us. We felt like a band of outlaws, out to rule the world, and that's how we acted. Case in point: Blue Thunder wasn't just good at racing. We were world-class pranksters too. We all recognized that these could turn out to be the greatest days of our lives, and we were seizing the moment.

One night before the Coca-Cola 500 at Lime Rock Park in Connecticut, I returned to my motel room and clicked on a light switch. The light didn't turn on. I had to go to the bathroom, so I hustled in there to take a piss. Flipped the switch. No light. It was dark and I had poor aim, so when I was done, I went to grab toilet paper to wipe the seat clean. No toilet paper. I was thinking . . . huh? I went over to the bed and sat down. There was no mattress, just a box spring.

"What the fuucckkkk," I said aloud. I picked up the phone and dialed.

"Hi, this is the front desk."

"Hey," I said, "this is Randy Lanier in room 222. Can you help—"

"Hello. Anyone there? This is the front desk. Hello?"

"Yeah, this is Randy Lanier in room 222. Can you please—"

"Hello? Hello? Anyone there?"

Someone had taken the speaker out of the telephone. That's when I realized: I'd been pranked. I went out into the hallway to walk down to the front desk, and that's when I heard Bill Whittington in his room, yelling. Turned out, our crew had pranked him too. They'd gone out and found the biggest, baddest, live Maine lobster they could find and tied it under his pillow, so when he lay down, that lobster started snapping at his face. Bill came running out into the hallway half naked.

"Those bastards!" he shouted.

Another time, at Road America in Elkhart Lake, Wisconsin, one of our opponents, Bob Tullius of the Jaguar team, lost the keys to his rental car. Our crew chief Keith found them, but instead of giving the keys back to Bob, we pranked him. He was on the phone with Hertz, pleading for help. Meanwhile, we turned on the ignition, took a big rock and placed it on the gas pedal, and then locked the keys inside.

So now the engine was screaming at top volume, and a crowd of people were surrounding the car. Right when the rental car guy showed up, the rental car's engine exploded and lit a fire in the grass. So much smoke poured from the under the hood, it looked like a bomb had gone off. (We paid for the damage, of course.)

The funniest thing I saw during the 1984 IMSA Camel GT season occurred in Oregon. We got out there a few days early for the G.I. Joe's Grand Prix at Portland International Raceway, a race that we won. Bill and I, along with Bill's brother Dale and our private jet pilot Nick, were staying in this executive suite with a bunch of bedrooms at the Thunderbird Hotel on the river in the city. Bill and I went to a restaurant we heard was good, but Nick and Dale stayed behind.

When we got back to the suite after dinner, I turned on the lights. Dale was in his room, sleeping. Nick, our pilot, was in the hot tub with a woman he had apparently just met. When I turned on the light, they both got spooked and jumped out of that hot tub. They were completely naked, except Nick was wearing his cowboy boots, and he was—let's just say—aroused. I did a double take.

I said, "Nick, why the hell are you wearing your cowboy boots in the hot tub?"

He said, "I needed traction. I couldn't get any traction. So I put my boots on!"

That's about the hardest I ever laughed in my life. He needed traction!

These guys were all larger-than-life, but none more than Bill Whittington. Bill was known to show up at races and fly a lap around the circuit at low altitude in a World War II–era P-51 Mustang fighter plane, shocking the crowds. Then he'd fly off and hide from the cops in a hangar.

Still, there were other times when the strain of everything happening in my life made me a sleepless wreck. The more attention we drew to ourselves, the more certain I felt that the FBI was following me.

Once, during practice for the Lumbermens 500 at Mid-Ohio Sports Car Course, I kept seeing these two suspicious men in sports coats wandering around. Big dark sunglasses. They were watching me—I could feel it. I was thinking: Who the hell wears sports coats to a race in ninety-degree heat?

The FBI does.

We had a catering area roped off next to our motor home, with chairs and tables under a big umbrella and servers dishing out salad and pasta and hamburgers. I pulled Pam aside under the umbrella.

"These two guys are following me," I whispered with my nose an inch from hers. "I don't like this at all."

"What are you talking about?" she asked.

"Look over there. Just pretend you're not looking at those two dudes in sunglasses."

She craned her neck. "Oh shit, Randy! I see them!"

Maybe it wasn't just paranoia.

That afternoon, at Mid-Ohio, Bill took out the Blue Thunder March during qualifying and set a lap record on the thirteen-turn road course, qualifying in first place. We'd been doing some research and development work for a company that made head sock cooling technology for race car drivers. This gizmo was a head sock with tubes running through it that attached to a canister full of cooling liquid. The liquid was supposed to run through the head sock and keep your head cool as the car's interior heated up to searing temperatures during a race. But I was so worked up over being followed by the FBI that, when I got in the car for my first stint, I forgot to switch on the canister that cooled the fluid pulsing through the head sock.

I started my stint in first place, dropped to second behind Derek Bell, but regained first when he punctured a tire. The track was slippery and the temperature in the cockpit was rising. It got so hot, my brain fried and—coming over a rise—I blacked out at high speed.

Something woke me right before I crashed into a guardrail. It was as if a soft whisper spoke to me. That split second of clarity saved my life. I managed to get the car back to the pit. A medical crew wanted to give me an IV. And there were those two dudes again, the mysterious sunglasses guys, staring me down.

"I don't need any IV," I said. "I'm fine, lemme go back to my motor home."

I was lying down in my motor home, cooling myself in the air-conditioning, when I heard the door open. Pam came in. She was holding a business card.

"Randy," she said, "those two guys who've been following you gave me this, and they said they wanted to speak to you."

She handed me the card. I saw the logo of Ford Motor Company and the name Michael Kranefuss, Special Vehicle

Operations. Those two guys weren't FBI at all; they were SVO. They were executives from Ford.

I came out still wearing my driving suit, and there were the two guys. We sat down in my catering area where a canopy blocked the sun. My head was still throbbing, but I kept it together. Kranefuss was German and spoke with an accent. The other guy did most of the talking.

"We have been following you, Randy," he said. "We like the results that Blue Thunder is having. We'd like to schedule a meeting with you in Dearborn. Great things are happening at Ford racing, and we want you to be a part of it."

I told them I was game for a meeting and that I wanted to bring my teammate, Bill Whittington, and my PR guy, Jim DeLillo. But, I told them, I wanted to stay focused on Blue Thunder so it would have to wait until after the last race of the season.

"Or," I said, "at least until after we've clinched the Camel GT championship."

We all laughed, but I wasn't joking. I was fully confident we were going to win the title. If the FBI didn't come and cart me away first.

Onward to the Grand Prix at Pocono in Pennsylvania. Mid-race, I was in the March in first place. At home, the fans watching on TV saw my car and a little window with my face in it. Announcer Brock Yates said to Steve Evans: "Randy Lanier is a very emotional guy. Boy, he just gets pumped up. When he gets in that automobile, he drives it as hard as he can. But around the pits, he's really a nervous, nervous man. Especially with two cars in the race today."

Evans: "Well, I think you'd be pretty concerned too, Brock, and a little excited if you were leading a world-famous series like this in your first year of serious competition. He has to pinch himself once in a while to make sure it's true."

Yates: "And of course he's got about a half million dollars' worth of race cars out there running around. . . . Those cars just have so much acceleration. . . . As we watch Randy Lanier threading his way through the slower part of the infield. . . . Now back onto the straightaway where that big Chevy [engine] gets up to full speed."

Evans: "In the early part of the season, Brock, there was a significant difference between the lap times of Bill Whittington and Randy Lanier. . . . But that margin has narrowed. Lanier's lap times are almost as quick as Whittington's now."

Yates: "He's been a really quick learner in this business. He's only been actively racing for about five years."

These guys were right about all of it, especially the part about me having to pinch myself. We didn't win the Grand Prix of Pocono, but I was still in first place in the championship standings, with Bill one point behind and Derek Bell in third trailing by nine points. One week after the Pocono race, we went to the Michigan International Speedway for the Michigan 500 Kilometers. Blue Thunder won, with Bill and me as codrivers. With two races to go, we were in a position to clinch the Camel GT title with one more victory.

Looking back on the sports world of 1984, it was an extraordinary time. Walter Payton surpassed Jim Brown to become the NFL's all-time rushing leader. Marcus Allen won the NFL MVP, and Doug Flutie the Heisman Trophy. The Detroit Tigers were World Series Champs. Thomas Hearns knocked out Roberto Duran in two rounds. It was a year of great rivalries: John McEnroe versus Ivan Lendl, the Celtics versus the Lakers in the NBA Finals. In American sports car racing, the big story was Blue Thunder. The news headlines announced our latest escapade after every victory.

"Whittington, Lanier Combine to Win Camel GT Race."

"The Iron Gambit: Lanier and Whittington Double Up."

Soon a toy company would put a diecast toy version of our car on the market. A toy Blue Thunder car!

I was twenty-nine years old. Living the dream, literally.

We rolled into Watkins Glen in upstate New York for the opening practice session of the New York 500, to be held on September 30. This was one of the oldest and most storied racetracks in North America—eleven turns, 2.42 miles. Coming into this race, a two-point difference was all that separated me and Bill, in first and second in the drivers' standings. If we won at Watkins Glen, we'd clinch the team title. I decided to field both of our cars. Bill was going to start in one, and I had his brother Dale set to start in the other. I could then drive whichever of those two cars was in front of the other to end the race. So I had an advantage in the hunt for the driver's title. That's the perks of being the team owner.

When this race started, I could taste that championship. We were so close. We couldn't afford any mistakes. Porsche was out in force, with the Coca-Cola-sponsored and Lowenbrau-sponsored 962s. On the ninth lap, Bill crashed so hard the front end of his car looked like it had been driven off a sky-scraper nose down into the pavement. He wasn't injured, but it was gnarly. We were quickly down to one car.

At the halfway point, the team of Brian Redman and Hurley Haywood—two of the best endurance racers of all time—were out in front in their Porsche 962. When I took over for Dale in Sweet Pea, our number 57 car, we were in second. I was all business, totally in the zone, peeling off quick lap times. I was far enough back that I needed a boost, though.

And then Redman slammed his Porsche into the guardrail while avoiding a car that'd spun in front of him. Just like that I was in the lead. But my old friend John Paul Jr. was chewing on my tail.

Over the final laps, John Paul Jr. and I battled with every-thing we had for every inch of pavement. We were taking cor-ners side by side, rubbing tires. We were like Rocky and Apollo Creed, throwing punches nonstop to the final moments.

Coming into a corner with a few laps to go, our cars scraped paint, and I felt my wheels ready to lose grip. My back end started to spin out, and I made a fast correction with the steer-ing wheel, catching it in time. Suddenly, John Paul Jr. slowed up, and I shot out in front. John Paul dove into the pits with a flat tire while I motored on.

When I crossed the finish line, it was sealed: I'd won the race and clinched the IMSA Camel GT title. It took time to sink in. I was cruising around the track slowly on a victory lap. Thousands of fans were on their feet. I couldn't believe it. National champion. Randy Lanier. I'd worked so hard. This is what all the smuggling was for. And it had worked. The more

I thought about it, the more it sunk in, and when I turned my head sideways—I swear—something amazing happened. I could see my kid brother Glen sitting next to me in the car. It was so real, I felt I could even hear his voice.

"Way to go, big bro. Way to go."

When I pulled the car into the pit, the whole Blue Thunder team gathered around. It was a team effort, and together we had made history. When I got out of the car, I felt all these hands hugging me and slapping my back, and there was my beautiful Pam in the middle of it.

On the chance that I might win, executives from R. J. Reynolds—owner of the Camel cigarette brand—had already created giant banners, so when Pam and I got on the podium, with all the fans going wild, the banners were hanging behind us: Blue Thunder, 1984 Champions. Outside of my wedding day and my daughter being born, it was the happiest day of my life.

We'd won over Jaguar, Ford, and Porsche. That a privateer team like ours would beat the big factories? As the racing writer Roy Hasty put it: "Little-known Randy Lanier shocked the sports car racing world."

"Let's go to New York and go wild!" I screamed to Bill. We were in our garage after the podium ceremony. I had a bottle of champagne in my right hand, my left arm draped over Pam's shoulders. The racetrack was 250 miles from Manhattan, and we were ready to party.

Bill was a furiously fierce competitor and, despite our team victory, finishing second in the series didn't thrill him. One thing about Bill: he subscribed to the theory that if you're not first, you're last. He was a little dejected.

"Nah," he said. "You go on, Randy. I'm flying back to Fort Lauderdale."

So Pam, myself, Dale, and his wife headed for the city. We partied at the 21 Club in Manhattan all night long. The day after, Pam and I lay in our hotel suite recovering, feeling on top of the world. We were living this crazy life that we could have only imagined back when we'd met as teenagers.

When the dust settled, not only had Blue Thunder won the team championship and I won the IMSA Camel GT driver's title, I was also the first driver in history to win both the series title and the Most Improved Driver award. Our guy Keith Leighton won an award for best crew chief. Because of us, March racing cars won the IMSA manufacturer's title. It was the first time in the eleven-year history of this series that Porsche didn't take that victory. We also won the engine manufacturer title for Chevrolet. We'd raced against many of the best drivers on the planet: A. J. Foyt, Derek Bell, Brian Redman, Hurley Haywood, Bobby Rahal, Emerson Fittipaldi, John Paul Jr. Nobody could beat Blue Thunder.

That same year, Ben's Apache team won the national offshore powerboat racing championship. I had T-shirts made for Ben, myself, and our friends, with the Blue Thunder and the Apache logos and the words "1984 Champions."

When I finally had a chance to clear my head and think, I decided it was time. My next move should be to IndyCar—one of the world's two top-rank open-wheel racing series (the other being Formula 1). IndyCar was different than sports car racing. It was about pure single-seat rocket ships on wheels, more like science experiments than road-going automobiles. IndyCar racing was also more dangerous, with significantly higher speeds, and it was incredibly expensive. All I could think about was that day in my grandparents' tobacco house when I first heard the Indy 500 on the radio. That dream had never left me.

In October, a couple weeks after the end of the 1984 season, I flew with Bill and Jim DeLillo to meet with Ford Motor Company. In a Dearborn office building, after the handshaking, we sat down for a two-hour meeting. They made Bill and me an offer to race for the Ford factory team in 1985.

I asked, "Do you have any interest in going to Indy?"

The Ford guys looked at each other, then back at me. "No," both said. Ford was not investing in IndyCar at this time. Ford, like Porsche and Jaguar, was investing in sports car racing because these cars held at least some resemblance to showroom cars that customers could actually buy. The whole "win on Sunday, sell on Monday" marketing model.

I turned the Ford job down. For starters, I wasn't really interested in working for a corporation. But the real reason? After winning the IMSA title, there was only one place for me to go to reach the next level. I wanted to win the Indy 500.

This effort would require a huge financial investment on my part. I was going to need more money, for real. Time to go to work.

19

The First Arrest

Winter 1984–1985

I was living multiple identities, and all of them were competing for my time and focus. I was a smuggler, and when I was living that identity, I was 100 percent in the moment. Same with race car driving. Total commitment when I was living that identity. Now after winning the IMSA Camel GT national championship, I wanted Pam and myself and Brandie to reconnect as a family. When you live life in the fast lane, you're not there 100 percent for your family. Your priorities get screwed up. There were things I did in my life and things about the person that I was that I didn't like. I wanted to be the best father I could, the best husband.

But I wasn't. I was on autopilot.

We validate our identity through our behavior. Change the way you identify yourself, and you'll change your behavior. That's what I needed to do—be a family man. The time I did have with my family—these were great memories, the ones I'd cherish the most in the future, in the darkest moments of my life in prison.

In 1984, I invested in a sixty-five-foot Hatteras, the most beautiful boat I'd ever seen and a perfect ship for our little family. I first saw it docked at an island in the Bahamas called Chub Cay. I was there fishing, and I asked the owner if he was interested in selling. He told me the only way he'd ever sell this boat is if he found a vintage P-51 Mustang World War II airplane to replace it. The P-51 was the most storied fighter plane of the war.

"Well, guess what!" I said. "I can make that happen for you!"

Bill and Don Whittington had a P-51 Mustang sitting in a hangar in Fort Lauderdale. Not only did they race cars, they also raced vintage aircraft. I bought the P-51 from Bill and traded it straight up for the sixty-five-foot Hatteras.

The winter after winning the Camel GT series, we took the Hatteras to Treasure Cay, on Great Abaco Island in the Bahamas. It was a different kind of life in the islands. The salty air frees you up. It's invigorating and calming at the same time. Brandie was five years old, and we played with her on the beach for hours at a time. At night, Pam and I would sneak off the boat and make love on the beach. Then we'd hide coins in the sand. The next morning, we'd take Brandie treasure hunting. We'd help her find these coins, and she would go crazy.

"Treasure! Treasure! I found treasure!"

Somedays, we'd take a Zodiac—the same kind of small rubber motorboat I'd used during my Beach Assault operations—to a private beach in an undeveloped bay. Some of the beaches had pink sand. It was surreal. Brandie loved to play with hermit crabs. We'd make sandcastles and dig a big moat around them, and she'd fill the moat with crabs.

One time she wanted to take some crabs back to the boat so she could keep them as pets. So we filled a shoebox with hermit crabs.

Early the next morning, she came running to us, crying. Somehow the shoebox had tipped over. We went hunting all over the boat for these crabs while she cried her eyes out. We found some of the crabs but not all of them. I keep a sign in my kitchen that says: "May your journey always lead you home." So that's what I told her: the crabs were safe. They'd just gone home.

We would take the Zodiac out to a reef and dive for conch and lobsters. We'd fish for mahi-mahi, yellowtail, and snapper. Pam loved to cook, and she spent a lot of time in the ship's galley, making fresh snapper and raw conch salad. The boat was as big as a mansion. I had a mechanic friend of mine working as captain of the Hatteras, so he was at the helm. He had his wife with him, and she did some of the cooking. We kept the Hatteras anchored at Treasure Cay, and some days we would fly in from Florida with friends on a little private plane. If we were hungry, we would circle over the Hatteras and tip our wing. That meant it was time to make some fresh seafood, so by the time we got to the boat, lunch would be ready.

When the holidays came, we flew Bill's Learjet to our place in Nederland, Colorado. I'd built a new three-story log cabin on an 8,700-foot peak. It was the third house I'd bought in Colorado in the past five years. We had the builder design the place to look like an old barn. But when you entered the central building, you saw an indoor racquetball court with a large plexiglass window where guests could watch the game. There was a full kitchen and lounge area, a gym on one side, and, on the other, a garage where we kept all the toys: dirt bikes for summer, snowmobiles for winter. Brandie started skiing that winter at five years old and picked it up right away.

Pam and I took Brandie to some stables to see if she'd be interested in riding horses. We got her a $50,000 white Welsh show horse named Brutus, and when we gave it to her on Christmas morning, the horse was wearing a red and white Santa cap. Brandie started competing as a jumper at equestrian events. She was fearless. For her next birthday, we went all out and threw an actual circus in our backyard, with the biggest elephant we'd ever seen.

Throughout these days, Pam had my back. I was a blessed man. She cared for me and loved me through all the bullshit that I'd created. Still, to protect her, I purposely kept her in the dark about most of what I was doing. She knew how I made money, but she never asked about details.

We were trying to live a life that felt normal. But in reality, it was far from normal. Because the clock was always ticking, and soon it was time for me to switch my identity again. When I look back on it, maybe I took things for granted—that those wonderful family times were always going to be there.

Early in 1985, a news story broke that stunned the motor-racing world. At age forty-five, John Paul Sr.—a legend in his time, winner of the 12 Hours of Sebring and the 24 Hours of Daytona—was arrested in Switzerland for attempted murder. The authorities had been closing in on him and his son on suspicion of marijuana smuggling. Apparently, Sr. got wind that a witness was allegedly going to testify against him. On a boat ramp in Crescent Beach, Florida, John Paul Sr. shot this guy five times and left him for dead. But the witness survived.

John Paul Sr. absconded to Switzerland but got caught in Geneva. The authorities then arrested John Paul Jr., who was twenty-five at the time. The feds claimed that the father-son duo was responsible for bringing in some two hundred thousand pounds of weed from Colombia (which was less than half of what I had brought in by this time).

When the alleged witness that Sr. shot recovered from five gunshot wounds, he told a reporter that he never had any intention to go to any grand jury about any of Sr.'s activities in the first place. "I knew he'd kill anyone who said anything about what he was doing," this guy told the *Los Angeles Times*. "But he got the wrong guy. I was too afraid of him to say anything, but I guess he thought it was me anyway."

This was the first shockwave in what would ultimately become a defining scandal of the 1980s sports world.

I always knew that John Paul Sr. and Jr. were in the business, though they were in deeper than I'd ever surmised. I also knew that Sr. had a serious temper. He was a dangerous man. People were scared of him—for good reason. But still, when I heard the news, I was stunned. If the feds could bring the Pauls down, who else were they gunning for?

Sr.'s temper made him dangerous not just to others but also to himself. The way I see it: he wasn't fully in control of what he was doing. I was convinced that I ran a tighter ship, that I was in a safer position. But the truth was, this first arrest was a sign. These different worlds I was living in—my separate identities—were going to collide.

Early in 1985, right around the time of the John Pauls' bust, I flew to England to shop for new Indy cars. I wanted the best, and I could pay for the best. The best was in the UK. I visited the March factory and the Lola factory and couldn't decide. So I bought two of each.

For each car, I needed a road course body setup and an oval speedway setup. For a road course setup, you want the car to be able to carry maximum speed through left- and right-hand turns, so you want bigger wings on the front and back of the car to create more downforce. Think about how wings on an airplane help the vehicle lift off the ground. An Indy car's wings do the same but in the opposite direction. They push the car onto the pavement for greater traction in cornering.

For an oval speedway setup, such as the Indianapolis Motor Speedway, there's less turning and higher straight-up speed. So you want a smaller wing in front and back for less downforce and more straight-line velocity.

I also spent tens of thousands of dollars on spare parts. I bought ten Cosworth V-8 engines, superb British powerplants at $75,000 apiece.

It wasn't vanity or excess: the more I spent, the more likely I was to win. In racing, having reliable equipment matters just as much as having talent.

IndyCar is different from sports car racing in so many ways, and one of them has to do with teams. In sports car racing, anyone could launch a team (though only the best can be successful or even qualify for major events). At the time, Indy racing was franchised, like the NFL or Major League Baseball.

You can't show up with your own team and go racing. You had to find a team in existence and join.

The sanctioning body (basically, what IMSA was to sports car racing) was at that time called Championship Auto Racing Teams, or CART, and the 1985 season was going to consist of fifteen races around the country. Like in sports car racing, you could rack up points with good finishes throughout the season in hopes of placing well in the national championship leaderboard. But the Indy 500—held every Memorial Day going back to 1909—was the race everyone wanted to win.

The toughest battle, the most glory by far.

The biggest teams in 1985 were Newman/Haas Racing (with two drivers, Mario Andretti and Alan Jones) and Team Penske (with three drivers, Rick Mears, Danny Sullivan, and Al Unser). I flew out to Los Angeles to meet with Frank Arciero, who owned the Arciero IndyCar team. I'd met Frank before; he was an admirable guy. He'd come to America from Italy after World War II with little money in his pocket. He was obsessed with motor racing. He built a successful construction, paving, and wine business, and then launched a racing team back in the 1960s.

Frank was known for giving young racers a shot and was responsible for helping to launch the careers of such legends as Dan Gurney, Carroll Shelby, and Phil Hill (the only American-born Formula 1 world champ to this day). Frank and I hit it off, and he agreed to sign both me and Bill Whittington for the 1985 season. The goal was to run a two-car team. One car for me, and one for Bill, who unlike me already had significant IndyCar experience. He'd run the Indianapolis 500 four times by that year, with 1982 as his best result—qualifying in sixth place and finishing in sixteenth.

Even though we'd be racing for Frank's team, he agreed that we would create our own crews and have our own home base in South Florida. So while our team name was Arciero, Bill and I were going to run our own operations, build our own cars, and pay for all of it. We needed a huge new shop in South Florida, two eighteen-wheel transporters, and a whole new crew. Bill kept Keith Leighton as his crew chief, and I hired a guy named Dennis McCormick, who was top notch.

My first test session in an Indy car took place at Road Atlanta early in 1985. I'd never been in one of these cars. It was cold that morning, so cold I could see my breath as I chit-chatted with the track officials working that day, joking to hide how nervous I was. None of my cars were ready yet, so I was borrowing one of Bill's.

The jump from a sports racer to an open-wheel machine is a big leap. My March sports racing car ran close to 190 mph. An Indy car will top 200 with plenty of speed still on the table. While my sports car racer had an enclosed cockpit, in an Indy car, your ass is inches off the pavement and your head is outside of the car. You're basically lying down, and the fuselage is as tight as a coffin. Your five-point harness is squeezed so tight around your torso and chest, you can barely take a deep breath. When the mechanics spark up the engine, the noise is like nothing you've ever heard. The engine sits right behind you, as rocket engines are situated behind astronauts. An Indy car's latent power is indescribable. So is the sheer volume.

I sat studying the instrument panel for a while, as the engine rumbled and warmed. The dashboard is kept simple, for split-second reads of vital signs. On the steering wheel is the radio button. Straight in front of you are two gauges. On the right, the tachometer, measuring engine speed. Maximum RPM: about 11,000. On the left: water temperature, in centigrade. There is no speedometer. Why would there be? You're going as fast as you can, always.

Slightly lower and to the left is the turbo boost knob. Turn it up for higher speed. But that also means faster fuel consumption. So higher speed is a trade-off for more time spent in the pit refueling. Two small knobs under the steering wheel control the stiffness of the shock absorbers, front and back. To the left are two levers that control the sway bar, which tightens or loosens the chassis. If you feel understeer (the car pushing forward in a straight line when you try to steer) or oversteer (the rear end wanting to swing out from under you as you're turning), you can adjust the sway bar and suspension to gain stability.

On the right is the gear shifter. On top of the dash, where it can't be hit by mistake, is a button that controls the internal fire suppression system. If you're on fire, you want to hit that button fast. Hope to God you never hit that button.

It can be overwhelming. But I was so excited to be in this position in the first place, and I was grateful to Bill for bringing his car out for me to test. You have to ask yourself when you first sit in one of these cars: Do I have what it takes to wring all of the speed out of this machine? Damn skippy, I do!

That first day, out on track, I started building speed gradually, heating up my tires to make them sticky. I was only a few minutes into the morning session when it happened. I should've known that, because the pavement was cold, I needed more time to get heat into the tires. At Road Atlanta, there's a blindingly fast short-shoot downhill that has a right-hand turn onto the front straightaway. I carried too much speed into this turn. I felt the tires lose grip. I tried to correct with the steering wheel, tried to regain control. But it was too late. I was spinning and the tires were shrieking.

The car slid off the track and onto the infield grass, kicking up a cloud of dirt and smoke. Unbeknownst to me, someone had left a motorcycle battery there in the grass. I ran over it and ripped up the side of the car's body. Indy cars ran on methanol fuel at that time because it was thought to be safer than gas. Sitting in the car, a little dazed, the methanol fumes started to overpower me. I had to unstrap myself, jump out, and shake my head clear. I was lucky that the cold weather had killed off the grass, so there was no fire.

I stood there looking at the wrecked car. "Shit," I said. "There goes practice." It was my first goddamn day in one of these cars. A humbling moment.

I had to get experience, and I didn't have much time. So that winter, we spent a boatload of money renting out racetracks and traveling in our motor home. We tested at Road America in Wisconsin and at Mid-Ohio. My cars still weren't ready yet—I had my team building them in our new workshop in Fort Lauderdale—so I was still testing in one of Bill's cars, and he came to most of the sessions. The more time I spent in the seat, the more time I spent honing my craft. The first time I nipped at 200 mph in an Indy car, the adrenaline level was off the hook. But then those speeds started to feel routine.

Then, it was time to switch identities again. Duty called in Louisiana.

I landed in New Orleans late in the winter of 1985 aboard Bill's Learjet. I picked up a rental car and headed for the Industrial Canal. That afternoon, I stood on the edge of the cement dock where the tug and barge would be coming in, alone, listening to the seagulls chirping.

Pretty quiet. No boat traffic. Perfect.

I went to check on the progress my distributors were making. I'd asked them to set up fake businesses outside the city in the warehouse district. One of my three distributors was named Sebastian—an easygoing guy and a pleasure to work with. He created a faux company set up to look like a shipping container conversion business, and when I showed up, I was impressed. He told the landlord of the twenty-thousand-foot warehouse he'd rented that he was going to convert shipping containers into living quarters for oil rig workers. Thus, it wouldn't look strange to have eighteen-wheelers carrying shipping containers on and off the property. He got a few shipping containers and put them in the yard on the side of the warehouse so that it all looked legit.

Another of my distributors rented a large warehouse on Tchoupitoulas Street across from the Coca-Cola warehouse. He set up a fake diesel truck engine repair service and put a sign out front reading "Diesel Repair." That way, it wouldn't look odd to see tractor trailers pulling in and out of this warehouse.

Gene created a company called Caribbean Imports, and he had business cards made for himself with an alias name and a telephone number that rang to an answering service. He had a front office by the gate of the fenced-in yard on the Industrial Canal with a Caribbean Imports sign out front and one of our guys at the front desk. Anyone checking up on the company could walk right through the door and talk to a real human.

He used this company to buy a million pounds of Venezuelan cement that was going into the barge as cargo along with the 160,000 pounds of weed in secret compartments in the ballasts. This was our biggest load, an absolutely massive haul of ganja. Enough smoke to keep the entire city of New Orleans stoned for a year.

The tug could pull this barge right to the fenced-in yard of Caribbean Imports. The plan was to bring the barge to the dock, use a crane to pull out the pallets of cement first, and then load the cement into the warehouses. Gene was going to have to figure out a way to off-load all that cement. Then we'd cut open the steel hiding the secret compartments in the ballasts, move the weed from those compartments into the CTIs sitting inside the barge's hull, and then use the crane to pull out the CTIs and place them on trucks. During the last California job, some of my distributors had made rookie errors with those bogus trucks. Now I was using the three best guys I knew—real pros.

This operation, from the time Gene told me about the unloading spot to the time when we were ready to load the barge in Santa Marta, took nearly a year. I sent Charles to Colombia to supervise the loading, and Ben sent two of his guys to help. I remained in the US. By this point, I trusted Charles to get this job done so that I could focus on IndyCar testing and getting ready for the season.

The racing, the smuggling, all of it was reaching new heights in 1985. But the heat was on us, and the feds were turning up the dial. Reagan's War on Drugs was claiming new victims. For the first time in history, the Colombian government agreed to extradite Colombian drug traffickers to the United States to be tried in American courts. In a two-week span early in 1985, right when we were readying to bring our load into Louisiana, Florida authorities seized two tons of cocaine. The newspapers reported how marijuana, cocaine, and opium crops in foreign countries were the largest in human history, while showing photos of American narcotics officers jumping out of helicopters and landing in pot fields to raid these operations and arrest the farmers in Colombia. Those photos looked like pictures of the Vietnam War.

The US now had forty federal agencies involved in the crackdown, and South Florida was crawling with undercover agents. "The problem has grown to epic proportions," a State Department official told newspaper reporters. "Drug traffickers have so much financial power now that they can undermine social institutions and stubborn political systems."

We had to be smarter than the feds. We had to be faster. Was I scared? Yeah, I was. But I was all in.

In March, the weed in Santa Marta was ready for loading and my partners and I gave the go-sign. Charles flew off to Colombia. I flew to California for my first IndyCar race: the 1985 Toyota Long Beach Grand Prix.

20

IndyCar

Spring and summer 1985

Before boarding my flight to the West Coast, I had my PR guy Jim put out a press release saying that I was gunning for the CART rookie of the year trophy and that I had every intention of competing with the top ranks at the Indy 500. The *Los Angeles Times* ran an item on me. "Randy Lanier, defending IMSA Camel Pro champion and winner of last year's six-hour race at the Times Grand Prix of Endurance [at Riverside], has announced that he will compete for the Vandervell rookie title in CART this year."

When I arrived at Long Beach and the crew unloaded my car, I wandered the pits wearing sunglasses and my fireproof Team Arciero coveralls. I noticed something right away. There wasn't the comradery you felt in sports car racing where it felt like, once you were out of the car, all the other competitors were your friends. This was cutthroat. In the pits I saw the guys I'd be competing against. Mario Andretti, Emerson Fittipaldi, Bobby Rahal—these were the gods of the racing world.

"Damn, man!" I said to one of my crew in the pit that morning. "It feels tense around here."

"Randy," he said, "these guys would sell their sisters to be a tenth of a second faster."

My crew and I had finished building my first car only days before we left for the West Coast. I chose the Lola chassis over the March for the first race, and I was nervous. I hadn't had time to dial in the setup. Long Beach is a tricky street course, mapped out on cordoned-off public roads. It was an easy place to make a mistake with big consequences. During a celebrity race on the qualifying Saturday that featured Tony Danza and the NFL star Mark Gastineau, Jackie Jackson, the oldest member of the Jackson 5, crashed his car and had to be taken to the hospital for X-rays.

When it was time to get in the car and go, I felt nerves like never before. For the first time in my life, I felt underprepared, even after all the testing I'd done. In racing, when you get in the car, you have to know: *You got this.* You have to! Confidence is everything. And I didn't have it. I went out and qualified twenty-third—not what I'd hoped. I wasn't comfortable in the car at all.

On race day, I arrived early in the pit with the crew. My car was painted red, and I kept my lucky number 57. Across the back was a big Apache Power Boats logo. I was running Goodyear Eagle tires, and I had the car configured with the bigger road course wing front and back, for max cornering speed.

At the start, the engines thundered, and the NBC TV cameras rolled. Grandstands all around the track overflowed with fans. We launched into the start, and I didn't feel right from the get-go. I was fighting the car. I was fighting the competition. Every muscle in my body was clenched, and the steering wheel in my hands felt so stiff it took all my power to turn it. I was out in the field, in back of the pack, in tight combat with cars all around me. Twelve laps in, I was coming into the hairpin corner that leads to the front straightaway. I got bottled up with cars all around me, and I clipped a cement barrier with my right rear wheel.

Bang!

I felt the jolt in my spine and the car spun, coming to a stop in the middle of the track with pieces strewn all over the pavement. I looked up to see a steward waving a caution flag. The safety car came out, and all the cars slowed. I got out of the cockpit and stood there, feeling like a friggin' idiot in front of TV cameras. Twelve laps into a ninety-lap race! A crane came out to pull my wrecked vehicle off the track. Bill didn't fare much better, dropping out after seventy-seven laps in sixteenth place.

That was it. That was my race. It was a rookie mistake, and I had to confront the fact that if I hadn't been spending so much time working on the Louisiana load, this wouldn't have happened. But then again, if I hadn't spent so much time on the Louisiana load, I wouldn't be here in the first place.

Mario Andretti won the 1985 Long Beach Grand Prix. We packed up and boarded a private jet for a grim flight back to South Florida.

Soon after Long Beach, I flew to Louisiana to wait for the barge. There was a lot of killing time in the office of the fake company Caribbean Imports. Gene, George, myself, some of our guys. Cigarette smoke. Magazines. To lighten the mood, we hit the French Quarter at night for some Creole food at places like K-Paul's and New Orleans Cookery. When we finally got word over the radio that the tug and barge were pulling into the mouth of the Industrial Canal, we all went out to the dock to witness what felt to us like a historic arrival.

That's when we saw it: a Coast Guard cutter following the barge.

At the same time, outside the front office of Caribbean Imports, an unmarked Ford LTD pulled up. I never had any training as an actor; this was trial by fire.

"How's it going, officer?" I said, opening the office door for these guys. "What can I help you with?"

We all played it cool. Immigration officers wanted all the passports of the men on board the tugboat. It was normal procedure for them but anything but normal for us.

"None of those tugboat crew can step on US soil," one of the customs guys told us, "until they've been cleared by us." He looked around and sized the place up. Nothing to see here!

"You bet, officer," Gene said.

The tugboat crew was made up of guys from Gene's salvage operation in Santo Domingo, and they had no idea they were pulling a barge full of weed. We had a manifest for a million pounds of cement, and if the customs officers checked, they'd find it alright.

The next day, they cleared us, and we began unloading all that cement into Caribbean Imports' yard facility. I had not planned to sell the cement or haul it; that was Gene's job. Gotta hand it to Gene. He was a crafty businessman. He did his research and found out what prebagged, powder Venezue-lan cement could fetch on the open market. Then he got on the phone and started cold calling all over the country, undercutting all the competition. He was able to sell it all for just a little more than he'd paid. We had to ask our weed distributors to use their eighteen-wheelers to move the cement to buyers in numerous states. They were not happy, nor were their drivers, but they went along. We couldn't move the weed until all the cement was gone.

At least the Caribbean Imports yard looked like it was doing what it was supposed to do: import work. After thirty days, we felt confident there'd be no heat, so we finished hauling cement and started hauling weed.

For me, the timing was terrible. I'd hoped this would all happen faster because I had to fly to Indiana for the Indy 500 rookie orientation day at the speedway. My car wasn't ready. I wasn't ready. I was worried there'd be strangers in suit jackets and sunglasses following my every move. Now I was headed to Indianapolis, the capital city of American racing. It sure wasn't how I'd always imagined it.

The Indianapolis Motor Speedway is a place where legends are made. It's also a place where dreams come crashing down and where people get killed. In the pantheon of sports meccas, the Indianapolis Motor Speedway tops the list in America. Older than Wrigley Field, Yankee Stadium, Fenway Park. Bigger than all those stadiums put together. It's still the highest capacity seating venue in the world, with seats for over 257,000 fans.

What other place could claim so much history? So much glory and so much death? Nowhere. And when you walk out onto that track, you can feel all that history instantly in your bones. You see it, hear it, smell it, embrace it.

Completed in 1909, it was America's first banked oval speedway, originally laid out in bricks—thus its nickname, the Brickyard. The engineers and entrepreneurs who put it together wanted the perfect laboratory to test the mettle of the most important new invention in human history—the automobile. At the first race ever held there in 1909, thousands of fans paid one dollar to watch the action. Race leader Louis Chevrolet, the namesake of the famous brand, was bloodied and temporarily blinded when a stone smashed his goggles. Another driver and his mechanic were killed in a fiery crash. That first race produced two land-speed records and only four finishers, out of fifteen teams. From its birth, this track has been about achieving the ultimate in human performance, bravery, and endurance.

The Brickyard has produced some of our greatest heroes: Wilbur Shaw, Johnny Parsons, Bill Vukovich, Roger Ward, Parnelli Jones, A. J. Foyt, Mario Andretti, Bobby and Al Unser— the list goes on. When I first stepped foot on the speedway, in 1985, nearly seventy drivers, mechanics, and spectators had been killed at the racetrack. Today, that number is seven victims higher. Every year since the beginning, the velocity has kept rising. In 1982, the fastest qualifying speed (average speed of four laps around the oval) was 207.004 mph, set by Rick Mears. In 1983, Teo Fabi hit 207.395. In 1984, Tom Sneva broke the record again, at 210.029. That's where it stood the day my eighteen-wheel transporter rolled onto the infield with my car and engines aboard.

My team was the first to roll a car off the truck, and the first car on the track, at the rookie orientation day. When I pulled out of pit lane and began to motor around the 2.5-mile oval, with its banked turns and its long flat-out straightaways, with its hundreds of thousands of empty seats and that giant blue sky above, I used my meditation skills to put the Louisiana load out of my brain. I changed identities entirely.

Gene and George? Ben and Charles? It was as if they'd never been born.

The majority of drivers who attempt to qualify for the Indy 500 don't make the field of thirty-three cars. They spend all that money and time and never even make the starting line. The competition to make it is so extreme, guys are willing to take any chance to squeeze out that hundredth of a second out of the car—come hell or high water. I was determined to make a statement: nobody was going to beat me, certainly none of the other rookies.

It was all about getting into the rhythm of the cornering, using all the track, and setting up the car just right to get the most speed in the straights and just enough downforce so you could keep the throttle down entering the turns.

Normally, you have to be careful with the turbo boost to preserve fuel. During practice, however, you could turn that baby all the way up. I was so fired up, I imagined myself setting the fastest rookie time ever. That's where my mind was set—when the whole day was destroyed in one humiliating instant.

Indy has a track lighting system for safety: green means go for it, the track is clean; yellow signals caution and to slow up; red means come to a stop. I was hammering on the back straight—the only car on the track—and the yellow flashed on. In the pit, my crew was readying to use a tire thermometer to measure the temperature of my rubber. If I slowed up, I'd lose heat in the tires, and I wouldn't get the right readout. I looked forward; nobody was in front of me. So I kept my foot down. No worries. Right?

I came in and my crew chief approached the car to talk to me, while one of the crew started checking the tires. Just then, I saw an official come over and signal for me to get out of the car. So I did. He was an older guy, white hair.

"Randy," he said, "can I talk to you on the other side of the pit wall?"

I took my helmet off and followed him, away from my crew.

He said, "Randy, did you see the yellow caution light on the back straight, flashing?"

"I did."

"Then why didn't you slow down?"

I got a little cocky when I shouldn't have. "I was trying to get a good read on my tire temps. I looked forward. There was no one else on the track but me, so I stayed on it."

He said something about safety and track rules.

"What the fuck?" I said. "No one was on the track but me."

He didn't like that. I could see the look on his face change. "You didn't adhere to the rules of safety of the Indianapolis Motor Speedway. And now you're telling me that you don't have to. The way I look at it, you need more time in an Indy car, and I don't think you're ready for this."

He marched away, and soon other officials came to the pits. The next thing I knew, I was getting booted out of the Indianapolis Motor Speedway. They told me to go home. I was furious. I was also embarrassed. Some of the big-time drivers were there that day, and they felt bad for me. Even though I didn't know them that well at all, Tom Sneva, A. J. Foyt, and Johnny Rutherford all talked to the track officials on my behalf. These guys didn't want to hear it. I was out of line the way I spoke to the official, and he took it personally. I was wrong. We started packing up our things and loading up our eighteen-wheeler to go home.

It was a disaster.

At the same time I was in Indianapolis, big rigs were hauling weed out of our warehouses. One hundred and sixty fucking pounds of it. Our largest score to date, a historically massive haul, had gone off without a hitch. After all accounts were settled, I came home with over ten million cash, just from this one score. The herbal gods were good to me.

While I was at the top of my game as a smuggler, on the racetrack, things weren't going well. I missed the Milwaukee Mile in 1985 because I was working in Louisiana. I was back for the season's fourth race, the Stroh's/G.I. Joe's 200 in Portland, Oregon. But I only made it 46 laps out of the 104 before my engine blew up. Bill Whittington, in the other Arciero team car, only made it 10 laps before his engine overheated. Mario Andretti won.

Then it was on to the Meadowlands in New Jersey. In qualifying, I crashed my car into Michael Andretti's, taking him out of his session. He was not happy with me, and he let me know it. In the race, my engine caught fire after 53 of the 100 laps. At the 1985 Budweiser Cleveland Grand Prix, I ran 71 of the 88 laps before a tricky wheel-bearing issue knocked me out.

IndyCar wasn't coming naturally to us the way sports car racing did. We couldn't get the Cosworth engines to hold up. Our pit stops were shit. At Road America in Elkhart Lake, Wisconsin, one of America's most iconic tracks, I finally finished a race, placing fourteenth—nine laps behind. I blew up another engine at Mid-Ohio. The final race of the season was right near my house in Miami. My family and friends all rallied around the effort. A reporter interviewed me in the pit the day before the race.

"I figured this would be a learning year," I said, masking my disappointment. "This team has been very patient, and I'm very appreciative."

Why was the racing going so poorly? Where we put our attention, our energy follows. Well, my attention was on smuggling the largest load of marijuana ever into the United States without getting arrested. But I couldn't say that to reporters. Instead, I fed the sports pages excuses. "I've had to get used to a whole new crew, and that takes some time."

On race day in Miami, an oil leak took me out halfway through. Bill had his best finish of the year, with an eighth place.

The whole season proved to be a study in disappointment. Part of the problem was the car. It had been a mistake to buy two different chassis in the first place—the March and the Lola. I'd test in the morning with the March and in the afternoon with the Lola, and I'd end up with too much data.

I couldn't get either dialed in. The other problem was me. I wasn't living the life of a serious professional race car driver. On top of smuggling, I was spending a lot of time partying. I wasn't living my truth. I wasn't asking myself the most basic questions that we all should be asking ourselves about the way we're living our lives.

How are my decisions affecting me and my family?

Am I paying the most attention to the most important things—the people I love and who love me?

Am I living by my core values, or am I on autopilot?

Instead, it was a lot of cocaine. Pam and I had so many late nights. And it was no longer because we were having so much fun. The stress of living multiple identities, failing on the race-track—both Pam and I were starting to feel very strung out.

At the same time, I was managing so many business ventures and frequently flying off to Europe with legal briefcases stuffed with cash to deposit in Swiss accounts.

In racing, you have to be entirely focused. I wasn't. Arie Luyendyk won the CART rookie of the year in 1985. Al Unser was champion. Randy Lanier finished without a single point.

That summer, Ben and I flew out to California to check on the construction of our casino, which we were going to name The Bicycle Club. I'd been using Bill's Learjet, but it wasn't always available, and I wanted something bigger. So I leased a Sabreliner. Ben had gone even bigger. He bought a Jetstar. It was huge, with three jet motors, and he had the interior custom built, like a Miami mansion with wings. Etched mirrors, a sound system that made you feel like you were at a live con-cert—the works. There was nothing understated about it. On the tail, he put a massive Apache boat logo.

We'd come up with a crafty way of supplying the money for the casino construction. Lawyers on the island of Tortola in the Caribbean had helped us set up accounts there. We wired money from Tortola to an account in Hong Kong. There, we moved the money from one account to another. Then we wired money from that account to another in Liechtenstein. Then we wired money from there to pay for the construction in LA, so while it looked like we were borrowing money from Liechtenstein, it was actually our own cash.

At the same time, I had my restaurant, Hunky Dory's, on the water in Hollywood. I was also building a million-square-foot shopping center in Dallas, Texas, with some new partners I knew through IMSA racing. I bought a mobile home park in Florida. I invested in a winery with Frank Arciero. It was a busy year, and I was stretched too thin. But my intention was to get everything lined up in 1985 because I was going to come out in 1986 a new man—focused, determined. Make no bones about it, I told a reporter that year.

"I'm an Indy driver now, and I plan to run all the CART races next year."

21

The International Marijuana Smuggling Association

Winter and spring 1986

*O*ne day I got a buzz on my beeper. I recognized Bill Whittington's telephone number, so I called him. He told me to meet him at a diner in Fort Lauderdale. I knew as soon as I saw him that something was wrong. We sat under a ceiling fan with a couple of cups of bad coffee.

"A guy I know has gotten arrested," Bill said. "I think he's cooperating with the FBI. It's not looking good."

"I don't understand. What are you telling me?"

"Randy, I think I am going to be indicted. My attorneys are trying to work something out." He told me his brother Don was in deep shit, too.

"Damn, man!" I said.

This news hit me like a punch to the nose. Bill was my teammate and one of my best friends. Don was one of my closest friends too. Just like me, Bill had been in the weed-smuggling game for a long time. It wasn't like I didn't know anything about their business. We'd done some work together. In fact, Bill had invested half a million dollars in my Louisiana load, and I'd given him a million back. I was stunned.

"That's some bad fucking news, man," I said.

I felt so bad for him. I felt so bad for Don. But I also had business to think about. We had the 1986 IndyCar season coming up, and I had planned to run two cars again with the Arciero team—one for me, one for Bill. I was also part-nered with Bill in a mobile home park in Lakeland, Flor-ida. This was a very complicated situation.

After thinking it through for a moment, I came to a conclu-sion: "I don't think we should be racing together. I don't want that kind of heat around me. I'm sorry, Bill." And I really was. I feared for him, and I feared what would happen next, if he went down.

I went home and told Pam. "Bill's in trouble," I said. "It's not looking good." We were in the kitchen of our house, just the two of us. She got scared. Very scared.

"Randy," she said, "if Bill gets indicted, he and his attor-neys are going to want to negotiate a deal. You think he's go-ing to want to go to prison? How do you know he's not going to rat you out in a plea deal?"

"Pam, Bill is one of my closest friends. The things we've done together! It's almost like we've gone to war together! He would never take me down with him."

"You better get as far away from him as you can."

She started crying. She was wanting her voice to be heard. I was not capable of hearing it. It was a bad scene, and the remorse has never left me.

Sure enough, on March 11, 1986, the story hit the newspapers. The main paper out of Fort Lauderdale, the *Sun-Sentinel,* ran a front-page story with photos of Bill and Don Whittington under the headline, "Race Drivers Charged in Drug Case." The story opened:

> Veteran race car drivers Bill and Don Whittington of Fort Lauderdale, who gained international acclaim when they won the prestigious 24 Hours of Le Mans in 1979, have been charged with defrauding the U.S. government of millions of dollars in taxes derived from the profits of a large-scale marijuana smuggling ring.

Bill was thirty-seven, and Don was forty. Also charged was a guy named Gary R. Levitz, the grandson of the founder of the famous Levitz furniture store chain that ran all those well-known television commercials: "You'll love it, at Levitz!" Gary was a friend and even a small-time sponsor for the Blue Thunder racing team.

The Whittington brothers were using some local, very good lawyers, the same guys that Ben had used in the past. Over the next week, Bill and I remained in talks, and he told me that these lawyers were negotiating a deal. Bill co-owned the Road Atlanta racetrack. We agreed that I would give him a couple million under the table and a small amount over the table to buy the track so he could get out of that deal and bank some of that money before it was all seized from him. The day Bill told me over the phone that he was going to plead guilty, I hung my head and prayed. Pam did too.

Five days after the story broke that Bill, Don, and Gary Levitz had been indicted, Bill pleaded guilty to smuggling some four hundred thousand pounds of marijuana. He got fifteen years (he was hoping he would have to do only five), while his brother Don and Levitz got eighteen-month sentences. My name appeared in the coverage in all the newspapers because I was Bill's racing partner. As far as I knew, I wasn't under suspicion. But how could I know what the feds knew? I couldn't. My smuggling empire was considerably bigger than Bill's. I was scared shitless.

Everyone knew that motor racing was staggeringly expensive. Our team always had the best equipment, the best personnel. We didn't have any Marlboro sponsorship. People must have been asking themselves: Where was the money coming from?

First John Paul Jr. and Sr., now the Whittington brothers. Who would be next? The whole mess was becoming a major scandal, with a lot of publicity. After Bill and Don pleaded guilty, the *Sun-Sentinel*, my hometown newspaper, ran an exposé titled, "Auto Racing Faces Problem of Drug Money Financing."

"While some sports have a problem of drug use by athletes," it began, "auto racing may have a problem of a different kind—drug money being used to help finance participation in the sport."

A few days after this story ran, the feds busted my old racing teammate Marty Hinze, who lived right in my hometown of Davie. Hinze was thirty-nine years old. Same story. Marijuana smuggling, tax fraud.

I know what you're thinking: under this kind of heat, you'd have to be crazy to plan another big barge score out of Colombia. Right? Well, that's exactly what my partners and I were planning to do.

One day that winter, I came home from a trip to Los Angeles, where I'd been checking up on the casino construction, and the minute I walked in the door, I knew something was wrong. Pam was in our family room with some friends. The instant I saw her, my heart skipped a beat. I told her friends to leave. It was the middle of the night, and the conversation we had broke my heart. Broke hers too. She needed help. The life we'd been living had driven her to this point, and I had to accept my responsibility for that.

The next morning, she checked into a substance abuse facility for a thirty-day stay. That was the beginning of her sobriety, a beacon that would guide her for the rest of her life. I feel blessed that she had the strength to take that difficult first step. I am so proud of her to this day.

Meanwhile, I was in so deep, so tangled in the web I had created, I saw the year 1986 as the year I would do my final load. The last score. The big one. But also the year that I would contend for real in IndyCar. I'd done it in club racing with my 1957 Porsche. I'd done it in the IMSA Camel GT series, even as a rookie. I felt in my heart that I could do it in IndyCar. I felt so sure that if I had the right equipment and the time to dial it all in, I could be as fast as anyone.

But I also feared that I was going to go down. I had ample reason to believe I was in the sights of the FBI. The way I saw it was, *this could be my last chance to win in a race car. And my last chance to earn, to see to it that my family was all set, forever. No matter what happens to me, they need to be taken care of.* I was like the gambler putting all his chips on double zero, ready to watch the wheel spin.

I called a sit-down with my partners—Gene, George, and Ben. I asked them to meet me at Forge Restaurant in Miami. It was early in 1986. These guys didn't need their arms twisted. We were all in for one more load. Ben said that he was preparing to defend the offshore powerboat national racing championship and could use an infusion of cash. Gene and George said that the yard on the Industrial Canal in Louisiana was open and operating. We still had the warehouses for the distributors. Looking back, the level of hubris on all our parts was off the charts. But that's not how we saw it at the time.

"OK, one last score," I said. "Then the business is closed. Forever."

In late March, I had Charles go down to Santa Marta to work out the details with the Family. Once the barge was loaded, our tugboat crew brought it to Brazil, where they took on a shipment of Brazilian wood and nuts as a decoy. We had about 170,000 pounds of weed on the water, and the trip to Louisiana would take some time. Each of our last handful of loads, we believed, was probably the largest in US history; each time, we believed we were smashing our own record.

One afternoon while the barge was at sea, I was at my house in Davie packing my gear to head to Phoenix for the first IndyCar race of the season. I heard the doorbell ring. My house stood on 4.5 acres, and I'd spent $200,000 on the landscaping for privacy reasons. You couldn't see much of the house from the road. I answered the gate speaker and recognized the voice of a guy who used to be one of my distributors.

I was concerned. I hadn't seen this guy in a few years. His name was Johnny. He'd left the weed game and had given his slice of the distribution to his brother. He'd gone on to become a land developer, building houses. Now what was he doing outside my house? I opened the gate, and he drove in. I met him as he pulled up to my circular driveway.

"Hey Johnny," I said, as he got out of his car. "How you doing, man? What a surprise."

He said, "Good to see you."

"What's happening?"

"Not much, Randy. You know. Still building houses."

"Well, what do I owe the pleasure?"

"Wish I could say it is my pleasure, but it's not, Randy. My brother got arrested, and he's cooperating. If you have anything going on, don't do it."

"I don't have anything going on," I lied. "Sorry to hear about your brother."

As it turned out, Johnny's brother had set up a deal to sell six hundred pounds of grass. He brought the weed in a truck to a hotel to meet the buyer, who turned out to be the feds. This was bad news! Johnny's brother knew where our off-loading site was in Louisiana. He knew where our stash houses were. He knew a lot about our operations.

"Listen, Randy," Johnny said. "They're watching you."

"Who?"

"The FBI."

"How do you know that?"

"Trust me. I don't have any reason to come out here and talk to you like this except to say I still consider you a friend. I wanna tell you to be careful."

I realized: this dude was worried. His brother wasn't going to rat him out. But if I got busted, he was thinking, who knows whose names I would give over to the FBI? Maybe his.

The walls were closing in on me. The Whittington brothers, Marty Hinze, and John Paul Jr. and Sr. had all gotten busted. Johnny's brother had gotten busted. Pam was in rehab. I had a load on the water. I had the Indy 500 coming up. And now I could be certain: the FBI was following me. I started to realize that there was a good chance the FBI knew all about our barge coming into Louisiana. I had to move fast.

I jumped into my Porsche and hammered into Fort Lauderdale to a street pay phone. I called up Gene.

"We got a problem," I said. We met at a diner that afternoon. "Gene," I said, "the boat is already on the water. It's going to land in Louisiana in a matter of days. There's a good chance the feds will be scouting all over the Caribbean hunting for that barge. There's a good chance they already know about this whole deal, and they're waiting for us to head right into a trap. What do you wanna do? We can't bring the load into Louisiana."

Right then, George showed up at the diner, and I had to start my story from the beginning. As I spoke, I could see the blood vessels popping in George's eyeballs. This shit was real.

"We have to reroute the barge," Gene said. We were all leaning over the diner table and whispering. "We have to turn it around. We can send it back south, through the Panama Canal, and up the West Coast to Redwood City, to the rock quarry we used in 1984." He said he'd have to first check to see if the yard was available for us. Gene and George agreed that they would handle that part of the job.

For my part, I needed to let my distributors know we were changing our plan. I wanted to make sure they were OK with going to Northern California. I felt it was only fair to let them know that I thought I had the FBI on my heels. These discussions mainly took place through pay phones. But two of my distributors—guys named Scotty and Sebastian—I met in person in their car in a supermarket parking lot. I explained to them what was happening and offered them a million dollars cash plus seventy-five thousand pounds of grass to sell if they would go out to California and supervise the unloading.

My presence would only draw heat to the operation, and also I was determined this time to focus on racing. Nothing could get in the way! I was desperate to get in that car, to compete and win.

Days later, I heard from Gene and George. The owner of the rock quarry in Redwood City was game. He wanted $500,000 cash. I agreed to pay him a downstroke—half up front—then the rest once we had the load in.

It was going to take months to get the barge rerouted and to bring this operation to fruition. All that time, the weed would remain on the water. I believed the product itself would be safe—it was all trimmed and cured, so the shelf life wasn't an issue. Getting it on American soil safely was.

22

The Indy 500

Spring 1986

*I*n late March, I called my lawyer to find out if I was going to get indicted. He'd been my lawyer going back to when I started my jet ski rental business. I met him in his office in a high-rise in Fort Lauderdale.

"Randy, what exactly do you think you might be indicted for?"

"Well, where the hell do I start?"

I told him the whole story, all the facts. And how my old friend Johnny's brother had gotten busted and was cooperating. That case came out of a bust that had occurred in southern Illinois. So my lawyer told me he would contact the FBI in the Southern District of Illinois to find out if I was, in fact, being investigated. A few days later, he called me and told me to come see him. We met again in his office.

"Randy," he said, "I got bad news."

"OK."

"It looks like you're going to get indicted."

I felt like the whole building had just tumbled down on me. I thought of Pam. I thought of Brandie. "OK" was all I could think to say.

"I want to fly to Illinois and start negotiating with the prosecutors."

"OK."

That's how we left it. I went home. Pam was still in rehab. All I could do was wait to hear from my lawyer. I spent the next few days watching Brandie, but I was so preoccupied, it was hard for me to look her in the eyes. It was so heartbreaking to imagine her life going forward, growing up without her father. After a few days, my lawyer called me from Illinois. He explained that the FBI had ample evidence and prosecutors were going to charge me with running a continual criminal enterprise.

"I'm going to have to begin negotiations, Randy."

"What does that mean?"

"We will have to negotiate what you are charged with and what you might be able to do to lessen those charges. We help them; they help you."

"I'll never rat out my friends, if that's what you're saying."

"Lemme see what I can do."

Pam got out of rehab in early April, and I had to keep everything a secret from her. Then, a few weeks after she got out, she got pregnant. When the doctor told us, I was blown away. Not only was she pregnant, she was pregnant with twins. She was so excited. I pretended to be. I put my best face on it. I was trying to protect her from the truth.

Days later, my lawyer called me again. "Randy," he said, "it's not looking good."

"Ayyyight. What do you mean?"

He had offered prosecutors in the Southern District of Illinois a deal: If they'd accept a ten-year prison sentence and a $10 million fine, I'd plead guilty. They agreed—if I'd fully cooperate. Which meant they wanted me to rat out my friends. No way. Not doing it. We countered with twenty years and complete forfeiture, basically, all my assets. But still, they wanted full cooperation. Period. That's where things stood. I couldn't believe it. This was real. This was really happening.

My lawyer told me he'd won one tiny victory. He'd gotten prosecutors to promise not to arrest me until his negotiations with them were over. And he'd gotten them to promise they wouldn't raid my house or anything like that. When the time came, once negotiations were over, they would let me turn myself in. All of this bought me some time.

The second I digested the information, my future became crystal clear to me. I was going to have to stall so I could spend as much time with my family as possible. But I also wanted to stall long enough to race. My determination to win reached a new level.

Because I had nothing left to lose.

The same week I heard from my lawyer, Pam got sick. She ended up in the hospital, where we learned that one of the twins wasn't going to make it. One of the babies had died. She was crushed, and so was I. I remembered how my father had behaved when my brother Glen died. He'd tried so hard to be strong for the rest of the family. So that's what I did, for Pam. I told her everything was going to be OK.

"It's all going to be alright," I told her. "Trust me."

"The 1986 CART World Series for IndyCars begins today in Phoenix," fans heard at the top of ESPN's broadcast. In the opening IndyCar race of the season, the Dana 200 for Special Olympics at Phoenix International Raceway, I lined up on the grid in twenty-third qualifying position. It was not where I wanted to start the season: at the back of the pack. Mario Andretti had qualified fastest. Sitting in the car with the engine throbbing, I reached deep, trying to summon superhuman focus, so I could race at the highest level, even with everything that was going on. Pam. The baby. The law. And 170,000 pounds of weed still on the water.

When that green flag waved, I started weaving through the pack on the oval superspeedway. I had worked so hard in testing; I now had this car under control. It was a beast. With the racetrack's stands overflowing with fans, I passed car after car.

Past A. J. Foyt.

Past Bobby Rahal.

Past Al Unser and his son Al Jr.

Past Rick Mears.

Past Michael Andretti.

When the checkered flag waved, I captured my first career points in IndyCar. My eleventh-place finish was my best so far.

One week later, at the Toyota Grand Prix of Long Beach, I finished thirteenth. From there, the whole IndyCar world headed to Indianapolis for a month of testing, qualifying, and competition.

Practice for the seventieth annual Indy 500 opened on Saturday, May 3. I flew out there on my jet. This time, I passed the rookie test, no problem. I rented a town house in Indianapolis, and Pam and Brandie stayed there with me. At the track, I wore white fireproof coveralls with a blue stripe across the chest. Frank Arciero had negotiated with sponsors, so for the first time, I had sponsorship logos on my car—Southwest Paving Company, Bosch, Valvoline. I met a guy at the track who was the creator of Uno, a card playing game, and he cut me a check for $50,000 sponsorship, to put his Uno logo on my car. The car was painted bright red, with racing number 12.

Nothing can quite prepare you for the first time you head out onto the track at the Brickyard before a live audience. On weekends, practice for the 500 lured one hundred thousand fans. Just to watch practice! The race itself is the largest single-day sporting event of any kind in the world. Many of my childhood heroes were there in the pits—Mario Andretti, A. J. Foyt, Al Unser. I was getting to know them. Some eighty cars were in Gasoline Alley, the paddock at Indy. We were all battling for the thirty-three spots on the grid. Seven Indy 500 champions were there, and there were fourteen foreign-born drivers from eleven countries.

My intention was to beat all of them.

During the first week of practice, Rick Mears set an all-time Indianapolis Motor Speedway record of 214.694 mph average over the course of a lap. I hit 215 on the straightaways, but I was running a little slow in the corners. Still, I was the fastest rookie. Which meant that, for the first time in my life, fans were coming out of the woodwork asking for autographs. Reporters were turning up to interview me.

"You can't help but be in awe of the place the first time you see it," I told one, while standing in my garage with my crew. "The track is so huge. You don't realize how big it is, how long the straightaways are. You feel excited to get on it, but you also feel cautious. You know you have to respect the speed."

Three drivers crashed during that first week of practice. At one point I was running over 205 mph when I picked up a pebble that got wedged between a brake rim and a brake disc. It cut my front tire as I was entering turn one. I lost control, coming within inches of hitting the wall.

"I think I used up some of my luck," I told one reporter.

It can happen that fast. One second, you're busting 200 mph. The next, you're toast.

Practice speeds were going higher and higher. The Wisconsin-born driver Herm Johnson crashed hard, and while I didn't see it myself, the descriptions I heard of his shunt were horrifying. Johnson spun and hit the wall at such furious speed that chunks of his car rained all over the pavement. He suffered injuries to his back and neck and would have to spend weeks in the hospital. He would never race again. Mario Andretti also crashed in practice, hitting the wall so hard that two of his wheels went bouncing down the pavement.

These accidents were routine at Indy in that era. Not even boxing could compare to the kind of violence that Indy fans saw. Rick Mears, another driver I met in 1986, was competing while suffering severe pain in his ankles from trauma suffered during a crash at Montreal the year before that had shattered bones in both his feet. Danny Ongais carried the scars from a 1981 Indy 500 crash; watch that accident on YouTube, and you'll be shocked that he survived.

More than two hundred thousand fans showed up over the qualifying weekend. Was I nervous? Fuck, yeah. But I had trust in the car, trust in the team, and trust in myself. You have to wait in line to qualify, sitting in the car, engine rumbling, sun beating down. Then the track stewards give you four laps, and the average velocity of your four laps is your qualifying speed.

Waiting on the grid for your shot, you're doing everything you can to remain relaxed and to keep your thinking crystal clear. You're thinking about wind speed and direction, and you're looking at the wind sock to see how strong the breeze is coming in at turns one and three. You're thinking about the condition of the pavement, about getting heat into your tires as fast as possible, about the racing line and where the pavement is stickiest.

Breath.

Focus.

Then—go time.

Out on the track, I made my first lap, and my crew chief radioed in my speed: 207 mph. Time to bring it! I made my second lap, and again my crew chief radioed in my speed: 208. Not good enough! Then 209. Not quite there!

Here was my final qualifying lap. Go big or go home. I dug deep and put myself in the zone. There is a limit to what the car can do in a corner at Indy. If you can come close to that limit—within hundredths of a second in speed—you're golden.

You're a winner. Cross that limit by what would amount to a hundredth of a second, and you can hit the wall. Reading the car, reading the wind, reading the pavement, reading the racing line—do it all perfectly and that is how you qualify for the Indy 500.

I'm not thinking about the FBI or prison. I'm not thinking about my family. I'm thinking about finding that intangible limit and giving it a little kiss.

When I pulled into the pit, my whole crew was jumping up and down, punching at the sky. My qualifying speed was 209.964 mph. I had claimed one of the coveted thirty-three spots on the grid. My speed was faster than some of my childhood heroes that week—faster than A. J. Foyt, faster than Johnny Parsons. The 1986 Indy 500 was already looking to be the fastest 500 in history. The top qualifier, Rick Mears, and the second-place qualifier, Danny Sullivan, both broke qualifying records with speeds of 217.581 mph and 216.828, respectively.

It wasn't until later in the day that I learned I had also set a record: the fastest rookie qualifying lap in Indy 500 history.

The whole month of May, Indy hosted banquets and VIP events where the fans could meet the drivers. I got to know a bunch of them. A. J. Foyt was known to be the world champion of orneriness. But in person, he was a fun guy. I played racquetball with Tom Sneva. He was eight years older than me and already a legend. Tom was a math teacher turned professional racer, and he'd won pole position at Indy three times (1977, 1978, and 1984). He was the first to turn a lap at the Brickyard at over 200 mph. He was competitive at everything—racquetball, golf, racing—but he was also a caring friend.

All month it was practice and autograph signing. As an Indy 500 rookie, I was a curiosity. The reporters found it odd that I'd never raced a car until I was twenty-five years old. Most guys start far younger. Some at five years old in go-karts.

"I went to a car show in Miami in 1979," I told Cooper Rollow of the *Chicago Tribune*, "and SCCA had a booth. I thought it would be kind of neat to sign up and maybe do a little amateur racing sometime. It was just going to be a hobby, you know. . . . But I never imagined it would lead to an IndyCar ride someday."

My dreams were coming true, but not in the way I ever imagined. The whole time at Indianapolis—at the track, in the city, anywhere I went—I knew the FBI was following me. I could feel their presence. It was like the old saying: no matter how fast you run, the law is faster.

On race day morning, Pam and I awoke in the town house we'd rented, and we looked out our windows. Dark skies blanketed the whole Midwest, and the weather called for pounding rain. I got down to the track, and all the teams were setting up. Fans started turning out in massive numbers, but the rain came so hard, track officials were forced to call the whole thing off. In sports car racing, you compete in rain. In IndyCar, it's too dangerous.

We had to wait an entire week for the rain to stop. I spent a lot of that downtime alone with Pam and Brandie. I was still keeping my impending indictment a secret from Pam. I never told her of the comet flying at full speed that was going to impact our family life head on. But I'm sure she knew something was terribly wrong. That whole week—full of nervous anticipation for the 500 and nervous worries over our future—passed excruciatingly slowly.

Then, finally, Sunday came. When I drove to the track that morning, I saw a sight I will never forget. Swarms of people were everywhere. The crowds were so thick I couldn't get near the track. I ended up having to call the police for help. The irony! Here I was, an outlaw midway through what had to be the biggest marijuana smuggling operation in history, calling the cops on myself. I got a police motorcycle escort to the track. Otherwise, I might've missed the race.

I signed countless autographs that morning. It's amazing, the look on people's faces as they greet a real Indy 500 gladiator in the flesh. The TV cameras were rolling. ABC had, for decades, aired only chunks of the Indy 500 on *Wide World of Sports* because the race was so long. But in 1986, for the first time ever, the "world's most famous race" (as ABC announcer Jim McKay called it in his intro on air) would be televised live in full—all five hundred miles, which in 1986, would last three hours.

There's a parade before the race, a huge production with floats and marching bands and each driver in an open convertible car, going around the racetrack and through the city of Indianapolis. Pam, Brandie, and I rode in the back of ours. Looking out at those packed grandstands, everyone cheering for us, Brandie's eyes were as wide as quarters, and she held a melting popsicle in her hand. She was too dumbstruck to think to eat it. The whole thing was a wild celebration, but I also had to be honest with myself. All these fans don't just come out to see cars go fast and a winner crowned. It's an un-spoken truth that the spectators come out to see cars collide at hyperspeeds, cars hitting walls.

That's one of the race's allures—that the pursuit of speed and glory is worth risking one's life for, that anything could happen at any moment.

David Hasselhoff—star of the hit TV show *Knight Rider*—sang the national anthem, and Mary Hulman—chairwoman of the board of the Indianapolis Motor Speedway—gave the famous order over the loudspeaker system.

"Gentlemen, start your engines!"

Over a quarter-million fans at the track and countless more at home watching on TV stood on their feet as thirty-three drivers took off behind the pace car, which had Chuck Yeager, the first man ever to break the speed of sound in a jet plane, in the passenger seat as honorary driver. I'd qualified tenth. There are two warm-up laps. During the first, at slow speed, the drivers wrenched the cars from side to side to try to get heat into the tires. Then on the second lap, all thirty-three men lined up in eleven rows, three cars abreast, moving around the track at about 80 mph.

Suddenly, in my rearview mirror, I saw a flash and heard a screeching noise. I focused closer in the mirror: Tom Sneva, in the car directly behind me, had inexplicably cut across the grass and smashed into the guardrail. It was bizarre! I thought: My God! He's a veteran. And his race was already over before it started.

That's how twitchy these cars can be. That's how easy it is to make a mistake.

Again: more delay. The stewards had to come out to remove Sneva's car and clean debris off the track. The drivers were getting restless. The fans were getting restless. Again, we did our two warm-up laps. Again, the thirty-two drivers lined up in eleven rows. When the green flag waved, an explosion of 25,000 horsepower sent us all thundering toward turn one.

Fate had put me in the driver's seat. I knew that if I could win this race or just make the podium, no matter what would happen to me in the future, that would be one thing the law could never take from me. And so I set out to achieve my goal.

23

The Checkered Flag

Spring and summer 1986

*H*eading into turn one, I felt the acceleration pin my brain to the back of my skull. Turn one felt completely unlike anything I remembered. During practice and qualifying, you have plenty of room. Now I was packed in tight in a field of cars. Directly in front of me was Brazilian Emerson Fittipaldi—twice the Formula 1 World Champion—and the American Johnny Rutherford—a three-time Indy 500 winner. Directly behind me was Danny Ongais—"The Flyin' Hawaiian." The best drivers in the business were all around me, doing everything they could to defeat me.

The turbulence was extreme.

The noise was extreme.

The g-force was extreme.

Everything about this experience had all my senses as alive and alert as they'd ever been, so much so that the most minute impressions imprinted themselves on my mind vividly. A hot dog wrapper floating by me in the wind. A tiny stone flying out of a tire in front of me, pinging my helmet.

Once I got to the back straight after turn two, the field began to spread out, and I climbed up toward 200 mph. At the opening of the race, you shift up in gears, but once you hit fifth, you stay there. After that it's all brake and throttle management, cornering dynamics, and chassis adjustment. I worked on getting myself into the zone. *Stay calm, Randy. Breathe. Relax your muscles. Relax your hands, your fingers, your ass cheeks. Let the car talk to you. Feel its emotions, sense its strengths and its fragilities. Use your hands, your eyes, your smell, and your touch.* After one lap—2.5 miles—I found my sweet spot and slipped into the flow. Everything else melted away. My consciousness began to work with as much speed as the pistons in the engine.

Maybe I need to take a slightly different line through this corner. Maybe I should come in a little lower, so I can carry more speed. How is the grip of the tires? Is there more grip in one part of a corner than another? Is there more grip in the rear wheels than the front or vice versa? Where and when are the passing opportunities? When should I gun for it, and when should I lay off?

You have spotters communicating via radio, helping you understand where the cars are located around you. You have flag men waving flags as you go past—a blue flag if a faster car is trying to pass you, yellow for caution, white with a yellow stripe to warn of oil or water on the track. Your crew chief is communicating with you over radio about the car and what adjustments should be made for more speed. But when it comes down to it: you are alone. It's just you and what you got in your heart, what you got in your head, and what you got in your right foot.

I could feel my car pushing, wanting to understeer. I was turning and the car wanted to keep going straight, so I adjusted my sway bar and radioed to my crew chief.

"It's understeering," I said into the radio, trying to stay calm. "It's understeering." I had to lift off the throttle, entering turn three.

I kept trying to adjust the chassis, but the car kept wanting to go straight while I was turning. I realized: I had this car set up perfectly for qualifying, but we'd made adjustments for the race because I wasn't out there by myself for only four fast laps. I had to run five hundred miles now. When your car is understeering and you keep your foot on the throttle, the car will go directly into the wall. The only way to handle an understeering car is to get off the throttle a bit in turns and try to make adjustments. I started losing a second off each lap. I started fighting the car more than I was fighting the competition.

The tank held roughly enough fuel for thirty-two laps—eighty miles. Indy racing is a team sport. With my crew chief in charge, we'd practiced pit stops over and over. When I pulled into the pit for my first refueling, my crew jumped into action.

One guy pressed a hose into a fitting on the side of the car that raised it up off the ground with air jacks.

Four crewmen changed out the four Goodyear tires, while a fifth guy hooked the fuel hose to my tank.

The hose pumped three gallons per second.

For the driver, the pit stop feels like an eternity because you know that you could be covering the span of a football field every second that you're sitting still. In reality, my first Indy 500 pit stop took less than twenty seconds.

On the track, the clock hands wind, and nothing stays the same. As the car burns off fuel, it lightens, and the shedding of weight changes its cornering dynamics. As the sun moves across the sky, the view from the cockpit changes too. The track gets covered in marbles—small chunks of rubber sheared off tires, forming balls all over the tarmac. One wrong move—or one accidental slip into a pile of those marbles—and your race could be over.

"Wait a minute! There's a yellow flag! And there's been a wreck!"

That's what the fans heard at home as announcer Sam Posey shouted into his ABC network microphone. We were one hundred laps down, exactly halfway. Just out of turn two, I saw the carnage of a wrecked Indy car, with the driver still inside. An ambulance and a bunch of Chevrolet pickup trucks fitted with fire suppression systems pulled up to the crash, and the pace car came out on the track. The whole field lined up behind the pace car and slowed to a crawl, and for a minute, I could take a deep breath.

"Holy fuck!" I was thinking to myself. I was halfway home, already totally exhausted. My brain felt like a wet towel that someone was wringing out to dry.

When I came around turn two, I saw that the wreck was veteran Johnny Parsons, who'd fishtailed into the infield grass, his car punching the wall. Parsons wasn't injured, and the fans got some excitement. I was running in twelfth place, but I was the top rookie in the field, and there was still enough race left to catch the leaders. After a few laps behind the pace car, it pulled off and the track went green again. The whole field accelerated back up to speed.

175 mph.

185 mph.

200 mph and beyond.

I felt the car continuing to push in corners, wanting to go straight into the wall every time. I kept fighting it. I couldn't get it dialed in. Mile after mile, lap after lap, hour after hour.

With ten laps to go, something happened, something that had never happened in all my years of racing. I was sitting in tenth place. I was well ahead of any other rookie. My spotters were telling me over the radio that the eleventh-place driver was nowhere near me. It was as if I was suddenly alone out there, and my mind began to wander.

I started thinking about Pam and her being pregnant. I started thinking about the load and the law. I was hurtling around this racetrack in front of hundreds of thousands, and the identities I'd managed all this time to keep separate began to melt together. My worlds were colliding.

My wife was due to give birth in seven months.

I had 170,000 pounds coming up the coast of California.

The FBI was following me.

The indictment, my lawyer, the negotiations.

All these thoughts began to crowd my skull.

I was short a distributor, so I'd gotten Pam's brother-in-law to step in. Could I count on him, 100 percent? Bill Whittington knew I was doing a load. He was now in custody. Would he rat me out to save his own ass? Could the FBI know that the load was coming into California? How was I ever going to tell Pam about this impending indictment?

That's when it hit me: I was still in the car, racing in the Indy 500. Why was I suddenly thinking about everything else? *Because my love of motor racing was strong. But my instincts for survival were stronger.*

My crew chief snapped me out of it. "Ten laps to go Randy!" he shouted over the radio. "Hang in there. You're sitting tenth."

I kept my foot on the throttle.

With three laps to go, there was one final piece of drama between my number 12 car and the finish. Bobby Rahal was leading the race, and he came up behind me, ready to lap me, which was normal at this point toward the end of the 500. It wasn't going to throw me off: I held my racing line and my speed. He couldn't get around me right away though, and two other drivers gained on him—Rick Mears and Kevin Cogan. They got bottled up behind me, through no fault of my own, and that set up an all-out sprint race between the three for the final laps and the victory, in the fastest Indy 500 of all time up to that point.

I kept my speed through my final laps. I knew I was finishing tenth—if I could get the car to the finish line. When I saw the checkered flag wave, it truly hit me—that this little kid from Virginia who grew up with a dream had finished the Indy 500. But a profound sadness came over me too, while I was still in the car, motoring around the track in a cool-down lap. The fans were all on their feet. Hundreds of thousands of people cheering. But I was no longer thinking about the race or the glory. The reality I was living came to me for the first time, in crystal-clear clarity.

I was going to lose my family. And for what? I had wanted to win so badly; I had made choices that were going to destroy the thing that I loved the most. Life is not about competition. Life is about love and the people that matter the most to you.

I started to question everything I believed in and all the choices I'd made going back to when Glen died. I could see myself down there from above, as if I was stepping out of my body and watching myself in a movie. There I was, on the track. The most glorious moment of my life, outside of my daughter's birth, became my greatest moment of despair.

I also realized what I was ultimately going to have to do. The indictment was coming; there was no escaping it. The prosecutors were going to nail me with a long prison sentence. I was going to have to abscond. To disappear off the face of the earth. If I was going to lose my family, I might as well live life on the run. Better to live life on the run than to rot in a prison cell.

As these thoughts ran through my head, my crew chief's voice came through on the radio, loud over the sound of the engine. "Randy," he said, "congratulations. You were the only rookie to finish the race. You're a shoo-in for the 1986 Indy 500 Rookie of the Year. Well done, my friend. Well done."

Bobby Rahal won the 1986 Indy 500 in one of the most thrilling races in American history. It was the closest three-car finish ever at Indianapolis, with Rahal, Kevin Cogan, and Rick Mears taking the checkered flag within 1.8 seconds of each other.

Days later, at a banquet room at the Indianapolis Motor Speedway, Pam and I showed up for the Indy 500 Rookie of the Year ceremony. I was wearing a gray herringbone jacket over a white shirt, with a thin black tie that matched a black pocket square and black slacks. Pam wore a black dress. She looked as beautiful as the day I met her back in 1970. Even more so. Her belly was full and rounded, as the baby was on the way. The ABC announcer and former racer Paul Page presented me with the Rookie of the Year award. The president of the American Fletcher National Bank presented me with a check. My total winning payout for the rookie award and the race was $103,437.50. A lot of money—for most people.

Standing at the podium, I thanked everybody I could think of. My whole crew was there, and I thanked my team. Behind me as I spoke, mounted on the wall, rows of photographs showed the smiling faces of previous rookies of the year— Arie Luyendyk, Michael Andretti, Rick Mears, and the rest. Afterward, I sat on a couch, and reporters interviewed me.

"It's going to take me another year of running here, getting used to running at super speedways," I said. "Then maybe not next year but the year after I can be a contender." The press surely believed me—that my future looked bright, that Randy Lanier could be a future Indy 500 champion. But I knew as I spoke that I was full of shit. There was never going to be another Indy 500, not for me.

At the end of the banquet, we all gathered for a photograph. I sat in a chair, and Pam stood beside me. My crew chief

Dennis McCormick sat to my left with his beautiful wife. My crew was to my right. When I look at that photo now, after so many years and so many experiences, I feel overwhelmed with bittersweetness. This was everything I had worked for. I'd finished ahead of some of my lifelong heroes—A. J. Foyt and Mario Andretti. But what was I going to lose to make those dreams come true?

Everything I held dearest. All of it.

24

Crash Landing

Summer and fall 1986

*T*wo months after the Indy 500, I was doing 214 mph on the ninety-eighth lap of the Michigan 500, flying down the back straight. I was near the front of the pack, chasing Johnny Rutherford into turn three. I was feeling good in my car, feeling like I had a shot at victory. My right front tire struck a piece of debris and suddenly exploded. Just like that, I was headed for the wall.

Bannnnnng! Like a grenade going off in my lap.

I saw stars and flashes of light.

Loud buzzing in my ears.

Couldn't breathe.

Didn't know if I was dead or alive.

When my eyes refocused, I could see that my car was speeding down the racetrack scraping against the side of the wall and that the entire front end was smashed. As the car lost speed, it slid down the embanked pavement and into the infield grass. When it came to rest, the pain shot through me like electric currents. I couldn't move. All I could do was scream. The medics and the fire unit reached me fast.

"I'm hurt bad!" I shouted. "My leg feels like it's broken!"

The car was engulfed in smoke, and they had to get me out of there. One of the medics explained, "We're going to try to lift you out of the car." They unhooked my five-point harness, and two of them reached down to grab me, one under each armpit. When they started to lift, the pain ripped through my body. It was indescribable. I screamed and they let go of me. They told me they were going to put a belt underneath me and try to pull me out that way. They tried it, and again I started yelling.

One of the guys explained, "We're going to have to cut you out of here." I heard one of the medics say they were going to use the jaws of life. This was a giant shear that literally cut through the car's body like scissors on paper. When they cut me out and got me on a gurney, they took my helmet off and put a neck brace on me, loaded me into an emergency vehicle, and drove me to the infield hospital. I was in so much pain I didn't know if my leg was still attached. I thought: At least I'm cognizant of my surroundings. That's a positive.

The minute I saw a doctor, I started shouting at him.

"You gotta give me something for the pain, man!"

The doctor shot me with 100 cc's of Demerol. It did nothing. The medics then pushed the gurney to a helicopter. They lifted the stretcher inside, and when they shut the helicopter door, it slammed against the side of my stretcher. My whole body convulsed. They slammed the helicopter door shut a second time to try to get it closed. Again, the door hit the side of the stretcher. The cabin was too tight for it. It took them three tries to get that goddamn door shut.

The chopper took off. I could hear the whirling blades as I lay there. I tried to lift my head to see what was going on around me, but I was strapped to the stretcher and the neck brace kept me from lifting my head at all. When we landed at the medical center in Brooklyn, Michigan, several people in hospital clothing were waiting for me. They opened the helicopter door, and when they grabbed the gurney, it felt like it'd been dropped off a cliff even though it moved only a few inches. I asked for more pain medication. I was in agony.

In the ER, even before I had an X-ray, the attending doctor told me, "You have a compound fracture to your right femur bone—the biggest bone in your body. We want to fly you to a different hospital that has a trauma unit."

"I'm not flying nowhere," I said, "until something is done about the pain."

This time they gave me morphine. Finally, the pain ebbed, and I felt nothing in my body. I started to lose consciousness. I have no idea how long I was out. But I was awakened by a nightmare: That I was trying to run from something terrifying, only my legs wouldn't work. It was the FBI chasing me. I was a fly in their web—in the dream and in real life too.

They didn't end up taking me to another hospital, and I went into surgery right there, in Brooklyn, Michigan. I woke up with a big steel rod in my leg and endless question marks about my future.

"Will I ever walk again?" I asked the surgeon when he came to see me in the post-op ward.

"Yes," he said. "I think so."

"Can I ever race again?"

"Well," he said, "that's up to you."

I spent the next few days lying in a hospital bed. Pam was there. Charles Podesta visited me. So did my crew chief and some of the other guys. I read about my crash in the newspapers. It was reported nationwide how Johnny Rutherford won the Michigan 500 in a race marred by numerous smash-ups in front of seventy thousand fans.

"The Lanier accident was the most serious," the *Chicago Tribune* reported. "Lanier suffered a broken leg and other injuries, and his car was destroyed. He hit the wall so hard that debris from the car also struck two official race observers who were on a stand in the backstretch. Their injuries were not serious."

All I could think about was rehabbing so I could get back in the car before it was too late. The season was only half over, and I doubted that I was ever going to get another. So I wanted to get my body in shape.

Back home in Davie, I learned how to do aqua therapy in my swimming pool. I did all kinds of other therapy at the gym—leg lifts, squats, thrusts. Gene, my partner, asked me to meet him in Southern California for the soft opening of our casino, The Bicycle Club. So I called my Learjet pilot.

"Fuel up the plane," I said. "We're going to LA."

When I got out there, the place blew me away. There was a restaurant, a hair salon, the works. I gave my confidant who was running it a Swiss bank account number. "Just send the money there," I said. Soon enough, about a hundred grand started showing up in that account every thirty days.

When I returned home, I reached my house at 2 a.m. I immediately saw a car parked out front by the gate, and it looked like a government-issued vehicle. An unmarked car. I thought: *What the fuck is this?*

I was driving a Porsche 930 Turbo. I turned off my lights and rolled by as quietly as I could. I saw two guys inside the car, and both of them had their heads resting against the windows. They were asleep. They'd probably been waiting for me for hours. To get into my driveway, I had to open a gate that weighed probably a thousand pounds. It was going to make a lot of noise. I felt I had no choice. So I hit the remote and the gate started opening. *RRRrrrrrrr.* It was loud, alright. But these two dudes didn't even wake up.

Inside, I found Pam frantic. "Randy!" she screamed. "The feds raided our house. Those two guys are parked in front right now! They were here all day!" She started shaking and crying.

"This is bullshit," I said. "My lawyer told me that he had negotiated with the feds. He said that once we finished our negotiations that they would let me turn myself in. There wasn't supposed to be no raid!"

"Randy, what are you talking about?! What negotiations?"

"They weren't supposed to raid my fucking house!"

"Randy—!"

"I gotta get the hell out of here," I said.

I had a fight-or-flight moment. I ran out to the Porsche. I opened the gate and drove off with the headlights off. What do you know? Those agents never woke up.

From a hotel room in Fort Lauderdale, I called my lawyer at 4 a.m. "What the fuck, man!" I shouted.

"Calm down, Randy."

"Don't fucking tell me to calm down. I ain't calming down until you find out what the fuck is going on! I thought they said they would let me turn myself in once our negotiations were through. And that they wouldn't raid my house!"

"Let me find out what's going on."

I was scared out of my goddamn mind. I waited in my hotel room until that afternoon when my lawyer called me back. "Randy," he said, "this has nothing to do with the Southern District of Illinois. This is an entirely different case. This is an indictment out of Miami."

"Another case? And there's already a fucking indictment!?"

"Yes, I have it in my hand right now. I'll read it to you."

The indictment had to do with a shrimp boat weed smuggling operation out of South Florida. Several people I'd worked with years earlier had used these shrimp boats to import weed. I handled some of the distributing for them, but none of the smuggling, and I'd never had anything to do with their shrimp boats. And that was years earlier, back in 1982. In addition, this indictment had to do with a Drug Enforcement Agency investigation—not the FBI. It appeared the two departments were not talking to each other.

"This is bullshit," I said. "I had no involvement with those shrimp boats. Now the DEA is raiding my fucking house?"

I realized what was probably happening: Some people had gotten busted. They knew I was in the game on a large scale. So they gave the DEA my name because they thought it would help them get off with lesser sentences. But they were lying. I had nothing to do with the shrimp boat smuggling operations. I explained myself to my lawyer.

"What am I supposed to do?" I asked.

"Let me work on it," he said.

I was afraid to leave my hotel room. Anywhere I went, people might recognize me. They might recognize my car. I made phone calls from pay phones but never the same phone twice for fear of it getting tapped. I knew my home phones were tapped. My friends' phones were probably tapped. Meanwhile, I was still in intense pain from the accident.

After several more discussions with my lawyer, we decided that I would turn myself in to the South Florida authorities, on one condition: they would agree that I could get out on bond right after the arrest and that no announcement would be made to the press. I would turn myself in, they would arrest me, they would release me on bond right there, and nobody would know anything about it. Then my lawyer would try to beat the case.

Meanwhile, I had the Phoenix and Miami Grand Prix coming up. If the news hit the papers that I'd been busted, that would be the end of my racing career. IndyCar wouldn't let me compete in those last two races of 1986.

"Tomorrow morning," my lawyer said, "come down to my office. I will have it all set up. We will go into the Broward County Courthouse through the basement. You'll be arrested. We'll do the paperwork. And we'll walk out the way we came in."

So the next morning, that's what we did. We went into an office in the courthouse, where prosecuting attorneys met us.

There were no handcuffs, but they did read me my Miranda rights. They took a mug shot and fingerprinted me. I'd already filled out the paperwork for a $350,000 bail bond prior to showing up at the courthouse. My dad had put up seven acres of property for collateral because I didn't have $350,000 in legit cash that I could show the government. I left the building. It all went according to plan. Only, somebody tipped off the press.

A bunch of reporters were there at the door when I walked out. I was furious and so was my lawyer, but there was nothing we could do. I stood there like a deer in the headlights as the camera flashes popped in my face. Those pictures show a man at his absolute lowest, everything he'd worked toward slipping away in an instant.

The next day, I went to the bail bonds office with an attaché case holding $350,000 in cash and took my dad's property off the paperwork as collateral.

On October 17, 1986, all over the country, Americans sat down to read their newspapers. The sports pages were full of intrigue that morning. The FBI had busted open a plot to kidnap hockey star Wayne Gretzky and hold him for ransom. Mike Tyson was gearing up to fight James "Bonecrusher" Smith, and the Mets were set to take on the Red Sox in what would turn out to be a historic World Series. Then there was the story of Randy Lanier, race car driver, who just four and a half months earlier had won Indy 500 Rookie of the Year honors.

My arrest was reported in the *Chicago Tribune*, the *Hartford Courant*, the *Boston Globe*, the *Los Angeles Times*, and the *Atlanta*

Daily World, among many other papers. A thirty-two-count indictment named eleven individuals, myself among them. "Here we have a complete, classical drug ring," a spokesman for the Miami DEA office told the *New York Times*, "in which, as the indictment alleges, 11 people conspired and for four years carried out a large-scale operation."

This DEA-led indictment had nothing to do with any of my smuggling business, none of my work with Ben, Gene, George, Charles, and the others. The FBI was still after me for that other case in Illinois. This was just the shrimp boat business—small change in comparison to the barges.

The doctors had cleared me to finish out the IndyCar season, but now—just like that—my racing career was over. My family was going crazy. They were worried about me. I had long talks on the phone with my mother, and all I could do was lie to her. I felt so ashamed I had to force the words through my clenched jaw.

"Everything's going to be OK, Mom," I said. "Do you hear me? I promise! Everything's going to be OK."

Meanwhile, the tug and the barge, loaded with weed, had cleared the Panama Canal and were right at that moment cruising up the California coast. With all eyes on me, what was probably the biggest load of weed in American history was headed for dry land.

25

Rock Bottom

Fall 1986

Sometimes, when I needed to think, I'd drive by myself through Miami—this city that I loved, that had given so much to me. I'd get on the expressways and then exit, cruising through the alleys, passing the darkened storefronts, the teeming intersections. This was my time and place to figure things out, sitting in the driver's seat of my Porsche, trying to make sense of what was happening to me. I was constantly looking in mirrors, taking evasive maneuvers, always feeling like a cop was going to burst out of nowhere behind me with lights flashing.

I was now awaiting trial on the shrimp boat case, a trial that would be held sometime in the future. I still had the indictment looming, coming out of the Southern District of Illinois.

There's no Rookie of the Year award in weed smuggling, no champion trophy. But if there was, I think I'd have a room full of trophies. I had created an empire. It was born in an era of free love but came of age during the War on Drugs. There was a war out there, for real, and there was more to the story than I knew at that time—what would turn out to be a critical piece of the puzzle.

In 1984, the Reagan administration signed into law the "super kingpin" provision of the Continuing Criminal Enterprise code, and it was set to be enacted on November 1, 1986. This new law dictated a life sentence for major offenders if "the defendant was the principal or one of several principal administrators, organizers, or leaders, [and] received $10 million in gross receipts during any twelve-month period of its existence for the manufacture, importation, or distribution of a substance." They were going after the big fish. And the law stipulated that the federal government considered cannabis to be a schedule I narcotic, as evil an offense as heroin.

My last load was scheduled to come into the port of San Francisco and into Redwood City, right after this law took effect.

It was on one of those long drives through Miami when I made up my mind on the most difficult decision I'd ever make. Soon after, I came home to Pam and asked her to sit down with me in our living room. I loved this house. Everything around me was a reminder of the life Pam and I had built together. But it was time to lay down the gauntlet.

"Pam," I said, "I have been living a life out of control. I'm in trouble. I talked with my lawyer, and it's not looking good."

"What are you talking about? The shrimp boat case?"

"No. There's another case out of southern Illinois. Somebody got busted and ratted me out. My lawyer is trying to negotiate, and the DA won't budge."

"I don't understand."

I took a deep breath and looked down at my feet. "They're talking about a serious prison term and complete forfeiture of everything."

"What!?"

I didn't respond

Pam said, "That's bullshit, Randy. Bill and Don didn't get that kind of sentence. Why are you getting treated so bad?"

"My lawyer is trying to—"

"Then get a different lawyer!"

Pam started to shake all over. Tears rolled down her face, and her lips started to quiver uncontrollably.

I said, "Listen, we gotta be smart about this." Then I dropped the bomb. "We need to get divorced." A look of horror came over her face, like the last bit of hope had just crawled out of her. "I have been thinking about this," I said. "I need you to file for divorce."

It was all coming at her too fast. She looked confused. "Me?" she said. "Why should I do that?"

"Look, if I file for divorce, it'll look like a setup. They're going to try to take the house. If *you* file for divorce, you could take the house as part of the settlement. Then they can't get their hands on it. We have to do this, Pam. We have to do it quickly and quietly. For the sake of our children. At least, they'll be able to grow up in our home."

She was now crying so hard she couldn't breathe. She came at me and started to beat me on the chest with her fists. I tried to hold her arms, but she screamed. I was worried we'd wake up Brandie, and the last thing we needed was for our little girl to see us like this. So I grabbed Pam by the wrist and pulled her into our bedroom. I shut the door behind us. She sat on an ottoman and put her face in her hands. She was going through so much, and it was all my fault. She was newly clean and sober. She'd lost a child in pregnancy. She was still pregnant now. I'd never seen someone so distraught, and I worried about the health of our baby.

"Please try to calm down, Pam. Take deep breaths."

I hadn't even told her all of it yet—just how out of control my life had become. The truth? I was snorting a lot of cocaine, drinking whiskey, and I was unfaithful to her. I was living life with the philosophy of *drive it 'til the wheels fall off*. Now seeing her like this made me realize: I was not worthy of her greatness. I had let her down so bad. Too often, I'd let my outer priorities take the place of my inner priorities when, in actuality, it should be the other way around. I'd failed to make *her* my priority. I couldn't tell her that now, but I felt it in my soul. I felt worthless and for good reason.

I also hadn't even told her what my plans were. I was going to disappear in Europe, and my hope was that someday in the future we would be able to be together again, somehow. It may be a big planet, but it's a small world. I was hoping there was a future for us, together. I couldn't know for sure, but I had made up my mind. It seemed like the only path forward.

"You have to do this, Pam," I said. "I have a lawyer all lined up. You need to call him tomorrow morning and get this divorce done."

"Oh my fucking God."

"I have to go."

"Where are you going?"

"I can't tell you that. But here's what we are going to do. I'm going to give you the location of twenty-five pay phones in the area. When I give you a time and a place, you have to be at that phone, and I'll call you on that pay phone. Before we hang up, I'll give you another date and time and another pay-phone location. That's how we're going to keep in touch."

I left her there, the love of my life, sitting on the ottoman with her face in her hands. I've done some horrible things in my life. This was the worst. But I felt I had no choice.

Shortly after, I got a buzz on my beeper from Gene. I went to a pay phone on a street in Miami and called him, pay phone to pay phone.

"What the fuck is this shit, Randy!?" he shouted.

"I'm sorry, Gene, I didn't know it was coming."

Gene said he had George with him. "You get arrested," Gene said, "and you don't fucking tell us? We have to hear about it on the street?"

"I'm sorry."

"The load is coming into Redwood City any day now," he said.

"I know. Listen—I need to update you. I had to contract out all my work on the unloading. I got guys lined up to handle everything. I will send you all the beeper numbers, and you guys will have all the contacts. These are my guys, Gene. You can trust them."

"Uh-uh, Randy. No fucking way. You get your ass out here to California right now. We are not contacting any of your distributors. We don't want their beeper numbers, we don't want to know their names, we don't want anything to do with it. There's too much heat. My people are scared."

"Now listen—"

"We are not listening to shit over this phone. You get on a plane. We'll see you in California tomorrow."

Back in my car, I punched the steering wheel so hard my hand started throbbing. "Fucccckkkk!" I had no choice; all my partners were relying on me. If I didn't go, the load would be lost. Nobody would get paid. I couldn't let that happen to my partners. They had put so much trust in me.

I knew the FBI was still following me. I'd taken a room at the Charter House, a Miami condo building, using the alias John DeRusso. (I had a driver's license and a passport under this name; these kinds of fake IDs were easier to obtain, if you had money, back in the days before 9/11.) I went back to the Charter House and packed a small suitcase—a change of clothes, all my beepers, and a big wad of cash. Then I headed to the mall. I parked my Porsche and left the keys in it, the doors unlocked.

Inside the mall was a jewelry store where I'd been buying Pam gifts for years. I'd bought a few Rolexes in this place as well. I walked in there, feeling 100 percent sure I was being watched. I knew the manager of the store well.

"Listen," I said, "I have something to talk to you about. Can we go back in your office?"

"Sure, Randy."

I picked out some watches, so it looked like I was shopping, and we walked into the back of the store. I told the manager I needed to go out through the back door. He didn't ask any questions. I left the watches on his desk and went out the back door into the parking lot, where I had one of my guys waiting in a different car. He drove me to the airport, and he was instructed to then go back to the mall and make sure my Porsche got home safely.

In my private jet, I took off for San Francisco to supervise the unloading of our biggest score yet—right under the nose of the FBI.

26

Disappearing Act

Winter 1986–1987

I was in San Francisco, standing on a pier at Fisherman's Wharf, when the tugboat pulled the barge under the Golden Gate Bridge. I could see it through binoculars. The tug pulled that behemoth to the customs house on the north side of the bay. There, as I later learned, customs officials asked the ship captain to empty the ballasts of water so they could inspect. They actually lowered themselves into one of the ballast compartments, and finding the steel floor suspicious, one of them tried to drill a hole in the floor. The drill bit broke, so this guy tried another. Again, the drill bit broke.

That's how close we were to getting busted. Right there. A shitty drill bit saved our asses, for the time being.

The tugboat crew was legit, and they had no idea they were smuggling weed. Customs officials collected passports from all the crew, instructed them to remain on the tugboat, and told them they were not allowed to come ashore onto US soil. The officials then left. They came back the next day, gave all the passports back, and welcomed the crew into the United States. The tug and barge cleared customs and were free to go.

Just like last time, we had the barge head from San Francisco Bay up the Sacramento River Deep Water Ship Channel for the port of Sacramento, inland many miles. George and Gene had set up a warehouse there to take all the Brazilian wood and nuts, all the decoy manifest we had aboard. We took the legit crew off the tugboat and put our own crew on. Then they pulled the barge back down the river and over to the quarry in Redwood City.

As all that was happening, I was organizing my three distributors with their warehouses and trucks, as we'd done before. It was a massive operation, and I conducted it all by pay phone. I still had my rented apartment in San Francisco, where I could hide out. So I was able to get all this work done without anyone actually seeing my physical person. I never talked to anyone face-to-face, nor did I ever use the same pay phone twice. This way, even if I was being watched, I felt like I wouldn't bring the heat on my crew.

Because I was worried about bringing the heat and the FBI, Gene's crew was tasked with the unloading at the rock quarry, and my crew was to handle all the trucking and warehouses. Gene's guys started cutting out the steel plate to get to the secret compartments in the ballasts. That night, he called my beeper. I called him from a pay phone on Columbus Avenue near Ghirardelli Square.

"Randy, we have an issue," he said.

"OK."

"One of my guys started cutting out the steel plate and was overcome by a nasty smell."

"What the fuck?"

"He lit a lighter so he could try to see in there, and there was a burst of flame. So he left it and moved to another compartment. We're going to unload all the other compartments first and figure out what to do next."

The following day, after unloading the other compartments, Gene beeped me again.

"I have bad news," he said. "There's been an explosion."

"What?!"

"Yeah, a fucking explosion."

He told me that seawater had leaked into one of the secret compartments and, over the months the barge was at sea, the weed had fermented. Now the compartment was filled with methane gas. This whole barge had turned into a large explosive. We literally had a massive bomb on our hands. Already, there'd been one explosion and two guys injured.

"We got to get that barge the fuck out of here," Gene said. "It's not safe to go aboard that vessel."

I had to go down to the quarry dock to see for myself. But I was beyond paranoid. Who knew if the FBI would follow me? I didn't want to lead the heat right to the weed. It was a half-hour drive down to Redwood City, and I had a rental car. I drove down at sunrise, the next morning, checking my rearview mirrors every second. When I got down there, a guard let me through the gate. It was a warm, humid morning. When I got to the dock, the barge was gone. Nothing there. Nobody was around. I stood on that dock scratching my head.

In all my years in the smuggling business, of all the strange things I'd seen, the disappearance of this barge was the biggest mystery. There were rumors that the two men who'd been injured in the explosion aboard the barge had perished. This even came up in my trial. But nothing was ever proven and no witnesses to the explosion or the barge's disappearance ever came forward.

Gene had years and years of experience in maritime salvage. He told me that he took that barge out to sea, with twenty-five thousand pounds of rotted marijuana aboard, and sank it to the bottom of the ocean. He said he blew the fuck out of that barge with dynamite.

Was that the truth? Were there two dead men aboard? To this day, I don't know the answers to those questions. But there's another scenario to consider. Gene knew I was in deep shit with the law. This made me vulnerable. It might've been that there was never anything wrong with that twenty-five thousand pounds of weed. Gene's crew might've unloaded it and sold it off, cutting me out. We all knew it was our last load. We were never going to work together again.

Today, Gene is dead, and George hasn't been seen in years. We'll likely never find out what happened. What I knew for sure was that twenty-five thousand pounds of weed were gone. And I was going to have to answer to the Family for it. The Colombians were going to want to get paid. They were my people, so I was on the hook.

My plan was to get my things in order as fast as I could. I flew from California to Colorado to empty out my house there. I'd told a friend that if he met me at the house with a large moving truck, he could have everything that fit in it. We loaded the snowmobiles and motorcycles, the gym equipment, all the furniture. Before I left Colorado, I buried $400,000 in the back-yard. I put the bills in plastic bags, squeezed the air out, and then heat-sealed them. I put the bags in PVC pipes and buried those, telling no one the location.

Back on the East Coast, I buried $3 million and a whole bunch of five-gallon buckets of gold coins and gold bars in the flower garden in Slick's backyard. I also hid several floor safes in the basement of my sister's house and in my aunt's house, without their knowledge. I put money in antique furniture and put the furniture in a storage facility.

I had all my companies and all my cars registered under shell companies out of Panama, so if I got pulled over, the cops couldn't trace the car to me. I was living as John DeRusso. The only way the cops or the FBI could learn my real identity—even if I got pulled over in my car and I had to present license and registration—would be through fingerprints.

The money from the last load was coming in, via Charles, with whom I kept in touch by beeper and pay phone. By this time, Charles had handled over $200 million in cash, in less than five years. I still had five million yet to come in from the last load.

Then, amidst all this chaos, on January 21, 1987, Pam gave birth to our second child, whom we named Glen after my little brother. I was at the hospital. I was thirty-two years old. I was sure the FBI agents were walking the hallways, keeping track of everywhere I went. Holding Glen in my arms had to be the most bittersweet moment of my life. I knew I was going away. I was not going to be there to raise him and to be his father. I sat there in the hospital that day with Pam, holding the baby, crying harder than he was.

Seven days later, I walked out of my apartment at the Charter House one morning and went to a deli. "Give me a bagel with cream cheese," I said to the guy behind the counter. "Nova, tomato, and onion please."

He started making the bagel. Behind him was a television, showing live news. The screen caught my eye. I squinted to make sure I was seeing what I thought I was seeing. Could it be? What the fuck?! Right there, on live television, I could see FBI agents raiding my house!

I could only guess that prosecutors for the Southern District of Illinois had finally ordered my arrest. The FBI had tipped off the local news. A newscaster stood in front of my mansion in Davie, holding a microphone, talking into the camera. I stood there dumbfounded, watching the TV.

"We are live, in front of the home of the 1986 Indy 500 Rookie of the Year Randy Lanier," she said. "As you can see, the FBI is conducting a search of Mr. Lanier's home. Above, a helicopter is hovering. Once again: I am standing in front of the home of local racing hero Randy Lanier."

The guy behind the counter put the bagel down in front of me. "Will there be anything else?" he asked.

I took the order, paid for it, and walked out.

My heart was pounding like it was going to leap out of my throat. The fear was indescribable. I could never go back to the life I'd known. My life in hiding had begun. I was afraid to even drive my car, lest somebody recognize me. I was beeping friends and stopping at pay phones. I got ahold of one of my distributors who said he had the perfect hideout.

"One of my stash houses," he said. "It's in Central Florida. It's empty. I ain't even ever used it. It's a big piece of property. You can go there. Nobody going to find you."

So I drove up there. He was right. Middle of nowhere, no neighbors, nothing. There wasn't much furniture except a bed, a kitchen table, some chairs, and a TV set. That first night in the stash house, I rolled up a joint and smoked it while I sat at the table alone, wracking my brain, trying to formulate a plan. I did this for a month, smoking, thinking, waiting for my beard to grow out, getting so bored I couldn't stand it. Meanwhile, once again, my name was all over the newspapers, all over the country.

"Davie race car driver Randy Lanier has been indicted for the second time since October," the *South Florida Sun-Sentinel* reported, "this time on charges of heading a marijuana smuggling operation that used oceangoing vessels to bring multiton loads into New York, San Francisco and New Orleans harbors." That's how much the FBI and now the newspaper reporters knew—all the ports where we'd brought in loads, with the exception of Fort Lauderdale itself.

The scandal of my bust only added to the stain on the sport of racing. The press called me "Florida's greatest pot-smuggling race car driver." Others said that the 1986 Indy 500 Rookie of the Year was "smoked." Race fans started referring to 1986 as "the year they all went to jail," and the IMSA nickname as the International Marijuana Smuggling Association would become a permanent joke to this day. Between the Whittington brothers, myself, Marty Hinze, the father-son duo of the John Pauls—our escapades amounted to a full-on scandal. Books would be written. Documentaries made.

The same maniacal passion I'd put into racing, I now fun-neled into saving my ass and evading the law. I started cre-ating my alter ego. In addition to the beard, I cut my hair so it was spiked on top. I wore big, fake glasses that looked like they were heavy prescription. I was becoming another man.

One day, while hiding out at the Florida stash house, I was watching the news on TV when I saw my old friend Don Aronow's face on the screen. Then I heard the word that shocked me to the bottom of my feet.

Assassinated.

Don Aronow! The king of Thunder Boat Alley! I jumped to my feet. "Goddamn, man! What the fuck?"

The details were unbelievable. Aronow had been the tar-get of a professional hit. He was leaving his Cigarette boat factory on February 3, 1987, when a black Lincoln Town Car pulled up. Several shots were fired from inside this Lincoln into Aronow's car. The police had no leads and no suspects. I tried to imagine who would want to kill Aronow. As far as I knew, Don was never into any illegal operations. Later it was rumored that Don was linked to some bad people, but I never knew anything about that. Who could want Don killed? He was a beloved figure and, in South Florida, a full-on celebrity. His murder created a sensation.

The killing of Don Aronow would go on to become the biggest mystery of the South Florida crime world during the late 1980s. When the truth finally emerged, years later, I would learn that Aronow's demise likely came from within my own inner circle. It'd all happened closer to home than I could imagine or believe. But at that time, I wasn't thinking about that. I was planning my escape.

Soon after learning of Aronow's death, I looked in the mirror one morning and decided I was ready. I had a full beard, and with my spiked hair and spectacles, I no longer looked like Randy Lanier. I took my fake IDs and walked out the door as John DeRusso.

I'd decided to move up to New York City. There were eight million people there. I could get lost in the crowds and live under the alias. It had to be far better than living alone in an empty house in the middle of nowhere. Eventually, my plan was to fly to Europe. I needed cash to live on the lam and to execute my escape. I still had money owed to me—if I could get it—but I also owed Gene and George $400,000. I called another of my distributors, who had stash houses in rural Pennsylvania, near the New Jersey border. I asked him if he would put me up in one of them for a bit and keep it a secret from everybody. He agreed.

"I'll have a driver in one of my tractor trailers drive you up there," he promised.

"Deal."

When I got up to Pennsylvania, I got busy. I had to figure out how to get over to Switzerland, withdraw my accounts, and move the money into new accounts, in hopes of covering any paper trail. I had to figure out how to get the money out of the California casino investment—to sell my 10 percent stake before it popped up on the FBI's or the DEA's radar.

That wasn't all. I had to tie up the loose ends on the last load. I also had a shopping center in Texas, and I wanted out of that investment. Then there was my stake in the Road

Atlanta racetrack. I had no idea what to do there. (My brother Steve would become manager of Road Atlanta for decades.)

I had one of my guys dig up $400,000 out of the ground at my place in Colorado and drive it to New York. When the rest of the money came in from the last barge score, Charles met me in the city. When he saw me, he didn't even recognize me because of my disguise. I had a friend who was in real estate— who used to run a very high-end escort service—find me an apartment in the city to rent, on Broadway near Columbus Circle.

It was at this point that I got a call from Ben on my beeper. I called him from a phone on a street corner near Times Square. "What's going on, man?"

"Randy, we need to have a meeting," Ben said.

"You and me?"

"We need to meet with one of the Colombians, from the Family. The three of us."

This was bad news. I was terrified. I had explained to the Family that twenty-five thousand pounds had rotted on the barge during the last score and was now sitting at the bottom of the ocean. But who knew if they believed me? Maybe they thought I was ripping them off. They also knew that the FBI was after me. If I got busted, would I rat them out? I could see why the Colombians might want me dead.

All these years, our relationship had been excellent. But that's because we'd never had any disagreement about money. I was so paranoid I couldn't sleep for days. I agreed to meet Ben and the Colombian in an open area, a public place, so no one could come flying out of a closet with a sawed-off shotgun.

I picked a bar in midtown on the Avenue of the Americas—I wanted some control over the situation. The day we were to meet, I got there early and ordered a drink from the bartender. I was standing at the bar when I saw Ben and the Colombian enter. They walked right past without recognizing me.

"Hey, Ben, it's me."

Kramer turned and focused his eyes, scrutinizing my face. "What the fuck, Randy. Look at you."

"Yeah," I said. "Look at me."

I turned to the Colombian. He was tall, skinny, with a clean-shaven face and eyes like black holes. If he was capable of smiling, I wouldn't know it. We shook hands.

"Let's go for a walk," Ben said.

We went outside and around a corner. It was nighttime, and suddenly we were on a street so dark and quiet the hair on the back of my neck rose. I felt sure I was about to get whacked. I explained the situation to the Colombian, how there was a leak aboard the barge. "You understand," I said, "we've been doing business so long I have no reason to try to screw you over."

"But you've been arrested," he said in his thick accent. "That makes us all vulnerable. And it makes you capable of anything. You're a desperate man, Randy. Look at you, wearing a disguise, going by a fake identity. Why would I believe you? You'll do anything to save your neck."

"Yeah," I said, "but look at it this way. I have no need right now to make any enemies. I got enough to worry about. Do you really think I would try to pull something like this? Listen, twenty-five thousand pounds of weed is sitting on the bottom of the sea."

"And whose fault is that?" he asked. "We grow the stuff. You transport it. So if something goes wrong during the transportation, why should we pay for it?"

He had a point. We spent at least an hour walking and negotiating, and ultimately came to a deal where I would pay $10 million for the whole load. The Family was giving me a discount of about $2 million for my misfortune. Basically, we split the difference for the weed that we'd lost. It was a fair deal, and I was grateful. Grateful for the deal and grateful to still be alive.

The next day, I called Charles from a pay phone on the street near my apartment. "How much is in the stash houses right now?"

"Seven million," he said. That was on top of several million I had buried all over the place and close to $12 million in accounts in Switzerland and Liechtenstein.

"Hold onto that money," I told Charles. "Wait to hear more instructions from me."

John DeRusso flew out of John F. Kennedy, bound for Europe, the next day.

27

Busted

Winter 1988

My first stop was Heathrow, and while I usually chartered private planes once I reached London, this time I flew commercial with a fake passport. I went to Geneva, to Zurich, to Luxembourg. Liechtenstein had no airport, so I had an attorney rent me a Mercedes 500 and I drove there. To be as safe as possible, I closed all my bank accounts and opened new ones, all under Panamanian shell companies.

I met with maritime lawyers and set up a contract with a crew to bring my sixty-five-foot Hatteras to the South of France. From there, I was going to take it to Costa del Sol off the coast of Spain.

That was where I was going to hide out. That was my plan.

While I was in Europe, the Southern District of Illinois expanded my indictment. They were gunning for all of us. Gene was arrested while arriving at Miami airport on a flight from Venezuela. Ben was arrested in his apartment in Miami. They got Pam's brother Ronnie, who had worked for me quite a bit. He had a daughter who'd been injured by a dog, and he was helping her recuperate in one of the quiet stash houses. Bad idea: the feds were surveilling it, and he was arrested. Charles Podesta was busted too, with incriminating evidence found in the trunk of his car.

George made it out of the country, and I met him at Baur au Lac, a beautiful old hotel in Zurich. There we were, two fugitives sitting down for some fine dining, white tablecloth and good wine. We were plotting our futures on the run. George had good connections, and he was able to get me a new fake passport. I paid him $25,000 for it. I was now going under the identity of Trevor Worthington.

"Would you be interested," George asked me, "in smuggling a load of hash into Australia?"

"Are you fucking kidding me!? Hell no! I'm done!"

With all my documentation, I felt my identity was bulletproof, so I flew to Antigua, where I had a crew manning my Hatteras. This trip would turn out to be a big mistake and perhaps a window into how bad my decision-making was at this time. I was going to spend a few days aboard the ship and then fly back to Europe. My crew would take the Hatteras to Venezuela, where the European crew I'd contracted would pick it up at a specific marina and then bring it to the south of France. But before all that happened, I was going to cool off for a few days aboard the Hatteras in the Caribbean.

I had members of my old crew with me, including Slick, who was back in my good graces by now. Slick too was listed in the FBI indictment, and he was also on the run. I felt sure that the FBI wouldn't be searching for us in Antigua. We could be anywhere. Even if the feds knew we were in the Caribbean, finding us off the coast of Antigua would be almost impossible. My plan was to prepare for a quiet life aboard my boat, living as Trevor Worthington. As for Slick, I had no idea of his plans. I didn't share mine, and he didn't share his. We were going to go our separate ways, forever.

Then, on the morning of October 10, 1987, I stood on the transom of my Hatteras at sunrise when I saw that little airplane fly over, and the buzz of the engine broke the silence of that beautiful morning. I knew in my heart that airplane was bad news. I went about my morning. Diving for conch. Smoking a little weed. When Slick and I and the rest of our crew pulled our Hatteras into Falmouth Harbor in Antigua that afternoon, the cops and the FBI were waiting for me.

It's a lifetime ago, but it plays out in my mind as if it were yesterday. The chase. The Antiguan police with their big rifles. The severed finger giving up my identity. The cold metal of the handcuffs when they were first slapped over my wrists. The two FBI guys waiting on the dock. There was no escape. No comfort of any kind. And I could only blame myself.

Race car driver, weed kingpin, loving father and husband. Randy Lanier, Ray Lane, John DeRusso, Trevor Worthington. It was over for all of them.

"Have you ever been locked up before?" asked the public defender.

"No," I said.

"Well, you're fixing to go to the most dangerous prison in the world."

It was October 12, 1987. I was sitting in a chair in the public defender's office in a courthouse in San Juan, Puerto Rico, wearing the same shorts and T-shirt I had on when I got busted. My whole world had collapsed. I never imagined a human being could experience such depths of fear and loneliness. The public defender sat across his desk from me, telling me about Río Piedras State Penitentiary, the biggest and oldest still-functioning prison on the island, often called the Alcatraz of the Caribbean.

"Trust me," he said, "you do not want to go to Río Piedras. They just had a riot there. A couple guards got killed." He paused to let that sink in. "You're about to go into an identity and extradition hearing now," he continued. "I will be representing you. I suggest you do not fight extradition. You want to go back to the US mainland. Because if you go to Río Piedras, you may never get off this island alive."

The identification and extradition hearing lasted only minutes, and I did what the public defender told me to do. I agreed that, yes, I was Randy Lanier, and I asked to be extradited to the mainland. The public defender told me it would take a little time, so I would have to remain on the island for a while. I was going to Río Piedras after all. When I asked for how long, he shrugged.

"I don't know. It shouldn't be long." *Shouldn't be long* in island time could mean weeks or months, I thought to myself.

After the hearing, US marshals marched me through the courthouse front door. Outside, newspaper photographers converged on me, a rabid pack of paparazzi. Click, click, click went the cameras. It all seemed so surreal.

Later that night, I found myself on a rickety bus. There were a dozen of us prisoners, broken into groups of six, each group shackled together. We had our ankles chained so we couldn't run, and handcuffs attached to belly chains. Nobody said a word. Slick and I were the only white guys on the bus. It must've been midnight when we pulled through the gates of Río Piedras State Penitentiary. The building stood four stories high, a tall white-stone art deco structure, all lit up in the night. It looked like the kind of place Hannibal Lecter might be housed.

When we pulled into the sally port, I saw two prison guards dragging a man across an unpaved area leading away from the building we were pulling into, one officer under each of the guy's arms. He was covered in blood and unconscious, feet dragging on the dirt, his orange prison clothes torn. He'd clearly been beaten badly. He looked like he was dead and might've been.

"Damn, that public defender wasn't bullshitting!" I said to Slick. "Look at what we got ourselves into!"

Inside the building, officers unshackled us and gave us orange jumpsuits. Now it was about 2 a.m. On the fourth floor—the federal wing—a guard was waiting to let us through the steel door that led into a prison tier. He slammed the steel door shut behind us. The tier was all cement and metal bars, and there were men everywhere, all of them Hispanic or Black. It was so hot it seemed like the cement walls were sweating.

A group of men surrounded Slick and me. Three muscled Puerto Ricans came forward and told us to follow them down the hallway. One of them opened a door into what looked like a stockroom. He flipped on a light, and rats and cockroaches scurried everywhere. I wondered: *Is this the room where I die?*

Are these motherfuckers going to rip my limbs off for sport? The
men told us to dig around for anything we could find to sleep
on. All we could find were ripped pieces of foam mats.

I turned to Slick. "Is this real, or are we going to wake up
from this nightmare?"

He didn't answer.

There were sixty beds in this tier, for three hundred men.
Everybody else was sleeping on the cement. We couldn't
find a place to lie down because men were lying everywhere.
Finally, we came across a spot big enough for two of us. I
lay down with my head facing one way and Slick faced the
other, so we could kind of watch over ourselves. I tried to
fall asleep. Early in the morning, my eyes were closed, and
I felt this shadow come over me. I looked up, and four men
were standing there. I jumped to my feet, not knowing if
they were going to assault us.

Instead, they had a couple of newspapers, and they were
looking at the front page and then at me. They showed me one
of the newspapers. The whole front page was a photo of me,
and the headline was in Spanish:

"Campeon de Carreras de Autos y Contrabandista Tras las
Rejas."

Champion race car driver and smuggler, behind bars.

One of the Puerto Ricans pointed at the newspaper and
said in English, "Is that you?"

"Yeah," I said. "That's me."

28

Prison

1987 to . . .

*T*he first night you spend in prison can break you. Some guys, they just can't handle it. Emotionally, they shatter. Never the same again. The first night after I was handed a life sentence without the possibility of parole, I was placed in a small cell at the supermax in Marion, Illinois. There was no bed, just a bench with a foam mat to lie on and a blanket. There were no other prisoners in this section, and I didn't know why they put me there.

"Anybody out there?" I yelled.

All I heard was my own voice, echoing back to me. I lay down on the bench, alone.

That night hit me hard. I felt like I was falling into a timeless and endless darkness. I thought of my mother and father, their heartbreak, and how much I'd let them down. Mostly, I thought about Pam and our kids. I would never get to live with them, never enjoy simple things with them. Go for a walk. Hug them and encourage them in their hard times.

I had fucked my life up so bad. The pain was indescribable.

The next morning, an officer who worked in the prison walked by my cell and asked me if I wanted a cup of coffee. I said I would really like a cup of coffee. When he brought it to me, I was so overcome by his kindness I couldn't speak. This simple gesture literally saved my life. I decided that from that day forward, I was going to find a way to keep kindness and empathy in my heart. I was going to try to live the best life I could in this new environment. I made the conscious decision to try to survive.

I was eventually released into the prison population and assigned to a cell with a roommate. I was shown where the law library was and where the mess hall was. I got a job cleaning the showers. I signed up for every college class I could. I started running, and soon I was up to fifty to seventy-five miles a week, around and around in the prison yard. I started doing push-ups, quickly working up to a thousand a day. I meditated. I got physically fit; I got mentally fit.

I'd spent most of my adult life driving Porsches and Ferraris, drinking champagne, living in a mansion. Now, the most elemental comforts took on extraordinary importance. A clothing iron, for example. In prison, you can check out an iron from the supply room. You take that iron, flip it upside down so the flat metal is facing up, and on that hot, metal surface, you can make toast or heat up soup or coffee.

I made chess pieces out of toilet paper. I learned to make stingers. A stinger is anything that you can use to boil water. You can use a toe-nail clipper and any electrical wire that you might strip out of a wall. Rig that all up and bingo—you're boiling water. Even the tinfoil from a pack of cigarettes can make fire to boil water. Touch a sliver of that foil to an AA battery with the side of the battery peeled open, and that creates a spark that'll light toilet paper. Now you have fire.

Let me tell you, if you can get your hands on some weed in prison, you'll figure out a way to smoke it. You can make a pipe out of a cardboard magazine subscription card or an apple. The plant had a way of finding me. More than once, I found nuggets in a baggy on the ground. Every time, I thought: The eternal energy that creates all things, sustains all things, and never changes has just blessed me!

Another time, I arranged for the guy who brought in the newspapers to the library every morning to bring me an ounce of cannabis. Thanks to luck or grace or just plain commerce, I was inside the most secure maximum-security prison in America—smoking weed! I was grateful; after all, the plant heals, and I was in need of healing.

Some days, you feel settled into the rhythm of prison life. You find your small place in this society of controlled movement and strict rules. Among the many evil men and the many good souls you encounter, friendships can become tight bonds. Some days bring the darkness, and you have to fight the battle within your mind to keep sane. The loneliness comes in crushing waves.

The guilt over having put your family through so much trauma—that too comes in waves. One of the hardest things you experience is in the visitors' room, when your family comes to see you and then it's time for them to leave. You watch them walk out the door, and it's all you can do to keep on breathing.

Violence too is part of daily life in prison. Numerous times, I saw men beat other men and stab other men to death. It's sad how the value of life is so little in the eyes of so many. When I saw these things happen, my will to survive only increased. It was a choice: live the best life I could, or I wouldn't make it. I was going to run like I'd never run, expand my mind with chess and books, open my mind to spiritual paths. I was going to be as mindful of others as I could and be the best version of myself possible.

One time, at United States Penitentiary (USP), Terre Haute, Indiana, I was in the chow hall. Terre Haute was called Gladiator School. A lot of stabbings. A lot of gangs. A lot of drama.

On this morning, my unit was the first to be called to chow, so I was one of the first in the hall. I got my tray and sat down at a table by myself. Back then, they had salt and pepper shakers on the tables; they don't anymore because they can be used as projectiles. There was no salt and pepper at my table, so I went to the table next to mine. Four men were sitting there, white guys with shaved heads and tattooed necks—Aryan Brotherhood. I said, "Hey, do you mind if I use your salt and pepper?"

One of the guys knew me, so he said, "No problem, Randy, go ahead."

I reached over and grabbed the salt and pepper. Not one crystal of salt landed on my food before I felt a hand grab my chin. I turned and this skinhead said to me, "Motherfucker, you ain't using this salt and pepper."

People were watching. I was being disrespected: it's not safe to show weakness in the joint. I had no choice. I had to get up and say something to this dude. So I stood and as soon as I got to my feet, the first punch hit my face.

One second, I'm picking up a salt dispenser. The next, I'm literally fighting for my life. That's how quickly things can happen. I survived that day. That fight got broken up before any real damage could be done. The guy eventually apologized. Said he was in a bad mood.

It took the feds seven years to seize everything. All my bank accounts. All my possessions. My homes. The Bicycle Club. The feds sent bulldozers to my father's home in Virginia, dug up the backyard, and when they found PVC pipes filled with cash buried there, they charged my elderly father with obstruction of justice. There were buckets of gold coins, gold bars, and uncirculated silver dollars that never showed up in any of the seized property forms from my case. I'm not sure if they never found them, if somebody pocketed them, or if they're still buried in the woods of Virginia.

The feds seized my brother's house and charged him with obstruction of justice too, for not turning in money I asked him to bury. Both my father and brother got three-year prison terms. The feds showed up at my mom's house in Florida with a tow truck. They took her car and gave her thirty days to vacate the home she'd owned for over thirty years. The guilt I felt was nearly insurmountable.

To keep me from trying to escape, the feds moved me around the country. The authorities believed I was an escape risk, and they were right. I came up with plots to use a bow and arrow to create a zipline over prison walls, to sneak out by hiding inside a broken vending machine, to hide in food delivery trucks. Every prison presented different opportunities. Sometimes they put me in the hole—a single secluded cell for twenty-three hours a day, for months on end—to keep me from plotting my escape. My longest stint in solitary confinement was for two years for an escape investigation in USP Florence, Colorado. Two years! Alone in a cell for twenty-three hours a day. Often, it was twenty-four hours a day due to staff shortages.

Solitary confinement changes people. It can change you for the better or the worse. In prison you must protect yourself at all times—sometimes from others, sometimes from your own terrifying thoughts.

At times, I lived in the same prison as Ben Kramer, who was also doing a life sentence. But not all the time. I was housed in the Federal Correctional Institution, Marianna, in Florida when I heard the news of Ben's attempted escape. He was in a federal penitentiary in Miami at that time.

I always knew Ben had balls! But the story I heard—it was like something out of *Mission Impossible.*

On April 13, 1989, Ben was strolling the prison yard in Miami when a guy flew in with a helicopter and landed in the yard. Ben jumped on board, and the pilot took off. But the helicopter's rotor blade caught on concertina wire, and the chopper flipped over and crashed. Both Ben and the pilot were captured, both with broken bones in their legs. The newspapers showed a photo of the destroyed helicopter. The *Los Angeles Times* reported: "Instead of a flight to freedom, Ben Kramer—once a world champion powerboat racer—received a fractured ankle."

A couple years later, I was at Leavenworth, and Ben was there. One day, out on the yard, guards came to get me. They brought me to the SIS office, the Special Investigative Supervisor, which is like the FBI inside the federal prison system. Two Miami detectives were there waiting for me. They showed me a chair and I sat down.

"What's this about?" I asked.

One of the detectives said, "We're investigating a homicide. Did you know a man named Don Aronow?"

"Yes, I did."

"Do you have any information with regards to Ben Kramer and the killing of Don Aronow?"

My heart skipped a beat. "I don't know anything," I said. "Nothing at all. And if you ever call me here again, please have my attorney present."

When I got back to the cellblock, I found Ben in his cell. I told him that the Miami homicide cops just called me to the SIS office. Something about Don Aronow. "Yeah," he told me, "I know about that. My lawyer is dealing with it."

We never talked about it again. But in 1996, Ben pleaded no contest to manslaughter for ordering the hit on Aronow. The killer was a guy named Bobby Young; someone I'd never met. Ben's lawyers apparently advised him to plead no contest because (as I understand it) the state offered him a good deal. Did he actually commit the crime? No idea. Only Ben knows the answer to that question.

Days turned into weeks. Weeks into months. Years into decades. I taught myself how to oil paint and spent as much time in the prison art rooms as I could. I became a mentor to new prisoners, teaching them how to mentally endure the crushing realities of life behind bars. I even got remarried, to a woman named Maria who I knew well during my smuggling years. But that didn't last long. The feds raided her house and her sister's house. They charged her with money laundering in a case linked to my smuggling operations. She did eight years and nine months, and when she got out, immigration deported her to Chile. (She now has a beautiful loving family there, and we remain friends to this day.)

One day, in 2006, I was putting away yoga mats in the recreation room at the Federal Correctional Complex in Coleman, Florida, when the prison psychologist approached me. By this time, I'd been incarcerated for nineteen years.

"Randy, we're going to be opening a new kind of unit," he said. "It will be called the Challenge Program. The program will be all about change. I think you would be good for it."

"Ayyyight," I said. "Tell me more."

"It's a one-year intensive program. If you complete it, your custody may be lowered."

That's all I needed to hear. "I'm game."

So I moved to the Challenge Unit, and I made my home there. Right away, I saw why they called it that. It was a lot of work. But I didn't look at it as a challenge. I saw it as a way to grow.

Then my life took another unexpected turn. The opportunity came up to become what's called a suicide companion. It's a strange-sounding term, but that's what they call it. Some of the prisoners who'd attempted suicide were telling the psychology department that the guards were treating them like shit and taunting them. Like, *hey, do the world a favor and go kill yourself. You're such a failure, you can't even do that right.* So, the psychology department developed a program for inmates to help their fellow inmates.

I began training by reading a lot of books and watching a lot of suicide prevention videos. I did a lot of training on how to talk to people who were on the edge of existence. The most important thing I learned was how to listen. One of the greatest gifts we can give is to be good listeners. Then, one day, I was in my cell and the head psychologist came for me. It was time to go to the prison hospital to begin my new role.

Inside the hospital at Federal Correctional Complex, Coleman USP—and in many other prison hospitals—there's a special room, and the first time you see it, it takes your breath away. It's about ten by fifteen feet, and the walls are plexiglass. There's a cement block in the middle, about three feet high, seven feet long, and four feet wide, with a thin mattress on top. If you're in the suicide cell, that's your bed, and it takes up about half the room. You don't get to wear clothes. They give you what's called a suicide vest, a wrap-around smock that hangs down to your knees. Regular clothing can be used to form a noose; the suicide smock cannot.

There's a bathroom but no door. There's a metal slot so guards can bring food and medication. They used to bring plastic utensils at mealtimes, but they stopped after one guy tried to use a plastic fork to dig the arteries out of his arm. If you're in the suicide cell, you're living on bag lunches, three meals a day.

If you try to commit suicide in prison, you end up in this room, and they can keep you there for up to ninety days. If you're still a threat to yourself after ninety days, they send you to a psych ward in Springfield, Missouri. If they think you're OK, they send you back into the prison population.

My job as a suicide companion was to sit in a cell that was attached to the plexiglass room for four hours at a time and just talk to these guys. I had a chair and a desk, and there were holes in the plexiglass wall so we could hear each other. Every fifteen minutes, I had to take down a note on what the guy was doing and what he was telling me. Was he eating? Was he able to sleep at night? What was he dreaming?

Some of the stories of these men will break your heart. For real.

One night, the guards came to get me. It must have been 2 a.m. "Let's go," they said. "They need you in the hospital."

I loved when they came to get me at night. We had to leave the prison unit and walk outside to get to the hospital. Then I'd get to see the stars and the moon. The first time that happened, I hadn't seen the full night sky for about fifteen years. It was breathtaking and humbling.

When we got to the suicide cell, someone was lying on the cement block, facing up. I recognized this prisoner from the yard, and I'd already heard the story up to this point. For years, this person had wanted a gender reassignment surgery, what we called at the time a sex change. The prisoner had filed papers in court over and over, but the government kept denying it because they didn't want to pay for it. So this prisoner took matters into their own hands, using the jagged-edge lid of a vegetable can smuggled from the kitchen. The makeshift surgery was done in a prison cell.

I tried to talk to this person but got no response. That was the only person I met who stayed the full ninety days in the suicide cell during all my time as a suicide companion. They transferred the prisoner to the psych ward, and I never heard anything about them again. The cruelty of the prison system can be beyond belief.

Another time I sat with a man who had done thirty-two years. This guy did talk to me. He was not good with eye contact but at least he sat facing me so I could see his face in that weird light that beamed down from above. He told me that he was hearing voices, and they were telling him to do things. Bad things.

Turned out, he had severe PTSD, but he had never heard of PTSD. He told me that when he was six, his dad used to take him down into the basement of their home and chain him to a radiator. Then he'd turn the heat up all the way. I was thinking: *My God, this poor man.* Getting tortured in his own home, by his own father, and he was just a child. And then having to go through life. This man would never trust anybody. Would never love anybody. Wouldn't even love himself.

I truly believe that empathy is the most profound feeling we can experience on the planet. Putting yourself in another person's shoes, looking at things from their perspective, gaining insight and understanding. You don't need to know much about another human being to love them. They can be complete strangers. Because love isn't about what you give and take. It's about understanding and compassion. Pure love doesn't change. It is what created and what sustains us. It is energy.

It took me two decades in prison to truly learn that lesson, which means, to me, those years were not wasted. Eventually, due to my work with suicide cases while living in the Challenge Unit, I got offered a transfer to a lower custody prison, meaning a prison with less supervision. I turned it down. My perspective had changed. I wanted to help others, so I stayed. I lived in the Challenge Unit, serving as a suicide companion, for eight years.

Once a month, every federal prisoner is supposed to meet with a counselor. This is routine in every federal prison in the country. One day in mid-September 2014, my meeting coincided with a court hearing I was scheduled to have regarding my sentence. In the past, I'd gotten excited about these hearings. My lawyer would ask for leniency. But every time, the answer was no.

This time, however, I had reason for hope: The Obama administration had handed down an order to the Justice Department to look into nonviolent prisoners serving long sentences. Additionally, both Charles Podesta and my old partner Gene (both now out of prison) had been working hard to get me released.

At the time, I was in USP Coleman in Florida. On the appointed afternoon, I left my cell and headed for my counselor's office. Guards opened a steel door that led to a hallway past offices that were mostly empty. I walked down this hallway. It was quiet, and my footsteps echoed down the corridor. My counselor was waiting for me. He had pictures of his kids on his desk. We shook hands. He checked his watch, then picked up the phone, dialing into a speakerphone that was set up in a courtroom in Southern Illinois. I heard my lawyer's voice come through the speaker, addressing me directly.

"Randy," he said, "you are only to speak when spoken to. OK?"

"Yessir."

I listened as my attorney addressed the judge and the US district attorney. I'd already served twenty-seven years behind bars. Think about how much time that is, for a moment. Think about twenty-seven years. I had plenty of time left to go—the rest of my life. The supervisor of the psychology department had written letters to the judge and district attorney on my behalf. Certain prison guards that I had gotten to know had written letters as well. All my Challenge Program work and my monthly evaluations—that whole file had reached the US district attorney's office.

When my lawyer asked for a reduction to time served, the district attorney had no objection. They agreed that I did not owe any forfeiture. I was stunned. Shocked. Sitting in my chair, I dug my fingers into my thighs.

The judge addressed me directly. I was to serve six months in a halfway house, he said. I was to see a probation officer regularly for three years. I was not to enter any establishment that served alcohol. I could not be in possession of a firearm. I could not associate with convicted felons. As he was explaining all this, I struggled to come to grips with what he was saying.

I was going to be released.

I was going to be a part of society again.

Part of my family.

The judge hammered a gavel, and that was it.

My heart was pounding. My counselor stood and congratulated me. He had genuine joy in his eyes, and although I barely knew him, I hugged him. When I walked out the door into that empty corridor, the only sound the echo of my footsteps, I clenched my fists and screamed to everybody and nobody.

"It's happening! I am going home!"

The day I was scheduled to leave prison, I awoke at 4:30 a.m. It was October 15, 2014. I was being housed in a cell with no cellmate. I did my push-ups. I cleaned my cell one final time.

At 8 a.m., the head of my unit's psychology department, Dr. Moritz, showed up to walk me to the Receiving and Discharge (R&D) Unit. I'd given most of my possessions away, but I had some books I wanted to give my son and my daughter and some oil paintings I was still working on. The guards brought me a little cart to put my things on. I loaded it and pushed it out of the cell, crossing the threshold of the door for the last time.

A couple friends showed up. I was not expecting them because I'd played it close to the vest with regards to my release. I didn't tell a lot of people. In prison you have to be careful because guys can get jealous. Somebody might have a beef with you, sneak a knife into your cell, and rat you out. Boom: another two years.

But somehow, news had gotten around. A friend named Leather Face, who was a One Percenter—a motorcycle gang member—showed up that morning to say good-bye. A guy named Shawn, who had a life sentence for homicide, also showed up. They asked if they could walk with me to R&D.

"Ayyyight," I said. "Let's walk."

Suddenly, a couple more guys showed up. Then three more. And two more after that. Now we were a whole crew, and let me tell you, when you see a crew of guys walking with purpose in a prison unit, everybody notices. I felt all these hands touching my arms, touching my shoulders, touching the back of my neck. Handshakes, high fives, hugs. I tried to speak but I couldn't. The lump in my throat wouldn't let me. I kept walking.

Some of these guys? They weren't ever going to get out of prison. Ever. But they wanted to celebrate my freedom with me.

We went through metal detector after metal detector, and finally we got to the last one that leads to the R&D Unit. A guard was there with a clipboard, and he stopped us. He checked a record sheet and then said, "None of you guys can come through this metal detector except Randy Lanier."

I stepped forward and showed him my prison ID. "Can these guys come to R&D with me?" I asked.

The cop looked at me and paused. "OK, one guy."

"Leather Face," I said. "Let's go."

I hugged all the other guys one last time. Then Leather Face and I walked through that last metal detector and through the next door. When we got to R&D, we had to say good-bye. It was amazing to see a man as badass as Leather Face with this look of kindness on his face. He was one of the toughest One

Percenters I ever met in my life. But he was also a kind and generous human being with emotions just like everyone else. One last hug and I could only wonder if I'd ever see him again.

In the R&D office, a guard fingerprinted me and walked me through some identification paperwork. They handed me a box with some clothes in it, which Pam had sent. After all these years, Pam still had my back. Man! Some sweatpants. A T-shirt. I was so thankful for that T-shirt.

Then, some officers walked me down another hallway and past a holding cell. The Receiving and Discharge Unit is where prisoners come in and where they leave. I looked at the guys in the holding cell, who were just arriving at Coleman, knowing some of these dudes would be behind bars for the rest of their lives.

Dr. Moritz, the lead psychologist, walked with me. When we got to the last door, the feeling was surreal. I reached out my hand and opened it.

Here is my son, Glen, twenty-seven years old. My daughter, Brandie, thirty-four years old. Pam, as beautiful as the day I met her. We all melt together. It is like being born again.

Gratitude. Love. Thankfulness. Energy. God is shining upon our family.

We get in the car and drive away. When we arrive at my mother's house, she's there waiting for me. She is ninety years old and a double breast cancer survivor. I feel that she has willed herself alive long enough to see this day. She has all the fixings for steak and eggs, shrimp and grits. After hugging and crying, we sit on the couch and talk about things that have happened over the last twenty-seven years. The death of my father. The birth of my nieces and nephews.

Pam takes me home that night to the little house where she's living in Davie. She's working at a home for substance abuse patients, and she has a guy renting a room in the house to help make ends meet. She's been clean and sober for decades. Like me, she remarried after I went to prison, and like mine, her marriage didn't last. Here's something I haven't told you yet: Pam cooperated with the FBI, which led to the arrest of my father and brother. She had no choice. She had to do it. Over the years, I forgave her for doing what she had to do, and I forgave myself for what I had done to her. It was a matter of survival: let it go or die of sadness. I chose life, and so did she.

That night, I try to sleep in Pam's bed, but I can't. I get up and walk out the door. The cool air on my skin feels so good! The stars look so bright! I start walking down the street in the middle of the night. Don't even have shoes on. I walk for miles—because I can.

I have paid my dues and now I'm free. This is really happening.

Epilogue

The gratitude has never left me. I feel it every day. Not that it's easy to rejoin society after a long prison term. A lot of guys have trouble with it. How to get a job, how to find a place to live, how to get a loan or a credit card—these things are difficult if you are a convicted felon. During my six months at the halfway house, Brandie came to stay at Pam's house to help me transition into society, and Glen luckily lived nearby. I don't know how I would have gotten back on my feet without the help of my family.

My old friend Preston Henn gave me a job selling tickets for his swap shop and drive-in movie theaters for minimum wage—$8.25 an hour. I lived rent-free at Preston's guesthouse for a while, so I could save money to rent my own apartment. Following the drug overdose death of someone very close to me, I took some classes and became a behavioral health technician. I got a job teaching yoga on the beach at sunrise to people struggling with addiction. Some were war veterans returning from Afghanistan. Others were struggling with behavioral issues. These people ranged from age nineteen to eighty-two.

I taught them that in order to change your life, you must change the way you think. We validate our identity through our behavior. Change the way you identify yourself, and you can change that behavior. Practice mindfulness, live with gratitude, live with forgiveness, let yourself experience compassion and empathy.

One year after I got out, almost to the date, my son, Glen, and his girlfriend gave birth to twin boys. Which to me was amazing. Glen was a twin, but his brother died. Now Glen was the father of twins, and I get to help raise his children in a way I couldn't do with him. It was like life was coming full circle. Eventually, I moved into Pam's home. One of the happiest days of my life was the day we remarried. We invited a group of friends and said our vows with our toes in the sand on the beach in Fort Lauderdale, this place that we love so much. Pam was wearing a clip in her hair that I'd bought for her in Paris, back in the '70s.

My family never gets sick of hearing me talk about how blessed we all are to be together. So many people take so many things for granted. To be able to get up when you want to, go to a refrigerator, and pour a glass of cool water. To be able to meet a friend for a cup of coffee, just to say hello.

Most of the friends I had when I was young are, for one reason or another, gone. In 2020, Bill Whittington came to the home where Pam and I live, and for three days we talked about old times and laughed our asses off. Just days later, Bill was in Arizona flying a small airplane, giving a ride to a friend who was terminally ill with cancer. Bill crashed the plane; he and the passenger were killed. I was heartbroken and so thankful for the chance to get to reconnect with him for one last time.

After serving fourteen years in prison, John Paul Sr. was released in 1999. He absconded in 2001 and is wanted for questioning in the disappearance of two women—his second wife and a girlfriend. John Paul Jr. served thirty months and was then able to get back on the racetrack for twelve years. He died in 2020 after battling Huntington's disease. My old partner Gene died of a heart attack. George disappeared, and from what I've heard, he's out there somewhere, hiding from the law. My old right-hand man Charles Podesta was forced to testify against me in 1988. I've forgiven him, and we remain friends today. Ben Kramer is still in prison. The racing boat company he cofounded, Apache Powerboats, still exists and remains one of the most legendary names in offshore speedboating.

There's a terrible irony to my story. For years, while I was in prison, I read about the cannabis industry. First, there was the legalization of medical marijuana and then the opening of medical marijuana dispensaries. First one state, then another. And now full-on legalization in a growing number of states.

Today, huge companies are making millions and millions of dollars growing and selling weed, companies that have HR departments, insurance plans, corporate offices. They're training farmers, training marketing and salespeople, training employees about different cannabinoids and strains. Reputable colleges offer programs in the cannabis business and in cannabis research—horticulture, health and well-being marketing trends, and chemistry. Colleges like Colorado State University Pueblo, Northern Michigan University, and the University of

Rhode Island. There's even a school in California called Oak-sterdam University entirely devoted to weed.

A $40 billion industry has sprung up, doing basically what I was doing—getting high-quality weed to the people. It's mind blowing to see how big this industry has gotten and gut wrenching to think what my life would've been like had I built my business now and not during the War on Drugs.

I've become a brand ambassador for two cannabis companies—MJ Harvest Inc. and Cannabis Sativa Inc. Both are publicly traded companies. The people who run these companies are good people. They go to work every day with little worry that the FBI is going to bust them and imprison them for decades. I get paid to help them spread the word, and I love the work.

But it's the work I do as a volunteer that I love even more. It's hard to fathom in this day and age, but there are still thousands of nonviolent cannabis prisoners out there, doing long terms and suffering unnecessary hardships. I'm vice president of a 501(c)(3) nonprofit called Freedomgrow.org, an all-volunteer organization. We have over two hundred prisoners that we help support, every one of them vetted as a nonviolent cannabis prisoner.

One of the things we do is called the Wish Program. We grant wishes for prisoners on important days like holidays and birthdays. We want them to know that they have support and that their lives matter. Fighting a cannabis case often bankrupts the families of these prisoners. So we help support those families. We send Walmart and Target gift cards to the kids. We run fundraising drives, do grassroots activism, and send commissary funds six times a year to these cannabis prisoners.

We also run a program to educate courtroom jurors on the process of jury nullification. It's all done through donations, and we won't stop until every cannabis prisoner has been released.

It's sad that, even as the cannabis industry is exploding and funneling vast sums of tax dollars toward our communities, cannabis prisoners are still doing time. The War on Drugs has been a war on the American people. We've been locking up our own citizens by the hundreds of thousands, and people of color have been disproportionally impacted.

Let me make this as clear as I can: nobody—*nobody*—should ever go to prison because of a plant.

When I got out of prison, everybody told me I had to sign up for an email address. So I did. One day in 2015, I got an email from a stranger named Mike Carr, who lived in Pennsylvania. He told me he raced a BMW and that he'd read about my story in a magazine. He wanted to know if I'd team up with him for an endurance race at Mid-Ohio, coming up.

I stared at the words on my computer screen for a long time, wondering how to respond. My prosecuting attorney's name was Michael Carr. So this stranger reaching out with the same name? I didn't know what to make of it. Finally, I typed the words: "Is this a joke?"

Nope. Not a joke.

I flew to Mid-Ohio, and there was Mike Carr with his BMW E30, a production car he'd outfitted as a racer. The car had number 89 on the side and a *Road & Track* magazine logo across the top of the windshield. I must have thanked Mike a thousand times for his kindness.

"You ready for this, Randy?" he asked me, in the pits at Mid-Ohio.

"Damn skippy!"

I had to borrow a helmet and racing shoes, which were the wrong size. My old IndyCar fireproof suit still fit, one of the few possessions the feds hadn't taken from me. I jumped in the car, fastened myself in. I sparked the engine. I sat there for a moment, listening to the song, smelling the fumes. How many nights had I lain awake in some god-awful cot in a prison cell, dreaming of this moment? To feel the pavement under me, the engine throbbing, the whole world outside the track disappearing—I sensed a whisper of the old feeling that I could conquer the world.

It was raining, and the pavement was slippery. I had to temper my approach as I was rusty as all hell. But I knew this track. I'd been here before, decades earlier, worshipping at the altar of speed. I began to drive and felt my mind-set shift. I slipped into the flow, and the gyroscope in my brain began to do its thing.

Hands soft and firm, fingers light and nimble.

Quick shifts, heel and toe.

Late brake dive into a right-hander.

Smooth on the throttle.

I'm roaring down a straightaway at one with the car and the road. Energy in motion. Being the best I can be. Setting myself up for the next turn. Realizing I am right where I belong.

Acknowledgments

*F*irst and foremost, let me say, I am the most blessed man on earth to have the family I have. I want to thank them for sticking with me all these years. It wasn't always easy. Pam, Brandie, Glen—I love you. Thank you.

I want to acknowledge my mother for instilling in me the ability to recognize compassion and empathy and my dad for passing along the wisdom that it's OK to be content with the unknown. I want to acknowledge all the people who helped support me during the twenty-seven years I was incarcerated. My brilliant attorney Steven Johnson represented me pro bono for twelve years, and his entire law firm (now called Ritchie, Davies, Johnson & Stovall) was behind me, including Karen, my attorney's assistant, who always made sure our communications went smoothly, which meant so much to me. Dr. Moritz, the Challenge Program supervisor at USP Coleman, has been a big influence in my life. Bob Ritchie, my original attorney, did his best for me. May he rest in peace.

I want to acknowledge my codefendant Gene, who helped me get out of prison and whose spirit still guides me. May he also rest in peace. I want to thank my brother Bobby and my brother Steve (rest in peace, I miss you so much) and my sister, Anne, for all the love and support. Thank you also to my buddy Mike Carr, who gave me my first crack at a race car after getting out of the joint.

Thank you to Keith Leighton and all the guys with the Blue Thunder race team who helped me win the 1984 title. Thank you to crew chief Dennis McCormick and everyone at Arciero Racing for all your efforts to win us all the 1986 Indy 500 Rookie of the Year trophy.

During my twenty-seven years in prison, I met some of the most amazing and brilliant men. Thanks to all you guys who made those years more bearable—Sean, Leather Face, Gary S., Mark Marks, Luis Rivera, Michael Mejuck, Dickey Lynn, Billy Deckle, and all the rest. I want to thank all my cellmates who kept it real. May you all find freedom if you haven't already.

I'd like to acknowledge all the people that I have mentored and counseled in the substance abuse treatment industry and all the people at Freedomgrow.org. One love!

This book says my name on the cover, but it represents the work of many people. Thank you, Sam Raim, my editor at Hachette, for your amazing feedback and dedication, your insights, and your patience. Thank you for believing in this project. Thank you to my agent and counsel Ted Baer and to Susan Canavan at the Waxman Literary Agency. And finally, thank you to my coauthor, A. J. Baime. We spent a hell of a lot of time together, bro! Should we do another book together? Damn skippy!